THE POLITICS OF
TOURISM IN ASIA

THE POLITICS OF TOURISM IN ASIA

Linda K. Richter

University of Hawaii Press / Honolulu

Library of Congress Cataloging-in-Publication Data

Richter, Linda K.
   The politics of tourism in Asia.

   Bibliography: p.
   Includes index.
   1. Tourist trade and state—Asia.   I.   Title.
G155.A74R53   1989   380.1'459150428   88–27698
ISBN 0–8248–1140–2

∞ The paper used in this publication meets the minimum
requirements of American National Standard for Information
Sciences—Permanence of Paper for Printed Library Materials.
ANSI Z39.48-1984

Contents

Acknowledgments

Authoring a book is rather like having a baby, in that it needs the cooperation of others, involves a certain amount of anxiety and discomfort, and rarely leaves one in the same mental or physical shape that they were in before. Unlike producing a baby, the gestation period is longer, the cooperation needed more sustained and varied, and the end result a bit anticlimatic.

In any event, I want to thank all those who made this book possible. Over 250 people were interviewed in the course of developing the book. Their generous gifts of time, files, letters, suggestions, and in some cases meals and housing were deeply appreciated. I am especially indebted to the many scholars, public officials, and tourist-industry leaders in the Philippines and Pakistan, where I spent the most time. Even during martial law, in both countries, I was treated with unfailing courtesy and assistance from all whom I sought out for information.

Funding was also critical. The initial work on Philippine tourism was supported by a Fulbright Grant. I was also a Visiting Research Associate of the University of the Philippines College of Public Administration. In Pakistan, I was under the auspices of the American Institute of Pakistan Studies. Travel to and support while in Thailand was provided in part by the Ecumenical Coalition on Third World Tourism and Kansas State University. My "home base" at KSU has also contributed to the project in terms of clerical support and a Summer Research Grant. The absolutely critical financial, clerical, and psychological support, however, came from the Alumni Office of the East-West Center in Honolulu. From September 1984 until February 1985, I was the recipient of their Alumni-in-Residence Fellowship. Beyond funds and clerical help, the luxury of time and the human and library resources provided by the East-West Center enabled this book to go forward. The East-West Center Institute of Culture and Communication (ICC) provided office space and many friends and researchers like Elizabeth Buck, Meheroo Jussanwalla, and Gregory

Triffonovitch with whom to share ideas and test assumptions about my work. At ICC and at the University of Hawaii Tourism Industry Management School, I also appreciated opportunities to present my research in progress.

Peter Holden, Ron O'Grady, and Kosong Srisang of the Ecumenical Coalition on Third World Tourism and Virginia Hadsell of the Center for Responsible Tourism have been major sources of inspiration and information. Special thanks go to Gordon Ring, Alumni Director, and June Saito of the Alumni Office, who facilitated research contacts and clerical support in the early stages of the book. Mary McCall, Dora Gerlaugh, Barbara Warren, and Angela Pearl deserve much credit for typing the manuscript during its several drafts. Yang Ning and Steve Jack have been super sleuths in compiling the bibliographical entries and in tracking down obscure citations.

Iris Wiley, Damaris Kirchhofer, and Eileen D'Araujo of the University of Hawaii Press and Linda Gregonis also deserve my heartfelt appreciation for their encouragement, suggestions, and thorough attention to details that a tired author would just as soon ignore.

Finally, I want to thank my husband, Bill Richter, for his love and encouragement coupled with an unswerving ability to discover split infinitives, ferret out non sequiturs, and demand that the book's argument answer his disarming but persistent query of "so what?"

Any errors or omissions that remain in this study are my responsibility and are *despite* the great effort and help of so many.

Tourism policy *can* be a vehicle for sound development strategies and the promotion of positive cross-cultural relationships. My association in the course of preparing this book with so many fine people interested in and committed to better tourism policies makes me quite optimistic that most political needs of policymakers *and* the public interest in thoughtful tourism development can be reconciled.

Abbreviations Used in Text

ADB — Asian Development Bank
AIT — Asian Institute of Tourism
ASEAN — Association of Southeast Asian Nations
ASTA — American Society of Travel Agents

BPC — Bangladesh Parjatan Corporation
BTTI — Board of Travel and Tourist Industry

CAAC — China's national airway
CITS — China International Travel Service
CTS — China Travel Service
CYTS — China Youth Travel Service

DAR — Department of Agrarian Reform (Philippines)
DOT — Department of Tourism (India)
DOT — Department of Tourism (Philippines)
DPB — Development Bank of the Philippines

ECTWT — Ecumenical Coalition on Third World Tourism

GATT — General Administration for Travel and Tourism (China)
GOI — Government of India
GSIS — Government Service Insurance System

IA — Indian Airlines
ILO — International Labour Organisation
ITDC — Indian Tourism Development Corporation

NTA — National Tourism Administration (China)

OECD — Organization for Economic Cooperation and Development

PACOM — Pacific and Asian Congress of Municipalities
PAL — Philippine Airlines

PATA	Pacific Area Travel Association
PIA	Pakistan International Airlines
PICC	Philippine International Convention Center
PRC	People's Republic of China
PSL	Pakistan Services Limited
PTA	Philippine Tourism Authority
PTDC	Pakistan Tourism Development Corporation
R&R	rest and recreation
RNAC	Royal Nepal Airlines Corporation
ROC	Republic of China
TAT	Tourism Authority of Thailand
TDC	Tourism Development Corporation
TEN	Tourism Ecumenical Network
TNC	transnational corporations
TOP	Tourism Organization of the Philippines
TOT	Tourism Organization of Thailand
UNDP	United Nations Development Project
WTO	World Tourism Organization

THE POLITICS OF
TOURISM IN ASIA

1

The Politics of Tourism: An Overview

'88 Olympics in South Korea Threatened by Political Turmoil
Soviet Missile Shoots Down Korean Civilian Airliner
U.S.-China Relations Thaw After 30 Year Freeze

WHAT do these headlines have in common? All were incidents with serious international implications in which tourism was either a significant element or a major political response. Tourism? It is very hard for many to believe that tourism is associated with anything more weighty than picking the right traveler's check ("don't leave home without them!") or selecting a destination at once "in," low season, with a recently devalued currency, and with clean water or cold beer. Yet as one investigates these events it is clear that tourism is involved.

The shooting down of the unarmed Korean airliner, for example, was a global outrage condemned by public opinion. It also revealed quite clearly the impotence of military arms as a response to such action. Retaliatory strikes, an embargo, tariff barriers, or a cut in diplomatic relations might have been options if the aggressor had been Fiji, but they were out of the question as a response to a superpower. In fact, when the rhetoric subsided, the only action taken was a short-term refusal by most Western nations to permit their airlines to fly to the Soviet Union or allow Aeroflot landings on their soil. The U.S. ban on the airlines was already in place having dated back to the Soviet invasion of Afghanistan. U.S. response to the invasion included denying landing rights to Aeroflot airlines, boycotting the Moscow Olympics, and establishing an unpopular grain embargo. Cancellations of numerous tours and exchanges to the USSR followed both Soviet actions. In 1984, political motives led the Soviet Union and most of Eastern Europe to boycott the Los Angeles Olympics.

The earliest public exchanges between the United States and the People's Republic of China (PRC) signalling improved relations came with the invitation to an American table tennis team to visit the PRC to play the Chinese team. Limited tours and exchanges have expanded and contracted according to the political relationship. The U.S. relations with

1

the government in the Republic of China (ROC) continue to be a sore point. Tourist flows in general can be seen as a crude but reliable barometer of international relations among tourist-generating and tourist-receiving countries.

The politics of international tourism are not only fought at the national level, however. Women's groups and church associations have made tourism a significant part of their agenda, especially in developing nations. The most prominent tourist-related issues tend to be associated with the exploitation of women, the advantages and disadvantages of tourism as a means of economic development, and the problems poor nations have in retaining control over their own tourism destiny.

Prime Minister Suzuki of Japan discovered how politically embarrassing church and women's groups could be when he took a tour of Southeast Asian capitals. It was a diplomatic fiasco. Everywhere he confronted noisy demonstrations protesting the ubiquitous sex tours by Japanese men. Though no one claimed the Japanese had a monopoly on seeking prostitutes, the affluence, mobility, and group travel of the Japanese made their all-male tours more conspicuous and objectionable. Their ability to pay vast sums to organizers for such "hospitality" also contributed to the expansion of prostitution.

Frequently, the politics of tourism are not played according to "the rules," as one discovers in the Philippines. The corruption and mismanagement associated with the acceleration of tourism in the Philippines under former President Marcos led to the industry's becoming a target of Filipino dissidents. Initially, the hotels bombed were those owned by President and Mrs. Marcos or those close to them. Later, the industry was literally shaken by an explosion just a few feet from the spot where President Marcos was telling the American Society of Travel Agents conferees that reports of unrest in the Philippines were media hype!

This book is written on the central premise that tourism is a highly political phenomenon, the implications of which have been only rarely perceived and almost nowhere fully understood. Furthermore, it matters a great deal whether the public and key policymakers are able to grasp the fact that, although tourism may have a frivolous carefree image, the industry is huge, intensely competitive, and has acute social consequences for nearly all societies.

The book explores—sometimes briefly, sometimes at great length— the amazing variety and complexity of political issues associated with tourism. In the course of this study tidy distinctions between levels of politics, government spheres of influence, and types of interest group configurations and public policies may be difficult to maintain. What may be missing in neat categories, elaborate model building, and sophisticated theorizing may be compensated for by an enhanced ability to understand and appreciate the many political dimensions of tourism that challenge and provoke decision makers.

Because this is a book about politics, it is organized around political systems and public policy. It is hoped that this arrangement will be convenient for those who are interested in a particular nation. It should be noted, however, that political issues discussed in one country or at one level of government are probably not confined only to that particular nation or level of authority.

Before turning to the country studies, however, it is important to put this research into a historical, disciplinary, and methodological context. Before we can assimilate the many political dimensions of tourism that affect national policy it is critical we know why it is so important to understand tourism in its full political complexity.

THE MAGNITUDE OF TOURISM

Today, tourism is the largest industry in the world and is expected to maintain that distinction until at least the middle of the twenty-first century.[1] In 1985 world-wide tourist expenditures were estimated at $1,800 billion.[2] Over 125 nations consider tourism a major industry, and in nearly a third of those countries it is a leading industry, a top earner of foreign exchange, and a critical source of employment. Even in a country as affluent and diversified as the United States, tourism is the second largest industry, the largest tradeable services export, one of the top three sources of revenue for 39 of the 50 states, and, as the employer of approximately 6 million Americans, the country's second largest employer.[3]

The magnitude of tourism means that its international political and policy ramifications need close and immediate attention. "This interest and recognition of tourism must take place today; tomorrow may be too late."[4] Yet this recognition has not occurred. Several years ago this writer documented the almost total inattention to tourism as a subject of political research or as a focus of national policy-making in the United States.[5] Regrettably that situation has changed little, either within the discipline of political science or at national policy level. At subnational state and local levels tourism development is regarded with great interest, though it is largely in economic development terms, with little awareness of its potential political impact.[6] Major changes in tourism's perceived policy impact have led to the establishment of ministries of tourism and other high government organizations in numerous countries.[7] Again, it was economics rather than a recognition of tourism's political potential that was ostensibly behind such moves.

Before moving specifically to the nation studies in this volume, it is important to consider generally how the politics of tourism affect international relations, public administration, and public policy-making. Often these are seen as separate and distinct political subfields. As this study illustrates, however, each offers insights into and examples of the politics of tourism. But as the nation studies will demonstrate, tourism politics is frequently a blend of all three.

INTERNATIONAL RELATIONS

The role tourism plays in influencing international relations is understudied but scarcely unimportant. It has numerous dimensions. First one can analyze tourism flow as an independent variable having political impact. One may be interested as Arend Lijphart was in his early study of the relationship between tourist flow and regional integration,[8] or in the symmetry or asymmetry of tourist relationships as in Hoivik and Heiberg's center-periphery studies between governments.[9] Some studies have hypothesized that tourism flows may be predictors of military and economic aid.[10] Others have found little or even negative relationships between the direction and magnitude of tourism flows and the likelihood of political support from the host country for the politics of the tourist-generating country.[11]

If causal linkages have not been conclusively determined between tourism flow and certain outcomes there does seem to be more impressionistic support that governments use tourism as a diplomatic barometer of their closeness and affinity for each other. As Robert Stock commented, "The flows of tourism between two nations can be used as a sign of the level of salience between the two nations and their people."[12]

Most nations have several policies toward foreign tourists that are based not only on anticipated length of stay but also on the degree of international cooperation existing between the two countries. For example, Canada requires no passport or visa from citizens of the United States or Commonwealth countries, but may require such documents from other nationals. Some countries refuse to issue visas to nationals of countries perceived as temporarily divided, such as the two Koreas, rather than appear to take sides in recognizing regimes.

In the international arena, where most relations between nations have a political component, it would be naive to assume that tourism development would not have strong political implications. For example, the People's Republic of China, Cuba, and Vietnam have in recent years sought a judicious blend of capitalistic profit and socialist political advantage from encouraging western tourism.

In the People's Republic that impetus has dramatically accelerated in the last ten years and is consistent with other pragmatic initiatives. Coming as it does in conjunction with normalization of relations with the United States and Japan and at the time when increased contact with the Republic of China (Taiwan) is desired, this policy is apparently directed at both its long-run economic prospects and the immediate political goodwill and publicity the new hospitality may garner.

The Soviet Union has similiar motivations in its efforts to promote tourism. On the economic side, the foreign exchange potential is obviously significant.

> A painstaking analysis by Soviet statisticians has revealed that the average profit, if that be the right word, from one tourist is equal to the export of nine tons of coal, fifteen tons of oil or two tons of grain. Further, if Lake Baikal were exploited as a tourist center, it would earn twice as much hard currency as the total export of oil from the USSR—without depleting its stocks of raw materials.[13]

At crucial intervals, however, the political advantages of tourism are paramount. The Soviet preparations for hosting the 1980 Summer Olympics demonstrated far greater government commitment and investment than could be justified by economic advantages. Indeed few Olympic sites have ever broken even. The value of hosting the Olympics rests with the forum it offers for demonstrating the strengths and achievements of the host society and the value of participating is designed to do the same. The People's Republic of China gains something when Americans and others line up for hours in Knoxville to see their World Fair exhibit. The PRC could have used the money spent on creating this most popular exhibit on scores of other projects, but in terms of public relations, the money could hardly have been better spent.

Another group of politically motivated nations includes such authoritarian non-Communist regimes as the Philippines under Marcos, South Korea, Republic of China, and Indonesia. Like the socialist nations these countries see in tourism a means of improving their international press notices. The 1988 Olympics in South Korea were expected to do as much before political unrest surfaced in 1987.[14] Publicity goals were clearly seen in the Philippine tourism slogan under Marcos, "Where Asia Wears a Smile," a promotion specifically designed to defuse criticisms of martial law and allay the fear of potential visitors as to their security.

Unlike socialist regimes, rightist regimes tend to encourage luxury tourism and convey a sense of the pleasures of capitalism rather than of more ascetic virtues. They are also more dependent for their stability and capital on the very Western nations that are the most active in the tourist trade. Conventions are encouraged for their economic value but also for the sense of political legitimacy that high tourist arrivals convey.

Neither the socialist nor the non-Communist regimes expect the tourist to be preoccupied with freedom of the press or other civil libertarian issues. They concentrate rather on conveying a sense of law and order and an impression of economic progress.

The United States has sought to use international tourism as a political weapon against the Soviet Union. American efforts to mobilize a boycott of the Moscow Olympic games as an international rebuke to the Soviets for the invasion of Afghanistan were intended to deny the USSR global respectability and prestige. Advocates of the boycott also saw the Olympic protest as a means of penetrating Soviet censorship and encouraging the domestic population to question the legitimacy of the Soviet presence in Afghanistan.

The Soviet Union tried to deny the United States a successful Olympics in 1984 by refusing to participate and encouraging other socialist countries to boycott. The Soviets used as their excuse a fear of inadequate security, seeking to capitalize on America's high crime rate and Southern California's reputation for anticommunist extremist groups. The United States charged, on the other hand, that in contrast to the U.S. Travel and Tourism Administration motto, "Travel, the Perfect Freedom," the Soviets feared that they could not control their participants and were afraid that numerous defections would take place.

On several other occasions the United States has sought to use tourism as a political weapon. The United States demonstrated opposition to the regimes of the PRC and Cuba by forbidding travel to those countries for many years. Now it is symptomatic of the desired change in political relationships that the United States has lifted the travel ban to the People's Republic of China, allowed some travel to Cuba, and has imposed a travel ban with respect to Libya. The United States has also written specific provisions for tourism into its treaties with countries like the Soviet Union, Egypt, and Romania where it hopes that international travel may provide an incentive for improved relations.[15]

Other political objectives have made tourism an attractive policy area for Israel. Given the nation's troubled history it has been important for the country to attract young and enthusiastic immigrants. Therefore much of the tourism infrastructure was designed for youthful interests and modest budgets. Such planning has been an apparent success. During the 1970s, over 10 percent of all tourists visiting Israel opted to immigrate there. Tourism is also encouraged as a boost to domestic morale. The existence of tourism affirms the nation's legitimacy and a faith in its internal security. The presence of visitors then keeps the citizens from succumbing to a garrison state mentality. Tourists also help to support cultural facilities that soften the harsh political realities and which could not be sustained by a purely domestic clientele.[16]

Moreover, tourism has been viewed as an important factor in the willingness of the United States to give defense aid to Israel. Tourism from the United States is the largest single factor in services trade in general and U.S.-Israel trade in particular.[17] This is consistent with findings in other countries that aid tends to flow disproportionately to nations with high tourist arrivals as compared to other nations of similar size and political importance. Although much of the aid has been bilateral and multipurpose, several nations and international organizations, including the World Bank, the United Nations Development Project (UNDP), and UNESCO have been instrumental in providing aid for tourism.[18]

Much more imagination is possible in aid-giving to Israel in particular and the Middle East in general and tourism has a role to play in that development. Consider, for example, regional marketing:

> Israel and Egypt are reluctant passengers in the same Mediterranean tourist boat. Both countries possess unique cultural attractions and relatively well-developed travel infrastructures. Their major problem in the next decade is not domestic capacity, it is foreign marketing. . . . Both Israel and Egypt would benefit by cooperative marketing of Israel-Egypt tours, especially for long-haul tourists from Japan and the United States. The catalyst and partner in regional marketing could be the United States. Both nations receive billions of dollars annually in development assistance which mostly goes into building plant and training, some of this going to the travel sector. A shift of a fraction of one percent of U.S. development assistance funds into regional tourism promotion schemes would do more to improve the export performance of both Israel and Egypt than a far greater increase into traditional development assistance projects.[19]

Neither country has oil wealth and in each tourism is the largest export sector. Still, like those in the discipline of political science, few in the U.S. State Department recognize tourism's strategic trade and diplomatic potential. "They are not sure what tourism trade is, but they are sure it is 'not in my department'."[20] The travel industry is more savvy—it was among the first to ignore the Arab boycott of Israel.

Government leaders have perceived of tourism as a political bridge among nations. For example, the tourist trade to Israel is important because it is heavily ethnic. Over 70 percent of all tourists from the United States to Israel are Jewish.[21] Travel to Israel tends to reinforce political support for the nation. Also, both Israel and Egypt have used tourism agreements as a way to encourage political acceptance of some of the more controversial aspects of the Camp David accords. By allowing Israelis to travel to favorite vacation spots in the southern Sinai both sides hope to convince Israeli citizens that political withdrawal from the Sinai will not mean the loss of access to the region for holidays.[22] The United States also negotiated a bilateral tourism treaty with Egypt in 1983 and considered a similar one with Israel in 1984. These would become operative in conjunction with a free trade area.[23]

Tourism has also been most important as a means of initiating or enlarging the scope of cooperative alliances with other nations through such bodies as the Association of Southeast Asian Nations (ASEAN), and UNESCO. For instance, ASEAN has set up a permanent committee on tourism, which is exploring the idea of an ASEAN passport, eased intraregional currency exchange and special fares, as well as the development of region-wide policy on tourism promotion.[24]

Still other international organizations expressly concerned with tourism have been active in lobbying international organizations and individual countries and have also launched their own tourism development initiatives within some countries. The World Tourism Organization (WTO), the Pacific Area Travel Association (PATA), and the Caribbean Tourism Association are three such examples.[25]

Additional international organizations whose tourism politics have been largely overlooked by political science are those multinational corporations including hotel chains, airlines, tour companies, and credit facilities, which have come to dictate fashion and prices in the billion dollar industry. Their relations with individual countries are of tremendous political importance as many have more financial assets than any other interest in the country. In some cases they actually represent more capital and borrowing power than the countries with which they negotiate.

Like the American Society of Travel Agents, such organizations, national or international, are not neutral as to ways in which the industry should be developed. Their perspective tends to favor large-scale enterprises and global marketing techniques that see the consumer, not the host communities, as relevant clientele. Though rhetoric assures the policymaker of all the attendant goods associated with tourism developments, the theme of a past PATA convention is more candid, "The Consumer: The Only One That Really Matters."

This short-range view of tourism that unfortunately is widespread in the industry is encouraged by the tax holidays, import policies, and credit policies that many nations have adopted to lure the giants of the tourist industry. In fact, the entire incentive structure gives primacy to quick returns and virtually no incentives for the companies to stay or expand or maintain good regional and national relations.[26]

Few political scientists have investigated the international ramifications of the corporate transnational structure. Consequently, the important variations that exist in financing, managing, and controlling tend to be blurred in largely sterile debates about the "goodness" or "badness" of multinational corporations. This is true of the tourist industry as well, though so far those even broaching the question have not been political scientists.[27] An important exception is Harry G. Matthews, whose book, *International Tourism: A Political and Social Analysis,* explores some of those issues for the Caribbean.[28]

So many questions of potential importance remain not only unanswered but unasked. Under what circumstances can tourism promote reconciliation among nations? Why is it so often the earliest component of a normalization process between two nations? To what extent does becoming a host nation improve national understanding of other societies? Under what conditions does tourism intensify hostility, friction, and feelings of relative deprivation? How and by what process do travelers' views become politically important? Is the new leisure class, the tourist, politically significant?[29] If so, is it the social class of tourists, their numbers, their country of origin, or some combination of these that makes them a political force? Are empathy, contempt, noblesse oblige, and indifference fostered by travel in poor countries? Does political influence depend on the proximity of the country to one's own, for example, Americans in Mexico or Cuba, on cultural affinity, on the type of tourism, or on age and social background of guests?

Too many millions are traveling for the political importance of their movements to go unexamined. Indeed, it is ironic that one of the earliest groups to recognize the political importance of international tourism was the terrorist.[30] Tourists are particularly useful to terrorists because they greatly alter the political stakes by spreading the conflict beyond the terrorist's immediate quarrel with the political establishment. The countries from which the tourists come almost always become involved. Regardless of the nation's attitudes, this intensifies the pressure on the host government. The political views of the terrorists also get an exposure well beyond what they could otherwise anticipate. Since terrorism is often a response to limited alternative avenues for political expression, terrorism against one's own citizens may in fact go unmentioned by media controlled by the hostile government. When nationals of other countries are involved, news coverage is much more likely. Japan and the United States, for example, have heavily publicized incidents in which their nationals were held by terrorists abroad.[31]

Though acts of terrorism against international tourists increase political pressure on the government coping with them, terrorism actually reduces the pressure and potential for political backlash against the terrorists. This is because such terrorist actions have little or no direct

impact on fellow citizens. For example, the rash of arson attacks on luxury hotels in Manila cost the terrorists little in local goodwill, since few
Filipinos could enjoy such hotels. It was also a particularly adroit choice
because of the president's financial links to the hotels hit. Similarly, the
1985 TWA hijacking in Lebanon boosted the political prestige of the
Shiite faction responsible.

Even though many of those involved would be apprehended, the damage to the tourist industry was a telling blow. Unlike terrorism involving
other economic sectors, tourism is especially vulnerable, because there
are always alternative places to visit. Since what is being sold is relaxation or at least enjoyment, any hint of insecurity about a destination can
cripple the industry. A bombing in Manila of the American Society of
Travel Agents convention in 1980 sent a special convulsion through the
industry because it once again demonstrated the ease with which terrorism could disrupt a vital economic sector by precisely targeting those
most influential in tourist marketing.[32]

Research should also be involved in determining areas of potential collaboration for improved and facilitated international travel. Several areas
illustrate the potential for such involvement. First, governments have a
wide range of tolls that can expedite or impede international travel flows.
These need to be studied for their political and economic consequences.
Among these are (1) exit taxes, (2) passport charges, (3) visa requirements, (4) foreign exchange restrictions, and (5) exit and entry regulations.[33] Although some regional groups, such as the Common Market
and ASEAN, have studied these issues, few scholars have examined their
obvious relationship to international travel, protectionism, and immigration.

Second, national and international travel laws have not had much
attention.[34] Although admiralty law, aviation law, and hotel law have
been around for some time, most travel law is new and explosive. The
regulatory power of state, federal, and even international bodies will be
sorely tested in the next generation as legislation and the courts attempt
to keep up with the wandering consumer and the industry. As one author
noted, "by conservative estimate there are at least 100,000 solid travel
cases (in the U.S.) just lying fallow for want of interested and motivated
counsel."[35] With treaties like the Helsinki Accords, the Warsaw Convention, and hundreds of minor agreements and laws at stake, scholars are
missing an important arena of international and diplomatic significance
for research and employment.

Third, it is important to examine if, how, and in what ways international travel affects (1) parochialism, (2) stereotypes about nations, and
(3) interest and political activity. It has been one of the hardier myths of

tourism that travel encourages peace, goodwill, and international understanding, but little empirical work has been done to demonstrate the
validity of the myth or to determine under what types of touristic conditions cultural learning or understanding is facilitated or frustrated. Nor
do we know the extent to which receiving countries come to internalize
the stereotypes sold in the tourist brochures. Something may be happening, particularly in the developing nations where there is such a discrep-
ancy in the economic power of the tourist and the resident, but as yet little research has been done. With world spending since 1981 for domestic
and international travel now exceeding world spending for military purposes, someone should be exploring the impact of tourism on international politics.[36]

PUBLIC ADMINISTRATION

Tourism may appear an unlikely topic for public administration but it is
increasingly relevant to the public sector. In Europe and Asia, public
administration and management programs in tourism development have
been available for some time. As subsequent chapters in this volume will
demonstrate, the role of the bureaucracy in tourist planning, implementation, and monitoring can be critical in virtually all kinds of political
systems. But until quite recently in the United States, tourism was a subject academically housed, if at all, in the business schools, in departments
of leisure studies, or occasionally in hotel and restaurant management
programs.

Lack of government interest in tourism meant that public sector training in tourism was all but ignored. This is changing today. Cities, countries, states, and even national governments and international organizations are accelerating public programs of tourism development and
management. In many countries, in United Nations agencies, and in
other organizations assisting tourism development, there is an acute
shortage of administrative talent with any knowledge of both tourism
and political science.

Yet, as we examine what can go wrong and right in tourism, it will be
clear that where tourism succeeds or fails is largely a function of political
and administrative action and is not a function of economic or business
expertise. Faced with shortages of personnel with requisite backgrounds,
governments are forced to rely on the scarcely disinterested advice of the
travel industry. Although a reasonable source of information on promotion and development, the industry cannot be faulted for not considering
the social and political factors it was never equipped to examine. Indus-

try needs and the public interest may well be compatible in many instances, but the industry is not designed to think first in terms of the public as public agencies are charged with doing.

The stimulus to monitor as opposed to simply develop tourism policies must come primarily from government leadership, not the bureaucracy.

> A central intention of bureaucratic functionaries in any modern social or economic system is to achieve personal career stability. One rule of bureaucratic survival is to minimize risk by employing standard and accepted methods of administration, problem-solving, and decision-making. The dangers of being responsible for judgements can frequently be reduced by having what appear to be "hard" quantitative data to apply to a statistical set of decision criteria.[37]

Even government leaders need to guard against overly optimistic conclusions based only on arrivals and expenditures and promotion costs. The more difficult social measures will require more subtle analysis.

Some public administrative structures are better equipped to cope with the implementation of tourist policy. Public sector responsibilities for tourism, for example, have a more lengthy and elaborate history in Scandinavia and the socialist countries than elsewhere.

The basic ability of the public service to perform basic services may also have a telling effect on tourism.

> These are analogous to the *hygiene factors* in Herzberg's theories of motivation; that is there are some factors which do not positively motivate tourists . . . but where they are absent tourists will be put off. A good example is sewage facilities. Tourists are unlikely to visit a destination because it has good clean sewage treatment, but if that treatment is not there then tourists will vanish. This is exactly what happened along the Neapolitan Riviera coast in Italy, where the sea became badly polluted.[38]

Crime levels, friendliness of residents, safe roads, and beautiful parks are other examples of conditions that well-monitored public administered tourism development can effect to influence visitor satisfaction and resident acceptance of tourism.

For these and so many other reasons, public administration is assuming an expanding role in tourism development that is not yet reflected in commensurate training for public administration professions. There is no reason why tourism management should not be as credible and attractive as a specialty area for public administration majors as gerontology, public health, criminal justice, planning, and public finance. In fact, as governments, especially state and city governments, take on more responsibility for tourism development, there is a tendency to take on additional administrative roles for convention management, new taxation initiatives and expanded land use, and labor-management decisions specifically affecting tourism. Health, recreation, and security issues impacting on tourism follow. In developing nations, many of which have a general shortage of administrative talent, scarce "slots" for study abroad are being reserved for those who will study tourism administration.[39]

The absence of interest in the United States has prevented curricula of tourism administration from considering tourism as a public sector activity. Moreover, the failure to distinguish between public and private sector tourism administration has meant that the public interest in balanced and long-range tourism development has often been subordinated to policies insufficiently integrated with overall economic and political goals.

POLICY STUDIES

One of the fastest growing areas in political science is policy analysis, but, scholarly attention to tourism as a policy sector has been almost exclusively the domain of economists, anthropologists, and planners. Although it is in developed nations that tourist travel flourishes most successfully, it is also in developed nations that a base exists for domestic travel. Tourism is potentially elastic in character, making domestic travel all the more important to developed nations during times of economic recession, when overseas arrivals may drop. Moreover, factors encouraging leisure travel (degree of education, income, and urbanization) are on the increase in almost all nations. Room for growth is also indicated in the variance in travel by residents of affluent countries. Whereas 60 percent of Great Britain's and Scandinavia's populations take annual vacations, less than 50 percent do in the United States.

We need to know far more about the tourism policy-making process. What we do know suggests that it may share many commonalities with other policy sectors within a nation. This is not surprising. As Douglas Ashford tells us:

> One of the most intriguing findings of comparative policy analysis is that what a country is doing seems to have little association with how it does it. There is probably more similarity across policies for one country in how policies are found and implemented than there is for the same policy across several countries.[40]

There are also some interesting differences, however, at least with respect to the initial policy decisions regarding tourism development, particularly in developing countries. Conventional wisdom usually stresses the "hard choices" confronting beleaguered policymakers. The endless demands and the severe budgetary and political constraints make policy-making characteristically crisis-driven or the outcome of shared poverty. Policy is described, then, as something one must make decisions about. In most nations, tourism policy is not like this and therein lies a powerful reason for its appeal.

Tourism is a chosen policy.[41] It is not a policy forced upon a reluctant regime by political pressures like agrarian reform, language policy, or some industrial policies. This may be one of the reasons that tourism policy has been neglected by students of the policy process. In its initial stages there is often little apparent conflict over policy. Tourism is a policy with apparently substantial rewards and few interests to placate or offend. By manipulating visas, currency regulations, internal access, and export and import procedures one can theoretically control the clientele, the level of spending, and the type of facilities provided—all with little if any public reaction. Tourism tends to become a subject of political debate late in the implementation process when major social costs become apparent.

Still, not all nations are equally sanguine about the development of international tourism. Some, like Burma, Nepal, and Bhutan, open their doors only when their lack of alternative developmental options make tourism sufficiently palatable. Others, like Saudi Arabia, enjoy few economic constraints and being uneasy about tourism simply choose not to issue tourist visas. Tourism development then is a policy area only if political elites decide it will be. But the reasons for selecting tourism are not constant among nations or, from regime to regime, within a nation. Nor are governments agreed on a particular pattern of tourism development. This will become especially obvious when, in later chapters, we will consider the politics of tourism development in specific countries.

For many governments the explicit impetus for encouraging tourism is economic. Tourism is sold by the international travel industry as a noncontroversial way to accrue foreign exchange without losing nonrenewable resources. Tourism is as elastic in demand as most agricultural products are not and as a service industry it is assumed, sometimes erroneously, to be labor intensive.[42] It is argued that the tourist dollar, via the multiplier effect, infuses the economy with several times the original dollar's value before its impact fades. Unlike other economic policies, tourism supposedly attracts foreign capital easily, requiring only the kind of inducements most developing nations are willing to accept, for example, tax holidays.

Regardless of initial motivation, the political impact of tourism is extremely important—how important, social scientists are just beginning to discover. Systematic, empirical studies are still quite rare and tend to be focused on easily measured quantitative criteria such as arrivals, expenditures, number of complaints, length of stay, and crime statistics. Even when whole policies of tourism promotion are studied, the emphasis is on efficiency rather than effectiveness, and gross economic revenue rather than net economic value.[43]

The reason for this is not hard to find. It is far easier to tally gross receipts than to measure the net contribution or cost of a policy, tallying not only promotional and administrative costs, but also broad social and psychological costs and benefits.

It is also politically appealing, containing a pro-business bias that is hard to resist and a pervasive boosterism that is common in most nations and locales, particularly capitalist ones. Using numbers gives an aura of simplicity as well as objectivity. Finally, arriving at a consensus for alternative measures has had little attention and less success. In the chapter that dissects Philippine tourism policy it is particularly obvious that how one stands on such a policy depends on where one sits.

> No matter how great the tourist industry looks to the World Bank official from the twentieth floor suite of the Manila Hilton, the view from the bottom is something else again. Luxury tourist accommodations run by TWA don't promise any more in the way of adequate economic development than do copper mines run by Kennecott or Mustang assembly plants run by Ford.[44]

The perceived consequences of tourism vary tremendously and appear to be a function of the policy examined, the level of analysis, the time frame, and of course, the ideological, occupational, and disciplinary bias of the person doing the critique. This study will be no exception. It is hoped, however, that the reader will find the conclusions well-grounded.

Most of those writing about tourism policies and their impact in developing nations tend to be quite negative about tourism's effect, especially the anthropologists who seem especially partisan toward cultural continuity and quite hostile toward the travel industry in general and tourists in particular.

Yet even Dennison Nash, an anthropologist who most eloquently makes the case that tourism is imperialistic in developing nations, has acknowledged that many anthropological critiques "reveal a kind of 'knee-jerk' response to the 'imposition' of tourism in their favorite societies." He labels such conclusions "prescientific." He cites sociologists that have come to quite optimistic conclusions about tourism in some developing areas while others have found results mixed.[45]

Tourism policies are being adopted and actively pursued by virtually 99 percent of all urban areas on the globe and thousands of rural areas.

Even locales consciously opting not to promote tourism are in effect pursuing a type of policy. Given the incomplete record of tourism's impact and its potential for both negative and positive effects, it is clearly appropriate that political scientists examine this sector.

Policy recommendations of the World Bank, the United Nations Development Project, the Organization for Economic Cooperation and Development (OECD), and the World Tourism Organization are but a few places to begin exploring the political ramifications of various approaches to tourism policy both within and among nations.

What kinds of political issues may be subsumed under the rubric of tourism policy?—national free time policies for one. The flip side of the right to work guarantees of many constitutions is the right to leisure. Paid leave, holidays, and free time are actually written as rights into the constitutions of 65 nations, while others reflect rights to leisure and travel in their legislation.[46]

The variety among nations is striking. The generous West German approach, for example, is considered by some to be "a reaction against a history of domination by a strong centralized and totalitarian regime." As in the United States, with its very different political history, little national direction is involved, but both countries are noted for their active pursuit of leisure and travel. Sweden, on the other hand, "is probably the only western country where the educational objectives include the preparation for leisure. . . . Virtually all Swedish municipalities have special leisure departments."[47] In Norway, cultural, tourism, and recreational policy in general are integrated.

In socialist Eastern Europe and the Soviet Union, leisure and tourism, like work, are directed at the development of the socialist person. As such they are seen as too important not to be planned by the state. "The activities of the citizens' free time . . . must be planned and, wherever possible, executed collectively."[48] With all of these nations, the primary focus of leisure or tourism policy is the resident not the visitor. Unfortunately, the reverse is usually true in developing countries where tourism's role is to earn from foreigners, not to invigorate, renew, or strengthen residents.

Tourism policies in particular and leisure policies in general are also closely related to national and regional environmental policies. The U.S. experience is instructive.

> In the past, laws have dealt almost exclusively with the pollution of air and water and with the management of *publicly*-owned land. These laws have left virtually unregulated the 73.7 percent of the contiguous 48 states that is privately owned. . . . Second-home development along the California coast has cut off all but 25 percent of the state's 1072 miles of shoreline.[49]

Time-sharing vacation spots, convention establishments, and family second homes are playing havoc with the ecosystem. Why?

> The answer is simple: the states have delegated their authority to supervise land-use to 78,217 units of local government. These local units support themselves mainly by taxing land. As a consequence, they are constantly searching for opportunities to develop the land, increase its assessed value and make it produce more in taxes. Thus the basic fact of private land development . . . is that some of the very units of government that are charged with controlling land use may be the ones most susceptible to pressures not to control it.[50]

Just in this one area of tourism and recreational land use the possibilities for political science policy research are numerous. Shafer suggests several: What kind of quasi-public structures, taxation, and controls are needed to balance the needs of society? In what areas is compromise most appropriate and least damaging? How can touristic land use and other land use needs be integrated?[51]

The unfashionable but ever so useful case study undertaken at the local level is desperately needed if an appropriate data base is to emerge. Such studies also have the heuristic advantage of being relatively inexpensive to develop and affording students a hands-on experience in dissecting and analyzing a growing and exciting political topic.

Political scientists may fear that tax deductible research on Cancún or the World's Fairs may appear as junkets, but their concerns are misplaced. There is plenty of legitimate, exciting research to be done. Political impact studies in Gstaad are no less relevant than those in New Haven, for communities coping with tourism are in fact much more numerous and usually at least as complex as college towns.[52] In fact, they may be both, as are such American cities as Santa Cruz, La Jolla, and Tempe. Even those nations, states, and cities that are most laissez-faire in their attitudes toward tourism are still forced by the political, cultural, and economic magnitude of tourism to develop policies for its expansion, control, and contribution to the political system. Often the decisions taken generate too little interest until massive social effects are experienced. Research is critically needed if the public interest not to mention the public treasury is to be protected.

This book is intended as an exploratory study of the political dimensions of tourism development. It is designed to be neither exhaustive nor precisely comparative, but rather suggestive of the types of political considerations and policy dynamics often overlooked in economic or social impact studies of tourism.

Those studies have contributed a great deal to our understanding of tourism and this research benefits greatly from the insights of other scholars and disciplines on this topic. Because the interdisciplinary nature of research is so important to examining this little understood subject of tourist development, a lengthy bibliography of the sources used is provided.

Missing from other studies, however, have been explanations of tourism policy that evaluate success or failure except in economic or occasionally social terms. Typically, arrivals, receipts, length of stay, and market share have been the overwhelming criteria by which government policymakers, the travel industry, and the attentive public have judged tourism policy. If available, the number of jobs created is mentioned. Occasionally policies are judged in terms of environmental impact or in terms of foreign exchange, balance-of-payments perspectives.

Sometimes a policy is judged in terms of its impact on other policy sectors such as education, housing, energy, transportation, and historical preservation. Such references are usually impressionistic, nonsystematic, and not conducted by government request or support. Rarely is a policy judged in terms of resident satisfaction, and then such studies are usually done by academics unconnected to policy-making.[53]

Tourism policies frequently fail, especially in developing nations, in terms of contributing to genuine development of the country. Often they are expensive, capital-intensive, import-driven, seasonal, given to excessive foreign exchange leakage and subject to well-documented negative social effects. And yet these same policy "mistakes" are made over and over again.

In the 1960s, when mass travel began, Europe received the brunt of the new "hordes." European countries generally had diversified economies with a variety of tourist infrastructure with hard currencies, low unemployment, and a good standard of living. Developing countries tried to offer basic amenities but had little traffic and certainly little time to invest in research on tourism. Ignorance and inexperience were assumed to be the problem with tourism debacles.

In the 1970s mass tourism became a reality in a majority of developing nations and the horror stories concerning its impact began emerging. Once the problems were clear, policy should have improved, but it often did not. In the 1980s there has been precious little evidence that tourism policy, even if more elaborate, is any more likely to cope with the problems so often associated with tourism. Why is this so?

THE APPROACH OF THIS VOLUME

This book contends that research has bypassed the political reasons that tourism is pursued and developed in ways often seen as dysfunctional in economic and social terms. Seldom are policies scrutinized in terms of what Harold Lasswell says are the core issues of politics—who gets what, when, and how. Seldom is tourism considered in terms of the political needs of those who wield power or of the government as a whole. Such needs are not publicly articulated like economic objectives are, but that makes them no less salient in policy development, implementation, and evaluation. In all disciplines scholars of tourism have complained that their particular discipline has treated tourism research as frivolous. No social science discipline has evinced less interest in tourism than political science.[54]

Most political scientists have ignored the topic and only a few others have considered the political dimensions.[55] Because the political goals are usually covert and unarticulated and because data collection generally excludes taxpayers, political goals of the leadership, influence, public support, partisan or minority attitudes, opposition reaction, external political climate, or net value and allocation of tourism receipts, it is not too surprising that tourism failures and even tourism policy successes are poorly and inadequately evaluated.

As we will see in later chapters, the political interests are such that leadership does not ask policy analysts or outside consultants, "is it wise to develop tourism?" but rather "how can we develop it quickly to show-case our nation's attractions and bring in big bucks" (or yen, or francs). This was brought home to me when I was asked about consulting on tourism development in Belize. A cursory reading on the country led me to conclude that at that juncture it needed a sewage system for its capital city before it needed to develop tourism. I was not ready to answer the only question they wanted answered. Later I discovered that another tourism consultant from New Zealand had told them the same thing in an earlier full-scale report. It was shelved. Eventually, a tourism consultant will help Belize develop tourism. It is less certain when someone will help Belize develop Belize.

The point is that scholars, policymakers, the travel industry, and community leaders need to understand that there is often a political agenda— wise or foolish, benign or selfish, compatible or incompatible—underlying the explicit tourism program. It cannot be eliminated and in many cases is laudable in intent, but it should be factored into planning, implementation, and the monitoring and evaluation of tourism development projects.

When this happens, some disasters can be avoided, such as committing resources to developing tourism in politically unstable societies; some political posturing can be channeled into less showy but more cost-effective tourism projects; some tourism can be developed at a different pace and at a scale commensurate with local needs; touristic events can be planned with greater sensitivity to international reaction, and so on. The possibilities are endless.

To explore the many ramifications of political variables on tourism development, a number of organizing strategies were theoretically possible for this volume.[56] From a practical standpoint my options were more limited. Therefore, my first delimiting decision was to focus on government policies in developing nations. Poor nations are the latecomers to tourism development and the ones who pay the greatest costs for failed policies and who most need successful policies. The selection of Asian nations was based partially on the fact that growth in tourism has been disproportionately rapid in this area. Many such countries seize upon tourism (most too uncritically I fear) as a means of funding future development by capitalizing on the present underdevelopment of beaches, mountains, and historic sites. In terms of the theory of comparative advantage this makes sense. Countries are making their very underdevelopment an economic asset by selling unspoiled, exotic destinations.

In fact, in a tally of revenues (as opposed to costs) from international tourism David Edgell reports that international tourism was proportionately "more important for developing countries than for industrialized countries, accounting for about one-third of their services trade. It was the largest of four major service categories for the non-oil-exporting countries."[57] On the whole such nations had a surplus in their travel accounts whereas most developed countries had a deficit.

Since I have lived for several years in India, Pakistan, and the Philippines, it was also natural that I build on earlier tourism research work in those nations. Four other countries included here, Thailand, Nepal, Sri Lanka, and the People's Republic of China are ones in which I have traveled and conducted research. Only for Bangladesh, the Maldives, and Bhutan was I forced to rely exclusively on secondary sources.

The Asian countries chosen represent a variety of political uses of tourism, some ostensibly directed at important national goals of political integration, independence, cultural preservation, and economic development. Some policies are destined primarily for the political aggrandizement and power of the chief executive. Communist, Catholic, Hindu, Buddhist, and Muslim governments are represented. The countries range in size from the world's most populous to one of the smallest, from huge continental masses and landlocked mountain nations to islands and archipelagoes. They are, in short, a representation of two-fifths of the globe's people, with all its diversity and problems.

Assessing the politics of tourism development in 10 Asian countries has to be an exploratory task for a single researcher and I make no apologies for the fact that it is not definitive or comprehensive. What I hope the country studies will provide is a base for further political science research on tourism in these nations and an awareness of the complexity and multifaceted nature of tourism politics.

Although my research has focused on Asia, the examples of tourism politics within these countries are by no means confined to these nations. If massive overbuilding of luxury tourist infrastructure had political objectives in the Philippines, it is no less the case in both Koreas or in many U.S. cities. If Thailand's sex tourism is a political embarrassment for the monarchy, it is no less a political bombshell for Japanese leaders who face angry citizens in other countries where Japanese sex tours have been active. If tourism is a means of fostering national identity, as in Pakistan and Bhutan, it is also the case in the Dominican Republic and Andorra. If preserving political and religious culture is important to the Maldives, it is even more true in countries such as Saudi Arabia that allow only religious tourism but still have not been immune to its exploitation for political purposes.[58]

The "edifice complex" of convention centers, sports arenas, and exhibit halls is not a political aberration of banana republic dictators. Developed nations such as the United States are equally infatuated with mega-development, no matter how divorced from economic reality. Convention centers are but one example. Almost every U.S. city of any size has government officials or community leaders who see such centers as priceless in prestige. Never mind that in 1984 not a single convention center in the U.S. made money, in Honolulu and at least a dozen other cities officials were contemplating such an investment.[59]

The announced rationale is always economic. If revenues are not generated from the center itself, then they will accrue from the "spillover effect" of large conventions. The political objectives and pressures are usually not mentioned. The social costs and economic risks are pooh-poohed as the whines of no-growth naysayers. Yet, it takes no elaborate econometric model for policymakers to realize that less than 1 percent of the convention market needs facilities in excess of one large hotel. Most conventions rotate locales and there is such a glut of convention center space that most centers do the bulk of their business with smaller conventions that would otherwise be in a local hotel. Convention centers may generate public works and may be politically valuable to the leadership, but the economic rationale rarely holds water.

This leads to another aspect of this book—the activities and critique of tourism's loyal opposition. If tourism policy does not integrate or anticipate its political component, then policies and the people affected by them will suffer. Critics of current tourism policies are becoming aware and are more than a little cynical about the excesses and "mistakes" occasioned by national tourism development schemes. Some of these people are those directly hurt by government policies. Many have little power.

Others are policymakers, travel industry experts, philanthropic and development workers, teachers, social workers, and writers. Many are organizing in dozens of forums to challenge government assumptions about tourism policy and to suggest and develop alternatives to the status quo. They are using political techniques and strategies in many cases to confront what they see as unwise or incomplete policies. The final chapter of this volume documents the thrust of their critique and the response of one global network to it.

St. Augustine once said that "The world is a book. He who stays at home reads only one page." Similarly, those policymakers who make tourism policy by simply repeating a common formula may think they have provided an answer, but without comparing, searching, and probing the experience of other societies, that answer is surely limited and could well be wrong.

2

About Face: The Political Evolution of Chinese Tourism Policy

You can't go further than China.
—A Chinese proverb

NOT ONLY is it difficult to go further than the People's Republic of China (PRC) in terms of culture and political heritage, for three decades most travelers were forbidden from going there at all. Yet in the 1980s this bastion of communism has become the unlikely "hot" destination for tourists.

The political decisions that have led to this improbable tourism boom illustrate the volatility of Chinese policy-making and the massive re-evaluation of acceptable strategies that is currently underway.

The topic is not an easy one to investigate, because unlike most of the other countries this book examines, the PRC remains a closed society with information other societies consider totally innocuous treated as *neibu* (restricted materials).[1] Even the telephone book for the PRC (about the size for a U.S. town of 50,000) is not a public document. So-called public buildings are not, and even published accounts designed for foreign readers are often, as we shall see later, more cryptic than candid. Illustrative of the frustration many feel when attempting to use Chinese sources is one article on Chinese joint ventures entitled "Data: the Figures, not Necessarily the Facts."[2] Not only is information scarce, Chinese tourism policy is in a considerable state of flux, making it difficult for researchers and politically unnerving for those in Chinese tourism administration to say with great certainty what directions the policy will take.[3] This is a problem consistent with policy-making for other sectors of the economy.

This chapter is based on my travels and interviews in eastern China in 1981 as well as on dozens of accounts and analyses of Chinese scholars and tourism specialists who have been there either before or since. These form an interesting and complex mosaic, but scarcely a completed puzzle. Keeping those caveats in mind, I will boldly plunge ahead (one is tempted to call it in this context "A Great Leap Forward") to outline the evolution and probable impact of mass tourism on Chinese developmental goals.

BACKGROUND

Chinese tourism policy from the 1949 establishment of the People's Republic of China until 1977 can be summarized as cautious at best and characteristically negative in nature—the fewer outsiders the better. This attitude was not unreasonable. For most of the first two decades of the PRC's existence, major tourist-generating countries were unrelievedly hostile to the communist regime. Travel to the PRC was forbidden by the United States and many other western governments. China reciprocated by generally denying entry to most foreigners. Chinese opposition further hardened and enlarged when Chinese troops fought against United Nations troops in Korea.

By 1953, however, the government began the first of several tentative steps designed to allow travel to the PRC. The Beijing Overseas Chinese Travel Service was created to manage overseas Chinese who were seeking to visit relatives and friends.[4] The government continues to have a distinct organization, separate accommodations, and a generally separate tourism apparatus for overseas Chinese.

In 1954, China International Travel Service (CITS) was established to shepherd groups of "foreign friends" to a few sites. Although CITS branches were set up in several major cities, tourism of this kind remained essentially a public relations exchange with representatives of a few friendly countries.

In the early 1960s the PRC, it is now claimed by post-Mao tourism officials, was eager to increase tourism. A General Overseas Chinese Travel Service was set up in 1963 (no one ever explained what this new reincarnation was designed to do over its predecessor) and The China Bureau of Travel and Tourism, under the State Council, was established a year later. Still, tourism was scarcely in a "take-off mode," as figures show that, in 1966, CITS still handled no more than 4,500 foreign tourists.[5]

CITS was and is today essentially modeled on the assumptions that Chinese governments from the time of Confucious to the era of Mao Zedong have had about foreigners in general, namely that foreign access to Chinese society should be delimited. Some have seen this as a result of xenophobia or a fear of manipulation by outsiders. Others have seen the intention as more political than psychological. First, there was the overall belief that important travelers should not go unescorted, regardless of the regime. The language barrier was part of the reasoning, but more importantly, escorts assured that tourists would not have contact with Chinese who might offer contradictory interpretations of political reality.

> Historically, Chinese governments have gone to no end of trouble to keep foreigners and Chinese citizens apart, so the Communists cannot be accused of inventing the practice. They do, however, have a genius for coopting historical precedents like this and transforming them into rigid institutions.[6]

Second, these groups were screened for their sympathy to the regime, then billeted in quarters built for the huge Soviet aid contingents prominent in the 1950s. Until the mid-1980s, hotels built in the ponderous Stalinist style of architecture, often capped incongruously by traditional Chinese roofs, formed the core of the tourist accommodations in key cities.

The Great Leap Forward (1958–1960) and the Cultural Revolution (1965–1970)[7] made the expansion of tourism a non-issue. Priorities were elsewhere. The highly touted Nixon visit and the invitation to the U.S. table tennis team notwithstanding, the United States did not recognize the People's Republic of China until 1978, although it did drop its barriers to travel there in 1972. In general, only formal exchange visits, a few sympathetic writers, and some business people on specific assignments were allowed to visit the PRC before 1977.

In 1974, the China Travel Service (CTS) replaced the General Overseas Chinese Travel Service. Indeed about the only tourist activity seemed to be in terms of the overseas Chinese, about which little information is available in non-Chinese sources. The CITS, on the other hand, after 22 years of existence, had direct travel contacts with only six Japanese travel agencies and a handful of western organizations such as friendship associations.[8]

As late as 1976 Vice-Premier Li Xiannian told a visiting American political figure that the PRC was not planning to expand tourism in the foreseeable future. But, within months, the policy abruptly changed. The death of Mao Zedong ended the influence of Jiang Qing, Mao's wife, and three other leftist leaders. These activists, since branded the Gang of Four, had been credited with some of the worst excesses of the Cultural Revolution. They had also been harsh critics of Deng Xiaoping, whom they attacked for "capitalist tendencies." It was just those tendencies that resurfaced in the form of policy when Deng was made vice-premier, vice-chairman of the party and chief of staff of the People's Liberation Army.

Chinese sources simply announce that the beginning of tourism as an industry began with the third session of the eleventh Congress of the Central Committee of the Communist Party of China in 1978.[9] It was at that congress that the party officially endorsed the "Four Modernizations."

The new label signalled a four-pronged effort to rapidly modernize agriculture, industry, national defense, and science and technology. Although couched in party rhetoric, the Four Modernizations represented the latest and certainly the most pragmatic campaign designed to mobilize the billion-plus Chinese citizens. Tourism was one of the sectors most dramatically affected by the new program.

Though today it is fashionable in the PRC to date all positive change in recent years from the fall of the Gang of Four, such scapegoating distorts history. The PRC's isolation from global relations had been eroding for years. The 1971 admission of the country into the United Nations accelerated diplomatic recognition between the PRC and scores of nations. The thaw in U.S.-China relations had begun. The less ideological stance of Deng simply encouraged the West and Japan to feel that expanded trade was feasible. The PRC saw the expansion of tourism as a logical component of its post-Cultural Revolution normalization strategy. Also, tourism, as the *People's Daily* put it, "not only promotes mutual understanding and friendship," but "accumulates funds for the splendid plan of our Four Modernizations."[10]

Six months after Mao's death Western cruise ships were visiting Chinese ports for the first time in 30 years. The China Travel Service and CITS had begun to struggle with hundreds of thousands of visa requests. In January, 1978, the first national conference on tourism was held to formulate guidelines and organizational details to cope with the pent-up demand. Implementing them would, however, prove an incredible task. In 1978 CITS handled 124,000 foreign tourists, a figure equivalent to the total it had dealt with in the previous 24 years of its existence! Between 1977 and 1980 tourist arrivals doubled each year.[11] From 1980 to 1985 growth averaged 21 percent, slowing to a quite impressive 8.5 percent in 1986 (see Table 2.1). Between 1977 and 1986 there was little doubt that the PRC was making every effort to expand its tourist infrastructure and training capabilities. Crash courses in English and Japanese were set up to meet the needs of guides and for other commercial contacts. By 1987, 10 percent of all Chinese were studying English.[12]

Unprecedented joint ventures with Western capitalist firms were being established. Their guidelines, established by the Fifth National People's Congress, were rather strange from a Western perspective. There had to be a minimum 25 percent foreign ownership but no upper levels were specified, nor was there anything definite on taxation and profits. The vagueness was less a product of wily maneuvering on the part of the Chinese than a reflection of the country's lack of a framework for commercial law.[13]

Once the details were filled in, many of the early hotel agreements fell through. From the international travel industry's point of view, the Chi-

Table 2.1. Visitor arrivals (in thousands) in the People's Republic
of China, 1978–1985.

	1979	1980	1981	1982	1983	1984	1985	1986
Foreigners[a]	362	529	675	765	873	1,134	1,370	1,480
Overseas Chinese	21	34	39	43	40	47	85	
Hongkong/ Macau/Taiwan[b]	3,821	5,139	7,053	7,117	8,564	11,718	16,379	21,330
Total[c]	4,200	5,700	7,770	7,920	9,480	12,850	17,830[d]	22,800
Received by CITS	164	219	268	316	320	380	469	n.a.
Received by CTS	806	695	886	865	908	826	773	n.a.
Received by CYTS	n.a.	n.a.	n.a.	24	29	47	52	n.a.

NOTES: a. Non-Chinese.
    b. Chinese from these three areas.
    c. Figures are rounded off.
    d. Revenues were more than $13 billion.
    n.a. = not available.
SOURCE: NTA and Far Eastern Economic Review, *Asia Yearbook, 1987,* p. 130.

nese simply wanted to allow the hotels too short a time in which to recover initial costs and a modest profit. Now most agreements are in terms of management contracts.[14] Although the exact terms of foreign investment took an inordinate amount of time to develop, the amazing fact was that those investments were occurring at all in a country that for 30 years had forbidden foreign ownership or even much private Chinese ownership within its borders. Moreover, by 1980 hotels proved to be extremely lucrative investments for foreign capital since they combined high demand, low building costs, and cheap labor, with the ease of repatriating profits.[15] The latter advantage, however, suggests that the PRC may be losing foreign exchange in the process.

Another reversal took place in the training of personnel to staff the burgeoning tourist infrastructure. The Cultural Revolution had for years inculcated a hostility toward people and things western. That approach was unceremoniously junked. Maxims preaching friendliness, service, and courtesy toward "foreign friends" sprung up everywhere. Not only chefs but some waiters were sent to Hong Kong for polishing in cuisine and etiquette. Special schools of tourism were established near Beijing and several other cities and tourism representatives were sent abroad for courses on tourism or on fact-finding tours to learn from more established tourism centers, such as that at Cornell University in New York.[16]

Of course what was happening in tourism policy was only a microcosm of what was happening in Chinese society at large. The previous major thrusts in Chinese policy since 1949, the Great Leap Forward and the Cultural Revolution, caused convulsive changes and massive political strife. In hindsight they seem dismal failures. Though the Cultural Revolution had a high economic growth rate, its disruption of the educational process is even now felt in most sectors where people in their thirties and forties lack basic training. The Four Modernizations, although certainly a sweeping departure from the policies of the Cultural Revolution, seem by contrast almost totally lacking in ideological content.[17]

What surprises Westerners is, in fact, the result of our tendency to take a historical approach to politics. Sinologists, by definition a group used to the big picture, argue that even the communist system, let alone the Four Modernizations, does not represent a fundamental break in Chinese tradition. They contend that China has for centuries been a centrally directed bureaucratic state "given to abrupt and sweeping changes in policy and in its relations with the outside world."[18]

This period of dramatic economic change also ushered in a comparatively liberal era in domestic policy. Letters to the editor occasionally criticized the window dressing for tourists and chided the regime on its preoccupation with tourist needs. The Chinese were stunned by the famous *dazibao,* or big character posters, with their mild expressions of criticism and requests for regime action on several issues. But the Xidan Democracy Wall, where the posters flourished for several months, became in 1980 just another wall for advertising. By 1981, my Beijing guide professed never to have heard of the Democracy Wall. The thaw in regime attitudes toward dissent was brief indeed.

Perhaps that was to be expected. As Peter Moody, Jr. stated, "Liberalization in a non-liberal state will generally be a power play. It will be undertaken when it promises gains for those who cause it to be undertaken—one assumes by those with sufficient power to disrupt the status quo, but without sufficient power to be fully satisfied with it."[19]

By the end of 1980 many of the heralded reforms were being called "readjustments" and by 1982 allegations against liberal reforms as encouraging greed and speculation were commonplace. Chinese youth were cautioned to be careful of capitalist, bourgeois influences.[20] Yet by 1984, Communist party pronouncements appeared to be increasingly tolerant of Western influences in fashion, music, and even industry, as long as party control and civil rights were not issues.[21] By 1986, hotel discos, video games, and the latest Western rock cassettes were available to tourists as well as to many Chinese, and development plans included a golf course, horse race track, aquarium, and amusement park![22]

Even as the political atmosphere within the PRC waxed hot and cold depending on the specific issue, relations with the United States continued to warm. President Carter's decision to grant formal recognition to the PRC and to exchange ambassadors and consulor staff signaled U.S. approval of policies of the new Chinese administration.

By this time, Chinese tourism had experienced much more than mere

Table 2.2. Visitor spending in the PRC, 1978–1986.

In U.S. $ million								
1978	1979	1980	1981	1982	1983	1984	1985	1986
263	n.a.	617	785	843	941	1,131	1,250	1,530

n.a. = not available.

SOURCE: NTA—Travel Business Analyst

increases in foreign visitors. What happened represented an entirely different dimension in the visitor industry. No longer were grateful and excited visitors selected from hand-picked special interest groups such as farmers and teachers. Most foreign travelers other than overseas Chinese continued to need group auspices, but visas were no longer terribly difficult to get. There are still places on the individual visa applications for indicating one's religion, political party, and level of competency in Chinese, but to what use such information is put is unknown.

Some intrepid travelers even managed to arrange independent travel, though the government was generally reluctant to allow them many choices of places to visit.[23] Barbara Letson, the author of a how-to-do-it book described her travel alone through the PRC, but it is unlikely that many of her readers will be tempted to devote major portions of their travel time to confronting Chinese bureaucracy. In an effort to be reassuring about what to do, she manages to be quite convincing in documenting that China is not the place to be a maverick or even an individualist. Letson's account of writing paragraphs of self-criticism for being in the wrong place at the wrong time may make an interesting anecdote, but it is not likely to inspire others to have such adventures.[24]

China has been criticized for its massive and inconsistent price increases.[25] Costs to tourists were allowed nearly to triple between 1980 and 1983 as the original political emphasis on having foreign guests gave way to the more urgent need to accumulate foreign exchange for development projects, including the amortization of costs for investments in tourist facilities. A double standard in pricing has also been instituted, which means air, rail, and restaurant prices are two to three times as high for foreigners as for the Chinese people.[26] And yet the pricing policy is perhaps one of few remnants of a socialist ideology premised on "from each according to his ability. . . ." The non-Chinese mass tourist costs the government more in tourist infrastructure and has fewer financial constraints than either the overseas or domestic Chinese (see Table 2.2).

Also, the PRC is determined to make certain that incentives for the industry per se do not mean net losses for the economy as a whole, as it has in many developing countries.[27] Further, there is a conviction that because so much of the Chinese economy is deliberately subsidized for reasons of health, safety, and basic transport needs, such artificially low prices need not and should not be passed along to foreigners. Pricing policies have therefore been pegged at levels comparable to those in the West.[28] John Bryden's summary of a planner's attitude in one Caribbean country is characteristic of the Chinese view. "Whether . . . benefits for tourists exist is not our concern. It is not part of a developing country's responsibility to provide benefits to the wealthier inhabitants of developed countries, who make up the bulk of the tourist market."[29]

The most important development in terms of the PRC's willingness to open the country to tourism has been the striking increase in the number of cities tourists may visit and the variety of activities they may pursue. In the early 1970s less than a dozen cities were open to foreigners.[30] By 1979, that number had increased to 60, by 1984 over 200 cities were opened, and by 1987, 496 cities could be visited by foreigners, including many in minority areas like Tibet.[31] Whether, in fact, this represents any additional political risk of "contamination" from foreigners is, however, debatable. Contacts between tourist and citizen, beyond the most superficial, are quite exceptional and have in fact become more unusual after the slight thaw of 1977–1979. Anti-Chinese Tibetan nationalism led to riots in 1988 that abruptly halted tourism to Tibet for an indefinite period.

The PRC did not continue its tourism rate of 1977–1980 in the years from 1981 to 1988. Why this has happened is not entirely clear. Some contend that Deng Xiaoping's capitalist policies, of which tourism is a part, may have simply been considered too controversial. Others assert that the policies designed to get Deng into power were not necessarily created to be an ongoing program. Others, including myself, attribute the slowdown in tourism growth primarily to factors affecting the industry. Tourism had grown so rapidly that accommodations, training, site development, and transport could not keep pace. Even in 1987, hotels were running at 96 percent of capacity in most areas. Only Shanghai could forecast a future possibility of overcapacity.[32]

Tourism analysts, for example, contend that the laudable desire to defuse tourism gains around the country by opening up more and more cities simply over-taxed an already inadequate tourist infrastructure. The Chinese government had underestimated the needs and expectations of this new group of international tourists and overestimated the demand to be just anywhere in the country. For almost everyone in the early years of the PRC's tourism program, theirs was a first trip to China. Therefore, nearly everyone wanted to see the top five or six premier destinations. The geographical breadth of such attractions also complicated the administration of tourism.

The PRC, long accustomed to glowing and uncritical praise from its foreign guests, was shocked by the many criticisms as tourist conditions deteriorated. Both the tourist and the nation needed to allow time for the PRC to digest the first wave of tourists, assess the impact, and assure that control of the industry continued to be geared to Chinese objectives rather than tourist demand.

It is, however, a terribly difficult process for the Chinese government or the tourist industry to really appreciate. As the ancient Chinese proverb claims, "a way of seeing is a way of not seeing."[33] For an outsider it is important to understand the mindset of Chinese tourism policymakers. Almost none had traveled abroad; therefore there was little awareness of what the tourist expected in terms of such mundane things as plumbing, accommodations, cleanliness, or freedom to move about. The foreign guests of the fifties and sixties gave the Chinese little indication of what to anticipate. Most were either state visitors moving in rarefied political circles, social scientists, teachers, and writers picked for their associations with pro-PRC organizations, or overseas Chinese who were staying with relatives who seldom toured or made demands.

The Chinese, historically, have expected visitors to be so impressed with being allowed in the country that they would be unlikely to quibble over arrangements. As Fox Butterfield explains in his brilliant book, *China Alive in a Bitter Sea*, "The very Chinese name for their country, Zhong Guo, is redolent of the antiquity and the pride Chinese feel about themselves. It means 'central country,' the seat of civilization at the middle of the known world."[34]

For 4,000 years, the Chinese rested secure in their superiority. The Chinese empire was unquestionably the greatest in the world, the "Central Kingdom," its boundaries coterminous with civilization. . . . In the early legends of the origin of the universe in China, there is an odd omission. There is no hint of any hero who led the Chinese to China from somewhere else. It was assumed that the Chinese originated in China. The pride all this inspired among the Chinese is something beyond western experience and comprehension. "Nationalism" is too paltry a word for it.[35]

This sense of history and superiority is illustrated in the tribute system, by which Chinese allowed foreigners access to China upon receipt of gifts and expressions of loyalty. Even after a century of western penetration and humiliation of the Chinese, the communist government to this day spends an unusual amount of time in the formal (and televised) reception of outside dignitaries.

In no western country would most of these visitors be considered newsworthy; certainly in no western capital would senior officials devote so much time to greeting foreigners, however humble. But in China, it was a signal to the Chinese people that their country was again the epicenter of the world, a strong nation that respectful foreigners pay homage to.[36]

To the new tourist, the country's chief appeal might be the status it confers on those who "get there first." It may reflect a genuine interest in this huge poor country they used to hear about from missionaries, or the special interest of history buffs intrigued with World War II. A large segment are the dauntless shoppers who see a bargain in every new destination and the buy of the century only a store away. To people who spend more time in Friendship Stores (the foreign currency stores) than in the Forbidden City, creature comforts loom larger than the Chinese could possibly have imagined.

Despite the rhetoric about "foreign friends" the Chinese have never had a history of friendly, intimate association with other nations. China's fine twentieth-century writer, Lu Xun, put it this way, "Throughout the ages, Chinese have had only two ways of looking at foreigners, up to them as superior beings or down on them as wild animals. They have never been able to treat them as friends, to consider them as people like themselves."[37]

The stage was set for misunderstanding. Enter the travel industry, currently the chief and certainly not a disinterested source of information about how a nation should develop its tourism. They quite correctly assumed that the PRC probably would not know how to market successfully to the West. A case in point is their use of packaging, advertising, and symbols. A country with brands called Atomic Enemas, Fang Fang Lipstick, Pansy Brand Men's Underwear, and Red Flag Sanitary Napkins can anticipate some marketing and imagery problems with the West!

The almost knee-jerk reaction of the international travel industry is to westernize, homogenize, and develop luxury accommodations and tour packages for the PRC. Luxury facilities do little damage or little good (except for shopping) when confined to western cruise ships merely stopping at Chinese ports. Capital-intensive luxury facilities take a far greater toll on foreign exchange, training, and maintenance capability when they are expected to be financed and maintained by a developing nation. What is good for the travel industry is almost never the only criterion a developing nation should consider, though it is often the only consulting perspective the nation may get. Despite the fact that Chinese officials visited many training centers and often took tourism courses abroad, they were essentially only exposed to an industry perspective. Area specialists, anthropologists, sociologists, and political scientists are seldom advisors in such training courses.

As the government faced the question of developmental costs and benefits and industry advice, it reorganized its administrative structure and began a series of conferences on what Chinese tourism should be like.[38]

POLITICAL ORGANIZATION OF CHINESE TOURISM

"There are no experts on China; only people with varying levels of ignorance."[39] Efforts to unearth information on Chinese tourism policy are seldom rewarded in the PRC. "Not available" is the standard reply. Even the rare opportunity of being able to talk with key national tourism officials and the head of the Tianjin CITS yielded only the most meager results. Interviews followed with six CITS city guides and one CITS national guide, plus the Chicago-based tour escort of China Holidays. Despite their assistance the skeleton of tourism organization remained incomplete. It was encouraging, therefore, to find others also attempting —albeit with similar frustrations—to find out the kind of simple information that might appear on an organization chart in the West. "It has taken . . . over three years of working with professional trainees sent by the Chinese travel services to study abroad, and extensive discussion with Chinese officials and managers to verify the organization of travel services in China."[40] What follows then is a composite of the puzzle pieces various writers have found regarding the tourism structure and, more importantly, its political dimension.

In 1978, as a reflection of tourism's emerging role in the Four Modernizations the China Bureau of Travel and Tourism was upgraded to a ministerial level organization, the General Administration for Travel and Tourism (GATT) (see Fig. 2.1). As such the GATT is the organization with overall responsibility for the development and implementation of Chinese tourism policy.

It is not, however, a public office one can visit. Like its subordinate organizations, CITS, CTS, and the new China Youth Travel Service (CYTS), it is surrounded by guards. Nor do these offices give out information on their organization or activities. Until recently no budget figures were available regarding the size of the government's commitment to tourism and few figures have been released regarding the amount of foreign exchange earned.[41] There is a tourism plan, but it is not available to the public.[42] Presumably, it is easier to modify if few ever know what it is in the first place. It should be noted that there is no unusual secrecy surrounding tourism. It is simply the way the government usually functions.

The GATT has immense authority since few foreign companies can establish tour services in the PRC. However, the Ministry of Foreign

Figure 2.1. Organization of travel services in the People's Republic of China.

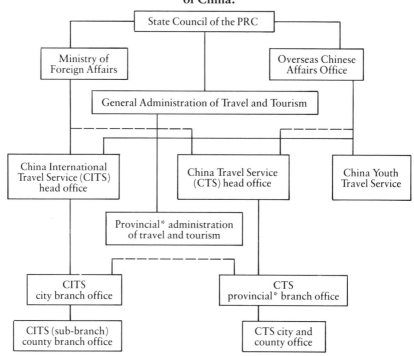

*Provincial here refers to not only the 21 provinces, but also the five autonomous regions and three municipalities of China.

SOURCE: Dexter S. L. Choy and Chuck Y. Gee, "Tourism in the PRC—Five Years After China Opens Its Gates." *International Journal of Tourism Management* 4 (no. 2): 116–119 (1983).

Affairs is involved in the status and clearance of foreign tourists, while the Overseas China Affairs Office does the same for all persons of Chinese origin, regardless of their citizenship. This distinction extends throughout the travel organization as will be discussed later.[43]

Tourist Categories

There are many categories—classes if you will—of tourists in the PRC, with separate policies and organizations for each category. The first consists of foreign guests who are usually with official or semi-official delegations. Short-term guests are housed in the finest Chinese hotels. Long-term residents in this category include journalists and embassy officials. Their travel is carefully planned with the Ministry of Foreign Affairs.

Figure 2.2. Organization of the CITS Head Office.

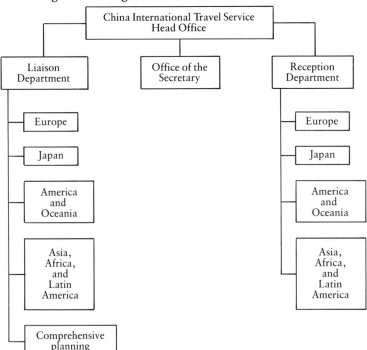

SOURCE: Dexter J. L. Choy and Chuck Y. Gee, "Tourism in the PRC—Five Years After China Opens Its Gates." *International Journal of Tourism Management* 4 (no.2): 116–119 (1983).

Until the mid-1980s permission for trips took months, even years, of official requests. By 1984, however, the process had become considerably shorter. Characteristically, this category of traveler may also meet key government and cultural spokespersons, provided they are currently in favor with the regime. As Leys bitterly observed, "Foreigners meet about 60 individuals. The literary world is represented by two or three writers, always the same, who take care of visiting men of letters; the same is true of scientists, scholars, and so on"[44]

The second category of tourist is the foreign, non-Chinese tourist whose visit falls under the auspices of the China International Travel Service (see Fig. 2.2). Tourists in this category constitute the most rapidly increasing element in Chinese tourism. They also are the ones targeted for bringing in foreign exchange. Consequently, most of the tourist infrastructure development is directed at this group. Since this category consists primarily of the affluent and experienced middle-aged traveler, this is a group with high comfort expectations and few proletarian sympathies.

Ironically and unintentionally, conditions are quite democratic for them in what is essentially an extremely class-oriented travel hierarchy. Once in the PRC, because of the present confusion in organization and the shortage of facilities, expensive and budget-priced tours are treated in essentially the same way. The only real variable is the group's itinerary and even it cannot be guaranteed. In the high seasons of spring and fall, tourists on the priciest tours may be housed as modestly as anyone, while the most humble tourist may enjoy fine cuisine and accommodations during the off-season.

The third tourist category and by far the largest is that of the overseas Chinese. Out of the PRC's 7,924,261 visitors in 1982 all but 764,497 were overseas Chinese.[45] This group is broken into several categories. The first consists of those from the Republic of China, though the PRC does not recognize the nationalist government in Taiwan. The political position is reciprocated by the government of the ROC. The one thing both sides agree on is that there is only one China. The second group of overseas Chinese consists of visitors from Macau, the third people from Hong Kong. Chinese from other countries make up the fourth group of what the PRC refers to as "the four kinds of persons."[46] Separate statistics are kept on overseas Chinese and in general they are not considered by the government as international tourists.[47]

For years, the PRC has actively competed with the ROC for approval, contacts, and financial remittances to relatives from overseas Chinese. Recently, commercial ties have also been encouraged. More modest facilities, separated generally from both other tourists and the Chinese people, are designated for overseas Chinese. Their travel is organized by the China Travel Service but additional and separate divisions for them exist in the visa departments of most Chinese embassies. As one writer recounts, an entire village may benefit from the PRC's public relations efforts to woo overseas Chinese:

> For a solid week prior to my family's trip to China, the village where my uncle and cousin live underwent considerable renovation in preparation for their arrival. Electricity was rewired, walls repainted, leaks repaired. Our "coming home" dinner . . . was an exceptional feast. Furthermore, a batch of color photos of our family that had been confiscated as "bourgeois" was suddenly returned. . . . The local authorities . . . are eager to make a good impression. . . . It's possible to arrange for (relatives) to accompany you on your travels through the rest of China. Our sponsorship provided our relatives with their first opportunity to tour their own homeland. They stayed in hotels for the first time in their lives, visited sites they'd never seen before, and ate food they'd never imagined existed.[48]

The fourth category of tourist is youth groups. Their travel needs are the responsibility of the newest of the PRC's three licensed travel services, the China Youth Travel Service (CYTS), which was founded in 1980. CYTS is the travel department of the All China Youth Federation, which is an organization with 300 million members drawn from Chinese youth clubs. The CYTS is to concentrate on the youth market and to develop hotels and camps targeted toward youth. Currently it has headquarters in Beijing and in 20 branch offices.[49] Although some see the formation of CYTS as a sign of competition in the Chinese travel industry, it is more likely an effort to reduce the pressure on CITS.[50]

The final tourist category consists of citizens of the PRC. Despite the fact that the Chinese consider their culture without peer, unlike many socialist countries where tourism is encouraged and even subsidized, the PRC has only recently devoted any of its scarce resources to domestic tourism.[51] This may reflect the fact that a country of one billion people has countless other more urgent priorities or that tourism is not seen as a particularly important means of integrating the PRC's minority groups into the dominant Han culture.[52] Ironically, foreign tourists have the greatest likelihood of visiting minority areas.[53]

However, as incomes have improved and political tensions relaxed in the mid-1980s domestic tourism has flourished. In 1986 there were some 27 million domestic travelers, and that number is expected to double in the 1990s. Although many are not tourists in the conventional sense, millions are and their numbers have created both opportunities and problems for tourism administration. Chinese forecasts made in the mid-1980s assume a 14 percent per annum increase in domestic tourism for the foreseeable future.[54] The increase in mass purchasing power has encouraged more discussion of domestic tourism and local governments have begun to organize tours, build facilities, and develop better transport for local use. It is a task well worth the effort, for in 1986 domestic tourism earned China 10 billion yuan (almost U.S. 3 billion dollars).[55]

Travel, even to see relatives, is still difficult to arrange. Separate hotels and hostels, plainer and more rustic than those for foreigners, are available for PRC citizens. Although such tourism affects only a tiny percentage of the population, with China's gigantic numbers, even a tiny fraction constitutes a great many. One excuse for traveling is to accompany Chinese relatives from overseas. Such travel is often quite in contrast to the official "classless society" rhetoric. "Minor complications may arise at restaurants when your relatives' meals have to be paid for with coupons; on trains, they may have to sit on 'hard seats' while you enjoy 'soft seats.' Restaurants or hotel staff sometimes become confused as to whether to accord your relative the same privileges as you receive."[56] High party officials and other well-placed bureaucrats have guest houses and sea resorts available to them. They also represent an exception to the otherwise segregated travel. They will often be on planes and in the best railway cars. Despite the relative inattention to domestic tourism, it has at least become an agenda item at the Third National Seminar on Tourism Economics, and an increasingly salient issue to tourism planners.[57]

CTS, CITS, and CYTS are not the only organizations in the tourism equation. CAAC, the national airways, is also an important element in the current and projected tourism development. Until recently, CAAC had the distinction of having the lowest utilization rate of any national air fleet in the world. The problem was a typical catch-22 for poor nations. Because planes are scarce, overburdened, and expensive, they are grounded in all but ideal weather. They then are even more scarce as a result. There is also little recognition of depreciation and a general feeling that money and gas are being saved when the planes are not flying. Unfortunately, many passengers and travel writers who have flown with CAAC can attest to far less concern for the safety of those within the plane.[58]

In 1985 the PRC spent over one billion dollars on new aircraft, making it the fastest growing aviation industry in Asia.[59] To introduce an element of competition and encourage greater productivity and better service, the CAAC is being divided into six regional carriers and CITS is setting up its own domestic charter.[60] The new approach is consistent with the increased attempt to integrate key motivational, administrative, and management styles of the West into the Chinese public sector. The government now argues that such pragmatism is overdue and in no way compromises the central tenets of socialism—public ownership of the means of production for public benefits.[61]

THE POLITICAL ENVIRONMENT OF CHINESE TOURISM POLICY

Discerning the politics of tourism policy-making is an even more subtle undertaking than ferreting out unpublished details of travel and tourism organization. In the absence of hard information two things occur: Western news sources speculate endlessly on each minor modification of structure, probably reading far too much into each change. The Chinese, on the other hand, attempt to depoliticize every discussion. Every action, no matter how different from what preceded it, is made to seem like the logical next step. Both sides are behaving rationally given the political environment in which they must operate. The resultant data, again not necessarily the facts, can be quite confusing.

An important policy decision was made in 1978 to decentralize the cumbersome process of having all tour operators go through central tourist services.[62] In an effort to promote market growth, provincial administrations were given authority to establish contact directly with tour operators. Branch offices were given control over the distribution of visas. Thus, individual travel agencies have courted branch officials with familiarization trips to the United States and elsewhere as they negotiated not only the scarce visas but also itineraries and costs.[63]

"We have to carry out the plan of the head office, but if we have done so and still have rooms, we can organize tours and receive tourists directly."[64] As a consequence, regional industrial towns like Tianjin also became incorporated into the tourist's itinerary, a sure indication that the Tianjin CITS office had been the one to release the visa. Naturally, most provincial administrators liked the new approach. This decentralization of tourism was part of a more general effort to diffuse decision making to provincial and sub-provincial levels to deal with foreign businesses. Foreign exchange allocations to local units were also doubled. The impact on one province is illustrative of the initial reaction.

> Intended to strengthen a sense of responsibility among lower level authorities, the de-centralized approach resulted in a perceptible increase in provincial initiative to promote tourism. This was especially true of Kwangtung province officials who took advantage of their geographic proximity to Hong Kong to make overtures to the outside world via the British territory.[65]

The term "responsibility" comes up again and again and indicates that lower levels are increasingly getting discretion over some management decisions. An example of one initiative introduced in some CITS branches in Gwangzhou, Shanghai, and Wuxi was a bonus system. Guides were evaluated and rewarded according to the amount their tour groups spent on extras such as shopping and special meals and in terms of the number of hours they worked, lack of complaints, and so on. The incentives, however, may have backfired, because by 1986 complaints of corruption led to crackdowns on guides and a subsequent drop in the quality of guide service.[66]

Responsibility is also in terms of allowing more private entrepreneurial activity among the people at large, some of which impacts the tourist sector. In nearly all cities and towns, night bazaars are springing up with vendors permitted to keep their earnings. This is particularly true in cities frequented by tourists, where private souvenir stands abound.[67]

Given the shifts in political fortunes and philosophies in China, there may be a serious question as to how much responsibility anyone wants.

Some managers feel that too impressive a performance may only raise expectations that become a higher quota next year. People also remember Mao's Hundred Flowers campaign in the late fifties when he encouraged everyone to express themselves freely and then locked up his critics. Already some imprisoned during the Cultural Revolution have been released and since re-imprisoned. Bureaucrats may be reluctant to take on responsibilities after years of seeing others pay severe penalties "for backing too enthusiastically a line which fell out of favor."[68] Tourism can be an especially political issue. "Any kind of cooperation between China and a foreign capitalistic country is a particularly sensitive issue, and those Chinese officials designated to administer such programmes are especially vulnerable within the Chinese political system."[69]

Policy-making in the People's Republic of China does not encourage real leadership, nor is this just a product of the insecurity of living in a communist society. As Fox Butterfield so aptly observes, "The Chinese invented bureaucracy over 2,000 years ago and their capacity for it is endless. Avoiding responsibility has been raised to a national art form."[70] Si-ma Qian, the great historian who lived from 145 to 90 B.C., had warned "Do not take the lead in planning affairs, or you may be held responsible."[71] One gets a feel for the sense of caution that pervades all writing. Today, for example, birth control is policy, but under Mao many respected scientists were banished for questioning whether sheer numbers in a society like the PRC were the production asset assumed by Marxist theory. The current guidelines of the Twelfth Central Committee, Third Plenum appear to dispel all doubts about the government's intention to encourage initiative and local responsibility, but it may be some time before the average bureaucrat can feel secure enough to implement the new order. China has a long history and the Chinese have long memories that make any government reforms appear ephemeral.[72]

It is little wonder, then, that Chinese accounts of tourism planning often obfuscate as much as they reveal. Although responsibility is still being urged on lower levels of bureaucracy, since 1981 there has been a reemergence of more central control.[73] How much was a response to power plays at the center and how much to specific coordination difficulties is hard to determine. Certainly, the center had an impossible task keeping track of tourists with hotels and even rural communes organizing tours. Delays, changes in itineraries, and overbooking were common complaints. Ostensibly, in an "image before profits" decision, the State Council of the PRC took back some responsibility and provincial and regional departments were no longer allowed to establish direct contacts with foreign tour operators. In the mid-1980s, decentralization partially re-emerged, ostensibly to create some competition for CITS but also because computers had made decentralization somewhat less chaotic than before.[74]

The agenda of contemporary tourism policy is indirectly indicated, however, by the Chinese. Foremost is a legitimate insistence that whatever tourism occurs should reflect China's socialist civilization. Among the criteria the government insists upon is that tourism contribute not only to the funding of the Four Modernizations, but that it contribute to mutual understanding. Apparently the Chinese continue to use tourism as a symbol of change in international relations. In 1983 Soviet and Eastern European tourists visited the PRC after nearly two decades of exclusion.[75]

Chinese style tourism must also include activities conducive to physical and mental health, so initially no casinos or brothels were permitted, although since 1984 a casino and a horse race track were approved. Opportunities for enjoying Chinese culture and obtaining quality information and appropriate hospitality at reasonable expense are also announced goals of the government. Diversification of tourist infrastructure includes the development of campsites. As an effort to integrate the tourist infrastructure with the rest of the society, Han Kehua, Director of the State Administration for Travel and Tourism, declared that Chinese regional architecture will be utilized, including structures such as yurts in Mongolia and bamboo structures in the South.[76]

Characteristically, Chinese policy-making on any subject is announced after the fact and very little indication exists of any debate over its features. Tourism policy probably would also be dealt with this way if it were feasible, but since it, by definition, involves outsiders—tour agencies, tourists, airlines, and even other governments—it has had greater publicity than its place in the Four Modernizations would indicate. At several national and international conferences on tourism one finds indications of the policy debate over tourism, though couched in language sufficiently cryptic to make it unclear which policy stand is likely to prevail. But that is, after all, a Western complaint. If one side of an issue was clearly the one to be adopted, Chinese commentators would not be reporting the other side anyway!

The Third National Seminar on Tourism Economics, sponsored by the Institute of Finance and Trade Economics of the Chinese Academy of Social Sciences in late 1983, was unusual in that problems of Chinese tourism not yet resolved were at least noted and reported and defects in earlier sanguine approaches were acknowledged. The seminar noted six areas of particular concern. First, the absence of special organizations charged with domestic tourism was deplored, because domestic tourism could be a way of fostering patriotism. But, later in the article, it reported that it would be unwise to develop domestic tourism at a time when the PRC lacked adequate infrastructure for even international tourists. Moreover, the PRC's enormous population might preclude such an effort.[77] Second, the seminar concluded that there was a lack of nationwide coordination and conflicting policies among organizations. The GATT, it recommended, needed more authority.

Third, the seminar report argued that the government administration of tourism and tourist business operations needed to become more distinct and separate.[78] This would be a complaint echoed by the Twelfth Party Congress in October 1984 when it called for the separation of government administration and business throughout the Chinese economy.[79] Fourth, liaison work with overseas organizations was considered far too centralized.

> The local travel services and tourism companies merely undertake the tasks assigned by the head offices, rather than act as tourism operators. Such highly centralized concentration does not fit China's conditions; the land is vast and tourist attractions are scattered, and the initiatives of various local organizations should be encouraged.[80]

Fifth, the PRC needs coordinating organizations among administrative areas so that tourist operation, development, utilization, and protection of tourist resources and construction of infrastructure need not be restricted by administrative area. Finally, "the system of personal responsibility within the tourist industry is not well exercised, and the principle of 'distribution according to work' is not fully carried out, . . . so that the enthusiasm of the employees in the enterprises is not fully taken advantage of."[81]

The above statement, written for a Western tourism journal, is the classic case of conveying words but no meaning. It is in a deliberately ambiguous bureaucratic code. Ambiguity is a form of freedom, allowing one to change specific meaning as the political tides change. Elsewhere in the paper there are other instances of adjacent paragraphs contradicting each other, as if it is enough to put in all views as long as they are not labeled as different from one another. This is, however, a characteristic Chinese approach. One exposes the contradiction as a way of resolving it.

Both of the authors are with the Institute of Finance and Trade Economics and have written frequently and with comparable opacity in other tourist journals. Only once in the paper did they openly suggest that there were two points of view. That was over the question of evaluating tourism's contribution to development. Some participants had proposed the use of scientific indices. "However, some participants argued that using indexes (sic) of e.g. averaged expenditure per visitor cannot reflect the *cost* of the tourist business." Per visitor expenditure could theoretically drop and yet benefits increase and vice versa. "Economic benefits from tourism must be measured by comparing both the cost and gain of the trade."[82]

Few nations attempt to measure the entire costs and benefits, preferring to stay with the easily quantifiable and always persuasive statistics the travel industry prefers. If China avoids that trap it will have a more sophisticated approach than most countries.

POLITICAL AND DEVELOPMENTAL PROSPECTS

Having examined the policy evolution and organization of Chinese tourism, it is now appropriate to assess the political and developmental implications of the current structuring of tourism in the PRC. If the effort at developing tourism does garner significant foreign exchange and result in expanded employment opportunities, Deng's reversal of nearly three decades of travel policy may pay off. The evidence so far is inconclusive.

Deng's own retreat from some of the early relaxation on restrictions of speech and press have made it difficult for his other more pragmatic economic reforms to succeed. There remains a basic tension between the need to decentralize and the tendency for both the center and the provinces to see any devolution of power as a sign of weakness at the center to be cautiously exploited by the daring or a source of anxiety to the timid. (If the center is not in control, the fearful do not know what course is safe.)

The struggle over currency is a case in point. In 1980, a decision was made to get control over foreign exchange losses to the black market by issuing foreign exchange certificates to tourists. Such certificates are the only currency accepted by the friendship stores, which are restricted to foreigners.[83]

The foreign exchange certificates have been used for local purchases by tourists, but their use in conjunction with local currency, the renminbi, is now contributing to the seepage of foreign currency into the local economy. As people seek out long-denied consumer goods and imports, such certificates may be abused. An example on a rather grand scale was cited when Shanghai customs confiscated four mini-buses and four cars that a Chinese construction firm bought from exchange certificates saved on an earlier deal with Japan. A black market is gaining ground between Macao, Hong Kong, and the mainland, as well as within Special Economic Zones like Szhensen.[84] In 1985, the PRC declared that Chinese citizens could hold foreign exchange and establish bank accounts in foreign currency. Where they will get such exchange legally and what limitations will be put on its use is not clear.[85]

The pattern of investment is another problem. The Third National Seminar on Tourism Economics made a wise decision in recommending that the government concentrate on site development and the environment, where returns are long in coming, leaving the accommodation sector to collectives, individuals, foreign businesses, and organizations abroad.[86] The government has, in fact, embarked on a major restoration of the Ming Tombs near Beijing as a part of a large resort complex being built by the Japanese.[87]

The government's ability to negotiate hotel agreements satisfactory to both the PRC and the industry appears to be improving after a number of hotel deals fell through in the late 1970s. Unfortunately, tourism has proved to be much more capital-intensive than the PRC foresaw. This is a common miscalculation among developing nations that assume a service industry will provide a cheap source of employment.

Although the travel industry would argue that it takes money to make money, the PRC has made some costly import decisions that have reduced foreign exchange holdings. West German railway cars have been imported for foreigners. One entire train of such cars now takes over 16,000 tourists a week to the Great Wall, a trip of less than four hours that could have been made in refurbished Chinese railway cars at a fraction of the cost while employing Chinese in the effort. Tour buses from Japan are exclusively used for "foreign friends."

Cooks are being trained in Hong Kong; travel experts are being groomed abroad. Bringing consultants to the PRC might have been more cost effective, but the government has had difficulty recruiting quality foreign expertise for the U.S. $100 to $150 a month they have been offering. More recently the government has accelerated in-country tourism training. The State Council turned over Beijing's Second Foreign Language Institute to the National Tourism Administration (NTA) to become the Beijing Tourism College over the competing bid of the Ministry for Foreign Trade.[88] The NTA has also been encouraged to develop a massive nation-wide training program designed to train up to 100,000 in tourism careers. The training will be implemented primarily through the colleges, though some in-service training on a rotational basis has started in the major cities.

Major difficulties include the fact that Chinese trained abroad are often pressed into immediate service rather than teaching. Also, there is the sad state of Chinese educational standards following the long years of deterioration during the Cultural Revolution. The Chinese government plans, however, to speed training by relying on a sort of snowball approach, where those trained are immediately expected to run classes for subordinates.[89]

Though the PRC is valiantly trying to professionalize its tourism sector, there fortunately has not yet been the wholesale kowtowing to Western tastes that has led scores of nations to spend up to 80 percent of their foreign exchange garnered from tourism on catering to the industry.[90] Cokes and cosmetics are available but they are not cheap. Goods sell at fair but scarcely fire-sale prices. To accommodate Western credit tastes, Visa and Mastercard are both available but the consumer—not the PRC —pays the commission. Until 1984 the rate of exchange was reasonable but no bargain. In 1984, the renminbi was devalued 30 percent against hard currencies, which will delight the international travel industry but is probably unnecessary and unwise in terms of tourism, since the PRC has all the tourists it can easily accommodate right now. It may, however, make sense in terms of other sectors of the economy.[91]

Whether the PRC will adhere to these policies and insist upon developing a Chinese-style tourism depends in part on whether advice is garnered from the international travel industry, intent on maximizing tourist and industry convenience and profit, or from the numerous developing nations and international aid organizations like the United Nations Development Project that have already had a decade or two of experience with tourism development.

As a sector providing employment, foreign exchange, and support for the preservation of Chinese culture, tourism is providing a much needed boost to the economy and the arts after years of depredation by the Red Guards. It is one of the genuinely positive side effects of using international tourism for modernization that cultural treasures like the marvelous clay army buried at Xian and the Ming Tombs are restored and other art forms are revived and appreciated once more.[92]

Although the PRC is doing many things right in its development of tourism, it has missed several opportunities to make the industry more labor-intensive. For example, many of the hotels have automatic doors and elevators. Moving sidewalks at the Beijing Airport eliminate the need for porters, but at a heavy initial cost and continued high energy consumption. If Chicago's O'Hare Airport has done without them, the compact and underutilized Beijing Airport scarcely needs them. The absence of porters or tipping is at least consistent with the country's ideological rhetoric of classlessness and self-reliance. Even these affectations seem misguided, however, when they lead to poor and indifferent service or to tourists curtailing their shopping beyond what they can easily carry.

This is especially so when every facet of the tourist sector, indeed the whole society, is riddled with class (now euphemistically termed "rank") distinctions. Cruise passengers may marvel at socialist tourism where the crew eats with the passengers, but such incidents are rare on land.[93]

The fiction that by abolishing first, second, and third class travel and instituting "hard" and "soft" seats one creates proletarian democracy fools no one. The familiar price distinctions and levels of comfort remain. Separate hotels, each complete with guards to make certain that Chinese and various tourist types do not mix, are a constant reminder that, whatever is happening on the economic scene, the political environment is still one of distrust and insecurity. The effect is to make the PRC needlessly more controversial and suspect in the eyes of outsiders and to make the citizens of the PRC increasingly more cynical about the Communist party being anything beyond a new ruling class.[94] As one critic put it,

> Maoist authorities run China like a restricted club. It is a colonial club, where meeting the "natives" is frowned upon. The only Chinese People one can talk to without getting into trouble are servants. . . . With its nightmarish obsession that foreigners may eventually . . . achieve unmonitored contacts with the people, the Maoist government has revived a great many privileges, special status rights, and waivers for foreigners in order to keep them even more isolated. It is a shameful legacy of the old imperialist-colonialist epoch.[95]

As one Chinese man bitterly commented when denied admission to the Peking Hotel, "It used to be 'No dogs or Chinese admitted,' now it's just no Chinese!"[96] His comments and those of Leys recall the row of enthusiastic spectators at a cultural show who were summarily removed from their seats to make room for our tardy busload of tourists. If the tourist attempts to bridge the chasm by deliberately sitting in a restaurant with Chinese patrons instead of in a curtained-off section or separate room, he quickly discovers that his audacity just means more inconvenience for everyone. All others near him will be moved away. Before long, the tourist grows into the role of privileged person and would not dream of going by public bus when a taxi is waiting.

This colonial mentality is a well-known side effect of tourism in developing countries.[97] Enclave tourism is also not unique to the PRC, but incongruously enough, a Club Med is being built there. What is and what is not bourgeois decadence and what is socialist development may not be rigorously definable but it would be interesting to hear it explained how Club Med fits into Chinese-style tourism. In one sense resort development does entail the isolation of the tourist where he can spend money but not impinge on the local culture, so perhaps in this regard such development fits the practice if not the rhetoric of Chinese tourism policy.

The gap between socialist pronouncements and their application is particularly disappointing to many of China's former admirers.[98] It is especially galling to those orthodox foreigners who decided to tie their fate to the Chinese Revolution and have been living in the PRC ever since. They were insulted and demeaned by zealots of the left during the Cultural Revolution; now they see the current regime kowtowing to the comforts of foreigners while relegating Chinese citizens to inferior conditions.[99]

What one finds in the PRC is a subtle variant of enclave tourism. Since tourists are not lured to the PRC by the promise of bacchanalian delights, they must have the illusion of seeing China without meeting Chinese. Again Leys is instructive: "Passing travelers see a changing landscape, and they are less conscious that they are being carried everywhere in a cage; the (foreign) residents who must stay put in Peking have plenty of time to count all the bars."[100]

Though the PRC has put more and more cities on public view, there is little reason to assume that informal contacts and actual mixing with Chinese is much more common than before. In fact, it may have been an effort to diffuse not only the money tourists spend but also the nuisance tourists had become in a few cities. The obvious enthusiasm many tourists have for shopping has meant that the Chinese guides have less obligation to be as didactic as in the early years when sympathizers were coming to appraise the revolution. Still even in Deng's China some factories, schools, and communes are usually included in tour itineraries. These must of course be only the Number One or Number Two quality establishments, so some of the best facilities are suffering from the constant tour groups interrupting their schedules. The more cities tourists can see, the more evenly this heuristic burden can be shared.[101]

The contradictions in Chinese policy are everywhere: classes in a classless society, responsibility without authority, centralization and decentralization, international understanding and friendship as a goal even as Chinese and tourists are kept apart under a system of portable apartheid. Even the teaching of English now going on throughout the nation, though designed for commerce not conversation, will undoubtedly facilitate the latter. Nearly every tourist has a story to tell of people who tried to practice English by talking to the visitor. This writer was approached several times by individuals for simple political conversations. Though conversations were brief and fleeting, they revealed that even in places far from Beijing and among people whose occupations were not academic there was an awareness of the reemergence of political controls and the end to the Xidan Democracy Wall, and they were willing to share their concern and critique of the current government with a total stranger.

Such conversations may be what the Chinese government is trying to avoid, but just as likely it wishes to prevent smuggling, black marketeering, and perhaps the awareness among the Chinese that the average tourist spends more in two weeks than 150 Chinese. The problems of relative deprivation have always existed in the south of China where comparisons between Gwangzhou and Hong Kong or Taipei have been generally unfavorable to the PRC. Deng claims that the more the PRC realizes its backwardness, the more likely it will be to accept the new pragmatism. Perhaps that is true. Relative deprivation in many other societies has, however, spawned violence. When that violence has turned on the tourist sector, the industry has proved to be extremely vulnerable, as it is in Lebanon, Jamaica, and the Philippines.[102] Tourists, unlike some entrepreneurs, do not need to go to a particular destination, and when there is a hint of insecurity, they do not.

Political backlash to Deng's policies is controlled as the whole society is controlled by the unhappy fate of dissidents at any point in Chinese history. The likelihood that public irritation with the favored treatment of foreigners or some other aggravation will change public policy is indeed remote. More likely, China's tourism backlash, if it does occur, will be a result of the Western tourist rather than the Chinese host. As mentioned before, the PRC is no longer receiving the uncritical admirers and those who identified with the Chinese Revolution. Such guests in the past generally wrote flattering articles and books even during the Cultural Revolution. "Chinese authorities are especially grateful to the willing visitors for their lack of untimely curiosity about the political somersaults of the regime. Here, since the travelers know nothing, nothing surprises them."[103]

The current generation of tourists is likely to be even less knowledgeable of China than those whom Leys ridiculed in 1972, but they are politically more inconvenient to the regime. They lack commitment and identification with the Chinese experiment and they are much less docile. Their very numbers mean they cannot be watched and organized as travelers could have been just a few years earlier. As the *Asia Yearbook, 1980* noted, the current foreign friends are curious but more demanding, more accustomed to international standards of travel, and less susceptible to regimentation.[104] Even here variation exists. Guides in all cities agreed that the easiest tourists to have are the Japanese.[105] They are more polite, are accustomed to group travel, and are less likely than Americans to indulge in political dialogues. The Americans are faulted as being noisy, demanding, hard to keep with the group, and somewhat rude and argumentative. A redeeming quality (though not valued very highly in Chinese society) was American frankness and informality. Best on balance are Canadians and Australians, who seem to have good reputations for aid to the PRC both through individuals and their governments, and who do not have a record to live down.

In a very different way, the Chinese have learned in recent years in a most unpleasant fashion that opening the country to visitors could be a less than perfect propaganda experience. The Chinese detained several American students and then expelled them for spying, but Western attention, for the most part, focused not on whether they were spying, but on a system that regards the innocuous kind of data each had as state secrets.

In 1982 another incident, the crash of a Chinese airplane carrying tourists to scenic Guilin, exposed the systemic difference between the PRC and Western news services. It was probably a political revelation to both sides. The Chinese were horrified that Hong Kong reporters would try to cover the story "without proper passes and permissions. Two systems, one boasting a relatively free flow of information, and the other in which information is a state monopoly, met in mutual non-comprehension."[106] The Chinese called a meeting, made a statement, and left to the rage of frantic relatives. "Once again the two systems were face to face. The Chinese mandarins, obviously used to cowed acceptance of their pronouncements were taken aback. . . . For a couple of days Chinese officialdom had been given a glimpse of what it would be like to govern people who demanded their rights."[107]

If and when the Chinese feel that accounts of the PRC are too unflattering or that the economic rewards are insufficient for the efforts expended, the "image before profits" philosophy could as easily spell the end of Chinese tourism as its expansion. This is especially likely if Deng's other economic policies are found wanting. If that happens, much of the stimulus in language instruction, cultural preservation, and the development of the scenic sites would also be probable casualties of any new order.

Opinions differ as to whether the PRC has received very much from its not-quite-open-door policy. The Reagan administration continues to propose arms sales to the Republic of China, which threatens to abort the improved relations between the PRC and ROC. In every country tourism is a part of its diplomatic strategy. The PRC's response to the Reagan initiative was to cancel several exchanges and visits of groups with the United States even as the CITS offered to facilitate travel for Taiwanese wanting to visit relatives.[108] On the other hand, the PRC now has World Bank aid, offers of arms sales from the United States, new export markets, and numerous technical and scholarly exchanges that did not exist before. By quickly linking the country with the international business community in terms of joint ventures, imports, and ties with the international travel industry, tourism has become an increasingly active policy sector allied to Deng's Four Modernizations campaign. Indicative of that is the fact that the central and local governments have budgeted Rmb. 13.2 billion for tourism development during 1986–1990, or over 30 times that provided in the 1978–1983 period.[109]

Though this alliance has given added impetus to tourism development, it also accentuates the sector's dependence on the continuity of Deng's approach. Budget deficits, inflation, food shortages, U.S. arms sales to the ROC, and increasing problems with the decentralization of business including tourism suggest that Deng's policies could easily fall into disfavor.

If this happens, the effect it will have on tourism depends on whether that happens sooner or later. If it happens before an elaborate tourist infrastructure is in place and while the problems of digesting tourism are more apparent than its potential, tourism could wither as rapidly as it blossomed. Excessive growth and spiraling costs are a real danger, given the whirlwind development. Tourism does, however, support other policies that enjoy strength less dependent on Deng's economic policies. Tourism is a way of wooing overseas Chinese, and Taiwanese in particular; a diplomatic link in which interest is likely to persist. Tourism's stimulus to the arts and cultural preservation may also be seen as subsidizing a source of national pride.

After the Third Plenum of the Twelfth Party Congress, there is no doubt that Deng Xiaoping's pragmatic views have prevailed. How long and in what forms his leadership will continue remain to be seen. His identification with the nation's opening to tourism is clear. As a consequence tourism policy in China may someday face a crisis based less on its own merits than on its identification with the policies of Deng Xiaoping. Its development will then hinge on whether it has demonstrated some intrinsic value to other factions of Chinese leadership. At this juncture decisive evidence is still lacking, but the potential for tourism encouraging constructive development is still great.

From an examination of the evolution of Chinese tourism policy, its political environment, and its organization, it is possible not only to see facets of tourism's developmental prospects that are not obvious in a strict economic analysis, but also to develop a greater appreciation for the culture-specific environment that can so greatly shape the implementation of any policy. Before one can compare the success or failure of any policy compared to its fate in other societies, it is critical to understand not only the design of the policy but the nature of the resources of the society and its administrative milieu.

3

The Philippines:
The Politicization of Tourism[1]

Welcome to the New Philippines
—Department of Tourism Poster, 1987

"PEOPLE POWER, the Unarmed Forces of the Philippines" means, as the t-shirts proclaim, a new era in the Philippines. Forced from office after he massively rigged the 1986 Presidential elections, Ferdinand Marcos now lives in reluctant exile in Hawaii and Corazon Aquino, widow of his assassinated rival, now struggles with the Marcos legacy of political and economic decay.

The events that brought Aquino to power made dramatic street theater—unarmed millions massed to protest the Marcos election fraud, to protect defecting military, and to promote the Aquino victory. Even long-time Marcos friend, President Ronald Reagan, was compelled to airlift the Marcos entourage to Honolulu and to recognize the Aquino government.[2]

Aquino inherited a bankrupt nation with a negative growth rate, a $26 billion foreign debt, 70 percent of the population at or below the poverty line, and a country that lost between 10 and 20 billion dollars to the systematic plundering of the Marcos government.[3] She assumed the office of the president even as Marcos still cowered in his bullet proof palace. Following his exit, Aquino moved into a presidential guest house near the palace. There was no transition; records were in shambles. A new constitution, new institutions, and new leadership were desperately needed to replace those discredited by the 20 years of Marcos rule. Eighteen months later these were in place.

Under such circumstances one might assume that tourism policy would hardly be a salient issue for the government but Aquino, like Marcos, felt that tourism policy would prove a useful political weapon. To understand how and why the Aquino government has shaped current tourism policy it is necessary to trace in some detail the unprecedented use of tourism policy as a political instrument by the Marcos government. It is also important to understand the many ways in which tourism policy was utilized for national and personal objectives, because other governments, particularly authoritarian ones, have used and are using tourism for some of the same political advantages.

TOURISM BY DECREE: THE POLITICAL USES OF TOURISM UNDER PRESIDENT MARCOS

No regime has more blatantly used tourism policy for political leverage than that of ex-President Marcos of the Philippines. Although tourism contributed to many of the regime's political and economic objectives, it achieved those gains at enormous cost to the Filipino economy. As time went on, the insensitive development of tourism in the midst of deteriorating economic and social conditions spawned a counter-use of tourism—opposition violence against the tourist industry. Thus one finds in the case of the Philippines a microcosm of the political uses and abuses of tourism.

Background

Although 20 years ago the Philippine economy was second in Asia only to Japan, tourism development was quite a lackluster sector until the advent of martial law in 1972. It is indeed ironic that as a democracy the Philippines lagged behind all other Southeast Asian nations in tourist arrivals while under the martial law New Society, and later the authoritarian New Republic, it was billed as a tourist haven. It did not happen by accident. Within a month after Marcos declared martial law, claiming that the country was seething with subversion and violence, ambitious government plans to expand tourism were already being announced. "The New Society, if it lives up to the plans and promises, may come to be known in our history as that era when tourism was in flower."[4] To understand just how tourism administration was converted from a prosaic little bureau in a nondescript building into the flashy, high profile, skyline-changing, priority sector it would become requires understanding a bit of history of the Philippine political environment.

Between 1946, when the Philippines became independent from the United States, and 1965, when Marcos was first elected president, two loosely organized political parties had alternated in holding political power. The Philippines had a reputation as a freewheeling, sometimes corrupt but always lively, democracy in the midst of the authoritarian nations of Southeast Asia. Its elections were always occasions for massive vote-buying on both sides, but the greed of the ruling party was to some extent checked by the free, often scurrilous, press, a strong opposition party and regularly held elections.[5]

President Marcos' first term in office more or less followed the characteristic pattern. In 1969 he became the first president since independence to be re-elected, in what was widely acknowledged to have been an unusually corrupt and possibly rigged election. The constitutional two-term limit for the president meant that Marcos was scheduled to leave office in 1973. During much of the president's second term he sought without success to have the constitution changed by encouraging a constitutional convention to develop a parliamentary system. That proved futile. At the same time, student protests, Marxist-encouraged agrarian revolts and the chronic (since Spanish times) violence of Moslem dissidents on the southern island of Mindanao made the Philippines seem unsettled at best. Critics would later argue that none of these events was particularly unusual for the Philippines. However, the president made them appear so. A terrorist bombing of a political rally (which was later discovered to have occurred at the president's behest) set the stage.

Using Tourism to Sell Martial Law

"Every visit is an endorsement of the continuation of the political, economic, and social stability achieved by . . . martial law."[6] On September 22, 1972, the president declared martial law, dissolved Congress, closed most papers, abolished the vice-presidency, arrested political opposition, and began what Marcos labeled the "New Society." It was during this tumultuous period, under the scrutiny of world opinion and with all competing political institutions neutralized, that the government began its massive tourism program.

In an open political system, heavy dependence on patronage and public works tends to take the form of projects like schools, roads, dams, parks, and health clinics. Some are purely pork barrel in nature, but they are designed to be relevant to popular needs, and to sway public opinion and with it the vote. In a closed political system as the Philippines was between 1972 and 1986 different political needs surface. The winning political formula then becomes not votes but the support of the key elements in the domestic and international elite. Tourism is particularly well-suited to assuaging elites and developing a clientele for authoritarian rule. Oriol Pi-Sunyer, in her study of Spain, documents the use of tourism in the 1930s as a way of countering hostility to fascist Spain.

> If Western governments were reluctant to support Spanish Fascism, Europeans could nevertheless be invited to Spain and, hopefully act as unofficial emissaries of the regime on their return home. Reports that the living was cheap (as it was for outsiders) and that the country was tranquil (as it appeared to be to the casual visitor) helped legitimate the system.

> For internal Spanish consumption, the hundreds of thousands of foreigners visiting Spain was offered as evidence that the dictatorship was accepted abroad. . . . The controlled media constantly reported on the growth of tourism and explained at great length how this apparently inexhaustible source of wealth benefitted the Spanish people.[7]

The parallels with the Philippines grow even closer when one notes that the later expansion of Spanish tourism flourished and was in part linked to U.S. economic and military support, which was in turn a reflection of the American-Spanish bases agreement of 1953.

Similar contemporary examples using tourism for political credibility could be found in the two Koreas and the Republic of China. But it was President Marcos in the Philippines who in 1972 demonstrated that tourism could be developed to convey and create regime legitimacy in ways and to a degree not attempted before. At the time martial law was declared, Marcos had two critical foreign policy problems. First, he had to overcome the shock and dismay in some Western circles at the unexpected imposition of martial law in order to neutralize opposition to his leadership. Second, he had to assure that martial law would not jeopardize the flow of foreign capital investment into the country, encourage cuts in foreign aid, or erect new trade barriers to Philippine exports.

Internationally, Marcos' problem was his own political legitimacy as well as the continuation and enlargement of the economic base for his policies. He met these challenges with characteristic articulateness and political skill. The imposition of martial law was treated as an entirely constitutional, hence legitimate, response to an emergency situation created by communist subversion and communal violence. Moreover, he insisted that an integrated series of policies was required to effectively curtail the situation. Marcos thus served notice to the nation that martial law was not to be a 90-day phenomenon. At the same time that he was building a case that internal subversion required the imposition of martial law, Marcos also managed to assure such international economic brokers as Robert McNamara (then president of the World Bank) and others that the Philippines was an ideal investment site for both international aid and multinational corporate development.

Tourism, which had fallen off dramatically in the period immediately before and after martial law, was quickly seized upon as a means to refurbish the Philippines' and especially Marcos' image. Tourism had not been a priority industry prior to the establishment of martial law and had, in fact, done very poorly during the first term of Marcos' administration. Yet within eight months of the declaration of martial law, tourism was a priority industry eligible for a variety of tax incentives and customs concessions. The regime had set up its first Department of Tourism (DOT) by May 11, 1973.[8]

Jose Aspiras, former congressman and presidential news secretary, was given the task of selling the Philippines as a safe and delightful destination thanks to the achievements of the New Society. He approached his job with customary gusto and a well-developed public relations instinct. In days, tourism went from a once-a-month news item to a daily media blitz. The impression was fostered that no visitor had had a good night's sleep in pre–martial law Philippines and no hotelier would have a good one ever again without martial law.

Aspiras had a formidable ally in First Lady Imelda Marcos. She is rumored to have been responsible for the creation of a cabinet level post for Aspiras. Though a longtime associate of the president, Aspiras began his most rapid ascent after he reputedly was among those who saved Mrs. Marcos from a would-be assassin.[9] This rumor gains credence from the fact that tourism had just been reorganized a few months before on the recommendation of a three-year study by the Presidential Commission on Reorganization. The new Philippine Tourism Commission was scuttled and with it tourism's longtime head, Gregorio Araneta, who was then given the position of undersecretary in the new DOT. Araneta contends that Aspiras' first choice was to be secretary of the Department of Public Information, but Marcos persuaded him that tourism would be a major responsibility in the New Society.

For some time, Imelda Marcos had nurtured expansive and expensive ambitions to see the Philippines, and particularly Manila, blossom into an international oasis for the luxury traveler. Her interest in the arts and in the general cultural life of the city had been ridiculed and frustrated by outspoken critics and a frequently hostile press. These constraints were gone after martial law began.

Nor was Marcos constrained in promoting tourism. Tourism, as a relatively new and heretofore harmless government function, had no real enemies. Unlike his key domestic program of land reform, with tourism policy the president had no need to perform amazing feats by juggling power interests. At the same time he could build a potentially important industry critically dependent on stability and relatively unconcerned about political freedom.

Tourists per se mattered less in the early years of martial law than did the publicity about tourism. The DOT launched an ambitious series of invitational visits to the Philippines for travel writers and tour operators, groups that could be depended upon not to bite the hand that fed them and who were not likely to be preoccupied with civil libertarian issues. In a friendly, beautiful country it was enough that the gun slingers were gone and no tanks patrolled the streets. To further the image of a peaceful, contented society, the DOT built a promotional campaign around the Philippines' most important asset—a cheerful, hospitable people. The slogan, "Where Asia Wears a Smile," was a particularly adroit choice for defusing criticism of life under the New Society.

Aggressive efforts were made to attract international gatherings of global appeal. Once these media events were secured, the mobilization required to assure their success began. The Miss Universe Contest in 1974 occasioned among other things such modern-day pyramid building as the construction of its venue, the huge Folk Arts Theatre, in an incredible 77 days of nonstop construction and at still unreported costs. The media event for 1975 was the "Thrilla in Manila," which pitted Joe Frazier against Mohammed Ali in their championship fight. Once again world publicity focused on the Philippines as journalists toured the country developing background stories for the spectacle. The government's tourism department promoted tourist events with a positively dazzling eclecticism that ranged from the "Miss Gay World Beauty Pageant" in Baguio to evangelist Rex Humbard's rally in Manila.

The IMF–World Bank Conference

But it was the International Monetary Fund–World Bank Conference in October 1976 that stimulated the most frenzied and politically motivated use of tourism. In late 1974, as soon as the Philippines learned that its bid had been accepted, all pretense at orderly and phased tourism development was abandoned. "In the rush to build the hotels, normal loan procedures were shelved. . . . Irineo Aguirre (Director of the Bureau of Tourism Services) says that 'the Government never planned for so many hotels to be built at one time.' The hotel construction had been planned on a staggered basis . . . but then the IMF came along."[10] The IMF–World Bank Conference offered an opportunity for both regime recognition and personal aggrandizement. No expense was spared to assure that this most prestigious international conference would find in Manila a showcase of stability, prosperity, elegance, and beauty. The tantalizing prospect of hosting 5,000 VIPs, even for just a week, led to a rush to complete 12 luxury hotels within 18 months, though the tourism master plan had not expected such accommodation needs for at least a decade.[11]

The opportunities seized for private gain became clear later. By 1976 the First Lady had become the first governor of the super-political unit known as Metro Manila. As the highest authority over the 17 constituent cities, Imelda Marcos was clearly in a position to monitor development. Her financial interests and those of her friends were not neglected. Enormous convention facilities and exhibition halls were rushed to completion. Round-the-clock shifts were utilized to complete her own hotel, the $150 million Philippine Plaza, conveniently located on reclaimed land in Manila Harbor alongside the lavish convention facilities. "Ownership" is rather a misnomer, as the hotel was built without Philippine Tourism Authority (PTA) approval and with 100 percent government financing. Friends, including the tourism minister, also borrowed massive sums with little or no equity of their own involved. Although the Central Bank looked askance at such risky ventures, the deal was struck when the Government Service Insurance System agreed to guarantee the loans. Some entrepreneurs reputedly borrowed far more at the concessional interest rates than needed for the hotels and used the extra funds for speculation.[12]

In any event, the IMF–World Bank Conference is still, over a decade later, the reference point for grandiose tourism development among international travel industry specialists. It is hard to exaggerate what occurred.

The skyline of Manila, indeed, part of what was once Manila Harbor, was drastically altered by the rise of more than a dozen luxury hotels. Depending on one's sources of information, in the 1975–1976 period, between US$410 and $545 million of government money became directly tied up in hotel financing. The relative size of this commitment can be compared from several angles: it was between one-seventh and one-fifth of the government's total proposed 1976 expenditures of $3.05 billion.[13] It is more than the nation's total 1976 borrowing from the World Bank of $315 million. The Development Bank of the Philippines (DBP) alone spent a "staggering $229.29 million" through July 1976 on tourism projects.[14]

From a development standpoint, the expenditure on hotel financing alone is between 30 and 40 times the amount that the government has spent on public housing. It could, of course, be argued that comparing government expenditures with government loans is misleading because, theoretically, the latter will be repaid. But one could make a similar case for such things as agrarian reform loans and low-cost housing loans. The government was not so zealous in those sectors. Further, with hindsight we now know that the massive loans were not repaid. Tourism was subsidized by the Filipino citizen through taxation and social security payments. The government now owns most of these hotels.

Though a spokesperson for the Philippine Hotel Association acknowledged that the hotels built in 1976 would "not be economically viable for the next 15 years," the government continued to extend their credit.[15] As of 1983, the Development Bank of the Philippines had acquired 80 percent control of 70 tourism related accounts that owed the DBP 4.5 billion pesos. Though 1.5 billion pesos in loans were converted into equity in the hotels, the total owed now far exceeds the value of the hotels as collateral.[16] The government lost the taxpayers' money with every move.

Nor was the hotel building the extent of the government-financed tourism infrastructure. The reclamation of land in Manila Harbor was a very expensive project. Most of the subsequent building on the reclaimed land was related to tourism. The First Lady's Philippine Plaza Hotel has already been mentioned. Its waterfront location was envied by competing older hotels that found their once waterfront locations disappear as vast acres of reclaimed land emerged in front of them.

Other grandiose projects included the Philippine International Convention Center (PICC), estimated to cost $150 million, and the Philippine Center for International Trade and Exhibitions. The convention facility spurred the creation of Presidential Decree 867 creating a Philippine Convention Bureau, which was supported by taxing all hotels big and small. The small hotels resented the tax because they had no convention traffic. The larger ones resented the PICC because it competed with their own convention facilities.[17] Airport, port development, and accelerated road building projects were also developed with considerable attention to their impact on tourism.[18]

The IMF–World Bank Conference was apparently a huge political success, despite the fact that only 3,000 of the 5,000 anticipated participants came. Few delegates seemed to note the incongruity of a New Society that was supposedly aimed at redressing inequities spending many times more for the construction of luxury hotels than for public housing and land reform. As was intended, most were impressed by the stability and attractiveness of the society, the tremendous growth in international investments, and the obvious improvement in law and order, at least in the tourist belt.[19] Military and economic aid to the Marcos government increased, in both bi-lateral U.S.- Philippines terms and in terms of IMF-World Bank aid. To most of the 138 government and tourism industry officials interviewed in 1976 and 1977 the tourism development effort was an enormous political success for President Marcos, though few would argue that it made economic sense. Secretary of Tourism Jose Aspiras even went so far as to conclude that Filipino Martial Law was itself a tourist attraction.[20]

Balikbayan *and Reunion for Peace*

Although the international beauty contests, boxing events, and wooing of VIPs garnered excellent publicity for the Philippines, a different approach was needed to counter the bitter criticism of many expatriates abroad and the ever-lengthening lines outside the U.S. embassy of those seeking to leave the Philippines. The Marcos government was extremely sensitive to charges of political torture, "salvaging" (killing) of opponents, repression, and corruption by the regime because they threatened to alienate the more than 1.5 million Filipinos living abroad, three-quarters of whom reside in the United States. Through consulate activities of sometimes dubious legality,[21] through referenda giving overseas Filipinos preferential treatment over local Filipinos, and through tourism, the government sought to influence Filipinos abroad politically and the nations in which they resided. There was an economic rationale as well. Filipino remittances grew in importance even as the Philippine economy deteriorated. Moreover, criticism abroad threatened to jeopardize the foreign aid and investment upon which the government grew ever more dependent.[22]

The government response was the *Balikbayan* (homecoming) Program. Begun in 1973 as a special project to assuage concerns about martial law among overseas Filipinos, it continued as an elaborate project to subsidize the travel to the Philippines of Filipinos living abroad. Over a score of national departments and provincial and local agencies are involved in the development of the program, as well as embassies and consulates abroad. *Balikbayan* initially was built upon the close Philippine family ties and what is the longest Christmas season in the world: All Saints Day (November 1) to Epiphany (January 6). Hundreds of thousands of copies of "Invitation to a Traditional Philippine Christmas" were sent abroad. School children were assigned to invite relatives home for Christmas. Local governments were charged with developing local festivals and immigration, tax, and customs officials were instructed to exempt *Balikbayan* visitors from most requirements. The icing on the cake was the Department of Tourism's 50 percent discount of airfares and concessional rates on accommodations and shopping.[23]

Although the DOT initially contended that the *Balikbayan* Program was an economic success,[24] fervent supporters of the regime would later acknowledge that it was very costly but well worth it in public relations value.

> The government of course, has lost and is losing a rather substantial amount of revenue from the program. But the benefits derived by the country are not only from the foreign currency spent here . . . it is also an effective means of rebutting through actual experience the lies they have spread about this country in foreign lands.[25]

Though the Philippine people bore the economic costs of subsidizing the tourism of more affluent expatriates abroad, the regime benefited politically from the program. By 1978 nearly a million Filipinos and their families had taken advantage of the government program. Even so, the government took pains to inflate the figures further, because they so successfully belied the "you can't go home again" claims of Marcos' critics. All overseas Filipinos and their families, regardless of their present or past nationality, who visited the Philippines were considered *Balikbayans* for accounting purposes. The effect of this was to inflate the number of Filipinos coming home and deflate the number of American tourists, for most *Balikbayans* came from the United States. This accounting procedure also made it impossible to compare the number of overseas Filipinos who were visiting in the pre–martial-law period with those who have returned subsequently. Statistics for the former do exist but were never cited and are not comparable, for the earlier statistics noted only Filipinos born in the Philippines, not whole families.[26]

The favorable comments on the cleanliness, beauty, and order that prevailed in tourist areas provided positive feedback to both the world and the local press. Like tourists in general, *Balikbayans* rarely were interested in the political details of the government but were impressed with the relatively relaxed atmosphere and congenial surroundings. Yet they were more credible for political purposes than ordinary tourists because they were in a position to compare the New Society on a temporary basis with the Old Society they had known more closely and had opted to leave. Encouraged by the success of the *Balikbayan* Program, the government developed other specialized homecoming programs geared to influential expatriate groups. Presidential Decree 819, in October 1975, established the *Balik*-Scientist Program, which included incentives for practicing professional skills in the Philippines as well as regular *Balikbayan* privileges.[27] *Balik*-UP was set up in July 1978 to encourage visits from University of the Philippines alumni, the graduates of the most prestigious university in the country. As an indicator of the coordination and high-level support these programs enjoyed, *Balik*-UP was promoted jointly by the ministries of Tourism, Foreign Affairs, and Trade as well as Philippine Airlines.[28]

Toward the end of the Marcos era there was some curtailing of concessions to non-Filipino family members, but the basic political objectives of the *Balikbayan* Program continued to overshadow the economic costs of the program.[29] Actually, in many respects the economic costs have decreased. Since the government now owned many of the lavish hotels for which it underwrote the construction in 1976, it was eager to get whatever tourists it could or face added empty rooms and an increasing drain on government reserves.

The "Reunion for Peace," launched in early 1977, was another attempt to bring back to the Philippines groups who could not help but compare the atmosphere under martial law favorably with what they had known before. The program appears to have been inspired by a similar initiative in South Korea, another authoritarian nation in search of better press notices. The political formula is astute: promote the return of former World War II servicemen and their families from America, Japan, and Australia for a nostalgic tour of old battlegrounds and memorials as well as a panoramic view of the New Society. Concessional fares and touring discounts sweeten the package. Meanwhile, the entire project complemented the president's initiatives in presenting the Philippines as an independent and vigorous society intent on reconciliation and relations with a variety of powers. Even for this small program the government developed a committee composed of the heads of the Departments of National Defense, Development, Foreign Affairs, Local Government and Community Development, Highways, the National Historical Institute, and the Veterans Federation.[30]

Both *Balikbayan* and Reunion for Peace have been programs that were generally well received at home and abroad. The United Nations' praise of both programs as innovative and constructive has encouraged the adoption of similar programs elsewhere.

Until about 1980 one would have had to credit the regime's tourism policy with general political success. For example, tourism was used as the basis for forging closer political and economic ties within the Association of Southeast Asian Nations (ASEAN). Marcos was interested in strengthening ASEAN for several reasons. First, it was showing increasing signs of becoming an important counterweight to Japanese and American influence in the area. Second, it offered an international forum for the Philippines and for Marcos, where Marcos could enhance his global reputation as a statesman while representing the Philippines as a genuinely nonaligned nation. Third, by initiating patterns of regional cooperation in such sectors as tourism, he hoped to avoid ruinous competition that could abort the Philippine tourism effort. At the same time, the campaigns for ASEAN cooperative efforts encouraged the general political support of the other member nations. Harmony with such ASEAN powers as Malaysia and Indonesia also reduced the likelihood that those Muslim nations would actively support the Muslim rebels in the Southern Philippines.

To further these objectives, the Philippine government worked tirelessly to develop closer communication and transportation links with ASEAN member nations. An air link was opened between the Philippines and Indonesia, thereby completing the air routes among ASEAN nations and facilitating regional travel and promotion. A permanent committee on tourism in the ASEAN was established and plans were made to develop a regional passport, for free exchange of currency among member countries, and to ease customs and trade restrictions.[31]

So important had tourism become as an ingredient in Philippine foreign policy that for a while every government employee going abroad had to take a departure course on both the policies of the New Society and the major tourism attractions in the country. In early 1977, the Department of Foreign Affairs went a step further and recalled the ambassadors and consuls from North America for briefings on tourism and a ten-day tour of the Philippines.[32] Even city governments were expected to use their mandatory tourism councils to initiate visits and exchanges with other foreign countries.

In May 1977, the city of Manila hosted its first international conference, the Pacific and Asian Congress of Municipalities (PACOM). Manila has been the site of numerous international conventions, but this was ostensibly the first international convention hosted by the city. The demarcations between municipal and national government, however, were certainly blurred under martial law. National government figures and departments were prominent in the planning, but most of the costs were borne by the Manila city government. The city had given "voluntarily" over 1 million pesos ($134,700) a year to the DOT since martial law began.[33]

Appropriately, the subject of the conference was national and local partnership in the development of tourism. PACOM is an apolitical body of local government executives from countries in the Pacific Basin. It has few resources and little influence, being largely a creation of rather particularistic political needs. The organization was founded by Honolulu Mayor Frank Fasi, who until the Manila convention had remained PACOM president. PACOM offered Mayor Fasi a forum that nicely complemented the variety in his Honolulu constituency.

The conference was also important to the Philippines. By giving this diffuse collection of local officials the VIP treatment, not only was the Philippines likely to be remembered favorably, but attitudes toward Filipinos abroad might be positively affected. It was mentioned, for example, during the planning for the PACOM conference that many politicians in a position to help overseas Filipinos would be attending. Moreover, a few of the mayors coming would be overseas Filipinos who would themselves be important in improving the Philippine image abroad. Philippine planners were particularly hopeful that Mayor Fasi would be elected Hawaii's governor in the next election so that his favorable record of appointing Filipinos to government posts could continue at a higher level.[34] They were to be disappointed.

It was also to be a morale booster for the local Filipino mayors who would attend and later help one of their own, Manila Mayor Ramon Bagatsing, become without opposition the new president of PACOM. Other nationality groups did not bother to put up presidential candidates when it became obvious that out of a total PACOM membership of less than 500, 300 were new Filipino members. PACOM planners were ready should there be a challenge to Mayor Bagatsing's candidacy, but their contingency plans were not necessary.[35]

PACOM was a small conference with fewer than 500 attending, but its keynote address was given by the First Lady and its closing speech by the President. This is an indication less of the significance of the convention than of the unstinting efforts of the First Couple to garner influence and prestige for the New Society.

The conference was executed with a precision and attention to detail that was most impressive. Thanks to the convention center and new hotels, the facilities were impeccable. The costs were enormous, however, and only a fraction of the investment was recovered by registration fees and visitor spending.[36] As several delegations remarked, the Philippine conference would be a hard act to follow for those national groups who have to account to the public for their expenditures.

Opposition Uses of International Tourism

Only two major tourism conferences have clearly boomeranged politically. The first was the Eighth World Peace Through Law Conference, which was held in Manila in August 1977. The theme of the conference was international protection of human rights. It was perhaps too much for the Marcos regime to woo jurists as successfully as it had wooed boxing and beauty contest fans, but certainly a Herculean effort was made. Marcos announced the lifting of curfew and the ban on international travel as well as the release of about 1,500 prisoners, and intimated that local elections would be forthcoming. They were not. The presence of the conference in Manila also encouraged local campus dissidents to stage antigovernment demonstrations. These the government gingerly confronted, reluctant to show its strength with American conventioneers in the crowd and with a stellar international gathering in the city.[37]

The second, which failed more dramatically, was the American Society of Travel Agents (ASTA) Conference. The Philippines had accelerated its tourism initiative by 1980 as hotel overcapacity became a major liability and public criticism of tourism policy grew. Overseas offices multiplied and a new tourism offensive was signalled by the opening of the Philippine Embassy's Special Services Office in Washington, D.C., to coordinate tourism, convention, and cultural activities. The effort was dramatic enough that even the industry press took notice.

The travel industry has been practically commuting to Manila in the past 12 months. The Philippine capital, with its superb meeting facilities and plethora of deluxe hotels, has managed to attract, like a giant Pacific magnet, a procession of travel industry conferences (PATA, the Pacific Area Travel Association, the World Tourism Organization) and this month welcomes the biggest annual industry event of them all: the ASTA World Congress.[38]

The American Society of Travel Agents convention was eagerly wooed and, once won, the Philippine government spared no expense in preparing a lavish conference for the more than 6,000 delegates expected at this important event. More than any other single tourism organization, this one influenced access and trade to the American and even the world market. This the government knew. But so did the President's opposition.

Despite elaborate security, no more than minutes after President Marcos opened the gala conference a bomb went off in the convention hall, injuring several delegates. The timing of the attack could not have been more adroit from the opposition's perspective, for it followed the president's ridicule of Western press accounts of the Philippines as unsafe.[39] The president was unhurt but politically stunned by his opposition's bold and successful breach of security. Moreover, the ASTA Conference was in chaos. The conference was cancelled despite Philippine government pleas. The Ministry of Tourism offered free stays, food, and travel to delegates who would remain, as it desperately sought to recoup its political standing. There were few takers.

With one bomb, the most important clientele group in global travel had been initiated into the state of domestic politics in the Philippines. Philippine tourist arrivals declined immediately by 10 percent and continued to decline throughout Marcos' tenure, despite the deteriorating exchange rate of the peso, which made the Philippines a very inexpensive destination for international visitors.

The tourist industry, developed in large measure by massive media promotion, had been undone by media events beyond the regime's control. Tourism had also been affected dramatically by the reports of general violence and political instability.[40] A case in point: the airport assassination of opposition leader, Benigno Aquino, as he returned from exile had an immediate impact on tourism.

> Reaction to the killing (and its consequences) among potential visitors to the Philippines can be illustrated by what happened in the convention market. Within days of Aquino's death, eight large international events scheduled for late 1983 and early 1984 were cancelled. Revenue from an estimated 10,500 high spending visitors was lost.[41]

Even business travel, which had been more resistant to bad political news, declined as the economic situation deteriorated.

This was not the first violence directed at tourism. Selective acts of terrorism against tourists and the tourist establishment had been increasing as the Marcos family and friends became identified as the prime beneficiaries of the government's expensive tourism development program. In the mid-1970s there were kidnappings of two Japanese tourists on the southern island of Mindanao. Since Japan assumes an unusually paternal role toward its citizens abroad, this event had severe repercussions. Japan, by far the largest tourism market for the Philippines, has a tremendous impact on Philippine tourism. The Japanese issued a warning to Japanese tourists to avoid the southern Philippines and almost all did, for years.

A beefed-up military police and stiff sentences for crimes against tourists were the government's attempt to keep lawlessness to a minimum in Manila's tourist belt.[42] By the late 1970s and early 1980s, however, a new opposition strategy targeted the hotels owned by the Marcos family and their associates. A series of arson attacks began that severely damaged or destroyed several luxury hotels and a floating casino. A group calling itself the "Light a Fire" movement claimed responsibility for the fires.

In mid-October 1984, a famous hill city monument, the Pines Hotel in Baguio, went up in flames. The hotel was filled with American veterans on a Reunion for Peace tour. Two other hotels burned in as many weeks. After over 50 deaths and 500 injuries from the three fires, the luxury hotels were forced to search visitors and their luggage, a decision scarcely compatible with the carefree ambience the Tourism Ministry spent millions to promote.[43]

If one tried to imagine the mindset of militant opponents of the regime, generally denied open channels of dissent, subject to preventive detention, not allowed habeas corpus, and frequently the target of torture and disappearances, the attacks become more understandable. After 20 years of Marcos rule, the radical opposition had correctly concluded that the president would not peacefully relinquish control and that foreign governments would not precipitate action against him.

Tourism was at once a highly visible, salient example of "crony capitalism" and of the grandiose pretensions of the Marcos regime. The tourist infrastructure was largely owned by the First Family or those close to them. Moreover, terrorist victims of arson or bombs were likely to be foreigners or the most conservative strata of the Filipino elite. Thus a backlash among the mass of citizens was unlikely. In any case, because foreigners were involved, there was publicity abroad, if not in the Philippines. Moreover, tourism is an important export sector that can be killed at little effort or expense. A pattern of sporadic violence can cripple it.

The government found that its very zealousness in building a tourism infrastructure simultaneously created new pressures to draw tourists even as it has developed new vulnerability to opposition violence. In June of 1984, the government announced it was putting 200 street marshalls in Manila with instructions to shoot to maim suspected criminals. By the end of July 1984, over 40 people had been shot dead by the marshalls and others wounded. Such law and order efforts did not inspire great confidence among tourists but for a time it had a chilling effect on dissident activity in the capital.[44]

The Domestic Uses of Tourism

Within the Philippines, the decision to rapidly expand tourism also had predominantly political objectives, though the rationale developed for explaining the importance of tourism was in terms of the economic benefits that would accrue from an accelerated program. Political legitimacy was no less important at home than abroad, and the spectacle of thousands of tourists visiting the Philippines supported the administration's claim to have earned the confidence and respect of the world. As in fascist Spain, tourist arrivals were hailed as personal endorsements of martial law.

Favorable comments of tourists and visiting officials were included in nearly every issue of the major newspapers since the creation of the DOT in 1973. Conventions, however, were a new variant on bread and circuses in terms of regaling the masses with lively details. Each was assured daily coverage and numerous feature stories.

The impression of an inordinate amount of newspaper space devoted to tourism was confirmed during my four-month content analysis of the three leading dailies, from January to May 1977. The three papers studied during the period were *Bulletin Today, Philippine Daily Express,* and the *Times Journal,* all Manila dailies. The first paper was owned by a friend of the president. The latter two were under the ownership of members of the First Couple's family.

By way of comparison, there were 12 stories on tourism for every one on agricultural policy, including the much heralded land reform. Another measure of tourism's prominence was the coverage devoted to it in the prestigious *Fookien Times Yearbooks* to which government and civic leaders contribute. In 1976, for example, tourism coverage (14 pages and cover) exceeded space devoted to agriculture, industry, or trade. This imbalance is even more pronounced when one compares the prominence, length, and accompanying photographs on the two subjects.[45]

Moreover, even mild criticism of tourism policy was dealt with more summarily than criticism of land reform implementation. Columnists who failed to be properly enthusiastic about government implementation of the tourism program lost their jobs. One such example, Frankie Lagniton, writing for the *Bulletin Today,* had his column cancelled without notice to him or his readers. Individuals in the DOT leadership felt he had been critical of their approach to attracting increased travel trade.[46]

Bernard Wideman of the *Washington Post* also ran afoul of the regime after a number of articles in the *Far Eastern Economic Review* and the *Washington Post.* His unpopularity with the regime was based, among other things, on his writing about the massive hotel construction and financing. Wideman was ordered deported, but a hearing shortly before the World Peace Through Law Conference led to a personal determination by the president that he could stay. Not so lucky was Associated Press Manila bureau chief Arnold Zeitlin, who the preceding November, after the IMF–World Bank Conference, was given 24 hours to leave the country without a hearing.[47] The decisions made no mention of the conferences, of course, but it seemed that the different treatment accorded these journalists was, in part, occasioned by the timing of the conferences and by the regime's awareness that such publicity could not be helpful to the image desired.

Tourism Implementation and Administration

Political legitimacy was only one of the president's domestic goals. Promotion of tourism has also proved to be a very flexible tool for selectively investing in the country according to political priorities, both personal and regime-based. Initially, the tourism master plan identified eight large priority zones for development. These reflected the stated desire to diffuse the investment, and thereby the benefits from tourism, as widely as possible. The eight priority areas were northern Luzon, Manila Bay region, eastern Visayas, Bicol region, western Visayas, Lanao area, Davao provinces, Zamboanga, and Sulu.[48]

The implementation of tourism development bore little relationship to that schema, which had been the product of more politically detached technocrats.[49] In an effort to accelerate development it was decided that government financing of tourism initiatives would go primarily to four much smaller areas where there was already sufficient demand to make such ventures quickly profitable.[50]

Two of the areas selected fit the critical mass criterion—the Greater Manila area and the Laguna-Cavite areas across Manila Harbor. The third, Zamboanga, was an area of potential rather than present mass demand. It was located on the troubled island of Mindanao and was developed as an international gateway to the Philippines in what proved to be a futile attempt to redress the years of neglect in the southern Philippines. Of course roads, airports, and improved communications facilities can serve military and tourist requirements alike. In fact, some military personnel suggested that rebel sanctuaries might be most effectively undermined by turning their rustic settings into tourist attractions, thereby bringing jobs and development to the area.[51] By 1988, it appeared that the tourists rather than the rebels were in flight from the area.

The fourth focus of tourism development was the popular resort area of La Union, the home province of the then Secretary of Tourism and the heartland of President Marcos' Ilocano supporters. There are many tourist attractions in this area, so that although it does not have the critical mass of a city like Cebu, which was ignored in the five-year plan, La Union is, nevertheless, a reasonable center for tourism development.[52] Patronage is a time-honored tradition in the Philippines that martial law only embellished. La Union is one of the smaller provinces in the Philippines, but it has the largest of the 12 tourism field offices and is the only province with a subfield office, in this case in Secretary Aspiras' home town of Agoo. The La Union Field Office is itself a tourist attraction, sitting as it does on a high hill overlooking Bauang, the provincial capital, and the ocean. The staff numbered 22 to 24, including 8 to 10 employees in tiny Agoo. The field office nearest in size was in the Philippines' second largest city, Cebu, where there was a staff of 16.[53]

La Union has also benefited from tourist-related infrastructure, including the Marcos Highway, which conveniently connects Baguio and Agoo. In the 1980s construction workers were also kept busy building a Mount Rushmore-sized bust of President Marcos along a mountainside. Despite the financial crises endemic to the Philippines that worsened each month, there were always funds for the Ilocano region.

Filipino politicians historically have furnished bountiful patronage for their home or linguistic regions. None, however, had the 20-year opportunity of President Marcos. In the 1980s, the First Couple had their greatest personal tourism patronage opportunity. They redecorated and in large part re-created an entire Spanish town, in the sleepy town of Sarrat. The architecture was circa 1800 but the amenities were strictly jet set. The motivation was not entirely political, because it was in the president's home province and the initial flurry of construction was for his oldest daughter's wedding. Sentiment and politics are not incompatible, however. Just as the cabinet and army, particularly the officers, have come overwhelmingly from the Ilocano regions, generally, patronage also tended to flow to the region.[54] Even in 1988, over two years after Marcos was unceremoniously whisked into exile and after hundreds of stories verified his plunder of the country, he retained the loyalty of many Ilocanos.

Tourism under martial law became an elastic source of patronage not only in terms of the private sector but also in terms of government employees. Just as only a fraction of the government's budget was strictly within the Department of Tourism, many of the personnel working on tourist-related activities were attached to departments and agencies with nontourist-oriented primary functions such as city governments, cultural bodies, banking and investment institutions, transportation, and planning and budgetary bodies.

The Board of Travel and Tourist Industry (BTTI), the precursor to the DOT, employed about 250 people at its zenith in 1972. By 1977, over 1,000 were on the Department of Tourism payroll, with an additional 300 in the powerful Philippine Tourism Authority.[55] Given the growth in tourism, such increases may appear reasonable. Not so easy to rationalize were the six people assigned to the DOT library, which at that time had 58 items in its cardfile—mainly speeches—and a clippings file. The library had no magazine subscriptions and no books![56] The Marawi City Field Office had a staff of six, but only five tourists had come by late May 1977. They were ecstatic when this writer's family arrived, nearly doubling the arrivals for that year.[57]

An intensive examination done by the University of the Philippines College of Public Administration of the administration of the Department of Tourism and its comparison with other departments is not possible to detail here, but there was an unusual amount of slack in the Department of Tourism and the Philippine Tourism Authority even by Philippine standards.[58]

There were also some rather bizarre wage policies. Most government positions are subject to wage standardization, but certain positions are exempted if the work is of a highly technical nature. The Department of Agrarian Reform (DAR) could not hire lawyers because of abysmal salary scales, and because, for all the government's rhetoric, it refused to consider DAR lawyers "technical" and therefore exempt from pay ceilings. Thus, landlords could abort most land reform decisions by paralyzing litigation to which DAR could not adequately respond.[59] The Philippine Tourism Authority, on the other hand, had not only its lawyers but 70 percent of its staff of 300 declared "technical," so their salaries were much higher than most in the Civil Service.[60]

Most DOT personnel receive salaries based on the wage standardization scale. Nearly a third, however, were employed as casual or contractual workers, which allowed them to bypass the civil service examinations and position ceilings in the department. This means that such employees are considered temporary, but Aspiras saw to it that most of the benefits of permanent government service accrued to them.[61]

An indicator of the importance the president attached to tourism is the number of former presidential assistants and military men heading key

tourism departments. In the field offices and in other central office positions could be found many former congressional aides, former politicians, and journalists supportive of Marcos. Despite the reforms
attempted by the Civil Service Commission, all levels of the department
exhibited the characteristic bureaucratic problems of nepotism and overstaffing.

The growth of tourism brought fresh hope to travel agents and other
sectors of the tourist industry, initially hard hit by the ban on Filipino
travel abroad. This ban was lifted, but in its place the Central Bank
established an enormous travel tax that made travel abroad prohibitive
for all but the most affluent.[62] Other Southeast Asian governments followed suit, despite ASEAN fears that such protectionism would only
hurt all regional tourism. For most Filipinos, the domestic tourism slogan "See the Philippines First" is incontestable. All travel agencies were
instructed by the government to develop and promote low-cost travel
packages, but no statistics exist on the response to such package excursions or on domestic tourism in general.

The government was hopeful that domestic tourism could be a means
of better integrating the country's scattered linguistic and cultural
groups, of broadening the support for the New Society, and preserving
the arts, culture, and antiquities of the Philippines. A promising start in
this direction was taken in 1973 by the DOT and the Department of Education and Culture. Student group exchanges and local travel clubs were
organized. Other small and politically interesting programs designed to
develop local support for tourism were the DOT familiarization tours of
the islands given to various farmers' groups and to selected local political
leaders.[63] Unfortunately, most of the government's domestic tourism
budget was axed in fiscal year 1977 in one of DOT's rare economy
moves. The disastrous economic decline and political instability since
then kept both citizens and the government preoccupied with survival.

In an effort to control and direct the industry more effectively, the government sought to incorporate tourism into its general policy of corporativism.[64] After a lengthy campaign, Aspiras succeeded in getting all
tourist-related organizations to band together in a single umbrella organization, which the department promised to utilize as an advisory body.
The Tourism Organization of the Philippines (TOP) operated, however,
more as a channel for communicating tourism policies than as a limited
forum of interest-group opinion.

Academics were drawn into the support of tourism. The prestigious
University of the Philippines College of Public Administration contributed to the administrative critiques of the Department of Tourism's personnel policies and members of its distinguished faculty have spoken

before a variety of domestic and international forums regarding tourism's relationship to other sectors of the government hierarchy. The government moved early in its departmental history to institutionalize tourism on the campus through its economic and political support for the Asian Institute of Tourism (AIT). The AIT was expected to draw and develop professional talent for the tourism industry from all over Asia.[65]

So multifaceted had the support for the involvement of tourism in the nation's developmental perspective become that even the highest planning body, the National Economic Development Authority, played no appreciable role in regulating the direction or extent of the commitment. As one official observed, "Tourism is a given."[66]

The effect of the decision to concentrate on luxury tourism was extremely costly from a developmental standpoint. Huge amounts of foreign exchange earned by tourism went to imports needed for the industry. Most of these items are for five-star amenities; for example, over 98 percent of the luxury transport, limousines, and air-conditioned coaches must be imported from Japan. There was also an enormous gap between what the Central Bank actually received in foreign exchange and what the department, on the basis of polls, estimated that visitors spend.

The gap, in part, reflected three other problems: the tendency of many tour operators to "salt dollars abroad," the unobtrusive but thriving black market, and the tendency, still unstudied, for a significant percentage of foreign exchange to remain in or be remitted eventually to the tourist's own country. In an interview with owners of small hotels, the complaint was made that many imports end up on the black market or are clearly superfluous, like imported detergents.[67]

Unnecessary expenditures are particularly common when luxury hotels are managed by multinational chains that use a central purchasing system for all supplies for the chain. The problem of foreign exchange leakage is more characteristic of luxury travelers who are apt to stay, eat, and shop in the multinational, five-star hotels while on tours organized in the guest's home country. If, for example, a Japanese tourist flies with a prepaid Japan Airlines ticket to the Philippines, where he stays at the JAL-owned Manila Garden Hotel and takes Japanese-language tours in Japanese coaches, what portion of his overall vacation expenses accrues to the Philippines?

Tourism Development for Personal Political Objectives

At the outset, it was noted that in a system as centralized as the Philippine government under Marcos the distinction between international, national, and personal political uses of tourism was often blurred. This section, however, explores those specific instances in which tourism policy has been used directly to affect personal fortunes without any apparent long-range considerations.

It is sometimes said that in the Philippines there is no such thing as conflict of interest, merely convergence of interest. The development of the tourist industry tends to substantiate that observation. Many of the top policymakers and close friends of the president have large economic interests in tourism. As mentioned before, the First Lady's holdings included the Philippine Plaza Hotel. According to individuals interviewed, former Secretary of Tourism, Jose Aspiras, had numerous investments in Manila motels, as well as hotels in La Union and in Zamboanga. Marcos' friend, Roberto Benedicto, Philippine ambassador to Japan and former president of the Philippine National Bank, was a major backer of the Manila Holiday Inn and the Kanlaon Towers. Nemesio Yabut, former mayor of Makati, owned the Makati Hotel. Jose Manzanan, Dean of the Asian Institute of Tourism, owns the Pagsanjan Rapids Hotel, and his wife has several handicraft and souvenir shops in Manila. Former Secretary of Public Highways Baltazar Aquino's wife owns the Mayon Imperial Hotel in Legaspi.[68]

Not surprisingly, then, many of the new hotel owners secured government financing far in excess of the generous ceiling the president endorsed, though small inns and pension owners often could not obtain even standard bank loans. When Manila became severely overbuilt with luxury hotels constructed with cheap and seemingly limitless credit, the president's friends complained in their role as hoteliers that they must renegotiate their loans or they would be unable to meet their payments, leaving the country's banking institutions with 14 hotels to manage.[69] It has since happened.

It must be kept in mind that the surplus of rooms was not unforeseen. DOT planners were right on target with most projections of accommodation needs. It was not mere error or oversight, therefore, that made the PTA unwilling to adhere to its own forecast of what was economic in the face of what was politic. The regime motivations have already been discussed. Relevant here, however, is that through pursuing massive hotel construction, Marcos could make himself and several strong supporters more affluent, and in the process create a prima facie government rationale for increasing tourist promotion and development to fill up the hotels.[70]

The government renegotiated hotel mortgages and launched several waves of new initiatives to help the hotels. What appeared to be a vicious if deliberate cycle, however, was not that at all. The new repayment terms were in fact arranged by financial leaders who were in some instances linked directly or indirectly to the ownership of the hotels.

Moreover, as one government official remarked in another context, "If you owe the bank 1 million pesos, you are at the mercy of the bank. But if you owe the bank 200 million pesos, the bank is at your mercy."[71] In this case the figure is over 4.5 billion pesos owed to the Philippines' major national credit institutions and guaranteed by the Central Bank.

An entirely different type of personal political interest involved the national carrier, Philippine Airlines (PAL). The government, in contrast with some other nations, did not own its own airline before 1978 but retained a 24 percent interest in it through the Government Service Insurance System (GSIS). Since 1964, PAL had been substantially controlled by Benigno Toda, who reputedly acquired PAL as a political concession from the pre-Marcos Macapagal administration. Since then, PAL's fortunes have followed rather closely the waxing and waning of friendship between PAL's owner, Benigno Toda, and President Marcos.

At the beginning of the martial law period relations were close. President Marcos announced a "rationalization" of the air industry in which PAL's two domestic competitors were absorbed and their routes taken over by PAL.[72] In January 1974, PAL became the sole carrier for the Philippines.[73] The airline's growth was steady despite a very small capital base of approximately P25 million (US $3.43 million). Relations between Toda and Marcos reputedly soured, however, sometime in 1975. The breach occurred when Toda presented the Marcos family with a U.S. $2.4 million flight bill for the "his" and "her" jets used by the family on their many trips abroad. The details of the dispute were confirmed by a high-ranking government tourism official interviewed in mid-1977.[74]

A none-too-subtle campaign against the management of the airline followed. A series of newspaper articles attacked PAL's service and administrative record, and in all disputes and petitions that appeared publicly, PAL lost every round. Among the defeats was the loss of the right to run the prestigious Manila Hotel. This left PAL, which had planned most of the restoration of the historic hotel, without a hotel to promote, unlike most national carriers. The next defeat came in 1977 when PAL appealed unsuccessfully to raise rates on the domestic routes, then among the lowest in the world.[75] This petition occasioned a spate of anti-PAL publicity that was in marked contrast to the usual laudatory comments about various sectors of the travel industry.

The final defeat occurred when PAL sought to keep the government from further liberalizing its air rights policy. The controversy pitted PAL management directly against the powerful Secretary Aspiras and the rest of the tourist industry. In the name of promoting tourism and protecting the nation's huge investment in tourist infrastructure, Aspiras vigorously pushed for an increase in flights to and from the Philippines by foreign carriers, a liberalization in policy that PAL could not expect to match by

reciprocal agreements.[76] Though there was an appearance of evenhand-
edness in the dialogue over air policy, there was little doubt as to which
way the government would move.[77]

Toda, who evidently realized his mistake in crossing Marcos, had
attempted as early as 1976 and again in 1977 to sell PAL to the government. The policy defeats of 1977 left him no options. Not only could he
not promote a hotel, raise uneconomic fares, or compete against foreign
air rights, Toda also could not obtain a loan from the Development Bank
of the Philippines for the purchase of additional aircraft. The reason
given by the government was PAL's small capitalization.

In October 1977, the government, which had twice turned down
Toda's selling price, decided suddenly to implement a 1966 board decision ordering Toda to increase his capitalization from pesos 25 million
(US $3.43 million) to pesos 100 million (US $13.72 million)—something
he could not do. Roman Cruz, who succeeded Toda as PAL president and
board chairman, insists that although the government and Toda could
not agree on a selling price, Toda had waived preemptive rights and
allowed the government to subscribe "wholly to a 900 percent increase in
capitalization." In the process, Toda's control went from 74 percent to 8
percent, and two weeks later Cruz took control.[78]

Since then the economic facts of life have remained as intransigent as
the political events have been mercurial. Most of the criticisms of PAL's
performance went unmet, though Cruz found several foreign multinational concerns willing to finance increases in PAL's fleet. Moreover, Cruz
discovered that PAL had to raise domestic fares, an argument not unlike
the ill-fated Toda's.[79] PAL continued to lose money throughout Marcos'
rule. Between 1981 and 1984, the airline, which had been profitable
before takeover, lost $167.5 million. Vindictiveness proved very expen-
sive.[80]

PAL's uneasy situation was resolved in a manner reminiscent of the ex-
president's financial dealings with other economic giants not firmly controlled by the regime until after martial law began. Exploring how these
takeovers took place offers insight into the way economic policy tends to
trail political objectives. The process proceeds cautiously, without any
nationalistic rhetoric that might frighten foreign investment, and is
implemented with minimum expense and maximum political leverage.[81]

TOURISM POLITICS AFTER MARTIAL LAW

Just days before the inauguration of President Reagan in January 1981,
President Marcos "lifted" martial law. The New Society became the New
Republic, but the political reality was that the Old Oligarchy of the Mar-

cos family and friends was still in control. As National Assemblyman Orlando Mercado put it: Marcos "facelifted" martial law.[82] Obvious controls on the press were loosened; subtle ones such as control of newsprint were not. Decrees issued under martial law remained in force, and the president was authorized to issue new ones. Writs of habeas corpus were gone; preventive detention was not.

One dismayed critic put it this way, "At least under martial law there was an illusion that it was merely a transitory stage . . . now we are locked into a system where the President possesses all the same sweeping powers with no end in sight."[83] Perhaps the most striking thing about the lifting of martial law from the standpoint of tourism politics was that, there too, nothing really changed. Resorts were still being built.[84] Lavish conventions, film festivals, and other activities were still being promoted.[85] The Department of Tourism was still opening foreign offices, and the personal political and patronage uses of tourism continued unabated. It was rather like having a gala dance party on the *Titanic*.

The Philippines was broke but *Balikbayan* and Reunion for Peace continued. The New People's Army grew daily, but so did the mountainside bust of the President. Malnutrition was on the rise, but luxury imports of food and vehicles for the tourist industry were exempted from taxation. Television public service announcements designed to alert some 50,000 estimated victims to the danger signs of leprosy were cancelled because they might cast a pall over visitors to the Philippines.[86]

Tourism development in the Philippines was not just a case of a government suddenly and belatedly deciding to cash in on the boom in world travel. If that had been the case the government had the data and the expertise to expand tourism prudently. The 1973–1977 DOT plan is a model of careful, phased, and diffused development.

It was not departmental error that led to the reckless edifice complex or allowed virtually unlimited levels of government financing to be diverted ostensibly to hotel construction but often to short-term speculation. The department simply acknowledged the parameters of its political authority. One could even argue that from a departmental perspective, DOT stood to gain from the hotel situation: it emerged as a potential savior of the national finances.

Ralph Waldo Emerson once remarked that "a foolish consistency is the hobgoblin of little minds." But President Marcos was no dummy. Unfortunately, where tourism policy is concerned, pervasive irrationality in terms of the national interest may be quite ingenious and lucrative at the individual or regime level.[87]

What happened with Philippine tourism under Marcos makes sense only in terms of the political objectives and personal taste of the First Couple. Too often the critics attempt to educate decision makers on the hazards of over-building, chide them on their folly, and call for better planning and information. Such critics miss the point entirely. They assume that if decision makers only knew better such debacles would not happen. This is not so. The policy-making structure must include an insistence on cost-benefit analysis, competitive bidding, and adherence to supply-demand factors and encourage public input. Otherwise, the debacles in tourism policy are almost certain to be repeated. Obviously, no decision maker is a prophet. Mistakes or lucky guesses do occur. But one must not be misled by rhetoric designed to persuade rather than inform.

Political elites do not generally opt to maximize economic rationality, at least not for the entire society.[88] That has been true historically in the Philippines as well as elsewhere. Martial law did not make the president more altruistic or better equipped to pursue the economic needs of the nation. It simply allowed him to proceed unchecked by democratic institutions.

Optimizing political benefits is not uncommon in politics, be they democratic or authoritarian. However, in developing or de-developing nations such as the Philippines under Marcos, the weak political institutions are rarely a match for political elites, particularly when those elites are immune from democratic repercussions or insulated from investigative reporting.

The administration created a veritable "stage set" of modernization and elegance that few development specialists at home or abroad saw fit to challenge. President Marcos got increased military and economic aid, international recognition, personal wealth, and the loyalty of relatives and associates who parlayed government loans for development into wealth and prestige. By the time Marcos was forced into exile in 1986 the tourist industry was in disarray, political instability was growing, and the Philippines had the highest per capita debt in Asia. Ironically, the Philippines owes so much that the country has a kind of reverse leverage on international banking circles. Thus the international finance community is forced to restructure loans, much as the Philippine government was forced to do with the hotels, to avert further decline and maintain hope of future repayment.

Though the IMF and the World Bank have forced some fiscal austerity moves on the Philippine government, the real costs are being borne by the government's banking, credit, and insurance systems and by the public as a whole. In fact, the very depressed nature of tourism is now being used as an argument for still more tourist initiatives.

Tourism probably could have been a successful developmental tool. The Philippines is blessed with both outstanding scenic beauty and a rich cultural heritage. The Philippines needed an alternative to the volatile commodity markets in sugar, coconut, and pineapples. The original

1973 plan might well have matured into a more gradually developing, but less import-dependent tourism program.

Investment decisions should have weighed tourism's economic and social costs and benefits against what an infusion of credit might have meant to other revenue-producing or developmental sectors. The National Economic Development Authority, as the government's highest planning body, should have been prepared to do this, but because of the First Couple's priorities it did not.

To the government, the immediate primary value of Philippine tourism clearly was not its economic value. The policy is consistent and credible only when tourism is evaluated against the critical and immediate legitimacy needs of the Philippine leadership, made suddenly vulnerable by the imposition of martial law, and the domestic and personal political advantages derived from tourism development.

Tourism development bought time, good will, and influence at home and abroad at a time when all three were in dangerously short supply. The administration kept hoping it could continue to do so, but that was wishful thinking. The debacle of massive luxury tourism development was too obvious. The spillover effects of enormous inflation, housing shortages, energy and water shortages, and the shame of the gigantic proportions of mass prostitution (over 100,000 prostitutes in Manila alone) made tourism a political liability to the regime, a source of controversy, and an avenue for violence.[89] But leaders have a way of staying with the formulas that initially brought them success, long after they have proved their declining utility.[90] It was too late for a new scenario. The third act was ending.

TOURISM POLICY UNDER AQUINO

In 1986, President Corazon Aquino had at least two of the same political motives in promoting tourism that Ferdinand Marcos had immediately after martial law was declared. She needed first to reassure her international constituencies, such as Japan and the United States, that she was in control, with a stable situation, and that she was a legitimate leader who enjoyed popular support. Second, she needed to guarantee that there was no interruption in aid or investment occasioned by her assumption of power.

Unlike President Marcos in 1972, however, Aquino was coping with a ravaged and impoverished nation as well as two serious and sizeable insurrections—one communist-led, one Muslim. Further, she chose to pursue her agenda in a turbulent democratic environment rather than one in which all opposition had been crushed.

Aquino also had a stark economic motivation for furthering tourism. She inherited over a dozen luxury hotels the government had taken over when President Marcos and entourage abandoned them rather than pay back their loans. These constituted a formidable drain on government coffers. Similarly, resorts, the convention center, and the 17 private homes of ex-President Marcos also needed to be put to good use. So Aquino not only needed tourists for their ordinary economic utility, but she also needed to stop the nonproductive and costly government-controlled tourist infrastructure from continuing to be a drain on scarce resources.

Still she accurately observed that the best way to promote the Philippines was to reduce the misery, filth, and malnutrition that pervaded the beautiful islands. Soon after coming to power Aquino made several key decisions that dramatically changed tourism policy from what it was under President Marcos. First, she made it clear from the outset that, however politically useful tourism was, the Philippines' tourism policy would be designed to subsidize national development, not to support tourism per se. That meant that the Department of Tourism would have a modest budget and would have to live on it, rather than raiding other agencies and levels of government.[91]

This has meant that in practice tourist revenues have also been supportive of projects impacting on tourism but not specifically connected to the industry. For example, the "Tourist Belt" of Manila is an exciting and important venue for most international tourists. It is also filthy, congested, and smelly. Under the Aquino administration the DOT is helping the city of Manila with garbage collection, since both bodies realize that the safety, health, and appearance of the Tourist Belt reflect on their own mission and effectiveness.[92]

Second, she chose as leader of the DOT an individual who, though a friend of her late husband, had entrepreneurial talent and marketing experience. Jose ("Speedy") Gonzalez has a reputation for executive skills and integrity. This contrasts dramatically with Marcos crony, Jose Aspiras, whose public relations zeal exceeded any administrative ability and who was also involved in some of the seamiest aspects of sex tourism.[93]

Under Aspiras, tourist brochures promised "a tanned peach on every beach," sex tours including those for pedophiles flourished, and his own notorious motels and massage parlors were exempted from the martial law curfew. Under Gonzalez it has been firmly announced that no government advertising exploitative of women will be tolerated, promotional exhibits at tourism conferences will be tasteful, and pedophiles will be prosecuted and protests lodged with their countries of residence.[94]

In fact one of Gonzalez's first acts as tourism secretary was to bring a tour of Japanese women to the Philippines as part of a new media effort to sell the country as a wholesome destination rather than a prostitution den.[95]

Gonzalez is also attempting to deal with the massive overstaffing that occurred under Aspiras. In January 1987, a 50 percent reduction in staff was contemplated,[96] but as time went on interviewers found Gonzalez and his undersecretaries increasingly vague about how much cutback would be feasible and politically tolerable. He has discovered that, in a country with massive unemployment and low wages, a lean public organization is not as practical or politically advantageous as it was when he operated in the private sector.[97]

Gonzalez, perhaps more than most of Aquino's Cabinet, is completely in accord with the government's new push toward privatization. The Philippines has a history of adopting U.S. management and budgeting fads of which privatization is simply the latest. (Actually one might argue that President Marcos was quite innovative in thoroughly blurring the distinction between what belonged to the Philippines and what belonged to him. He personally "privatized" many of the nation's public resources.)

The desperate financial plight of the government makes privatization less an ideological decision than a pragmatic necessity. This is especially true of the DOT, which manages lavish properties of little public utility that were sequestered from the Marcos holdings. Until they can be sold, the DOT has converted 3 of the 17 homes the Marcoses owned in the Philippines for use as VIP lodges and luxury tourist quarters. Other properties built and managed by the Philippine Tourism Authority are also up for sale as the government struggles to raise cash.[98]

One building not for sale is Malacañang Palace, the traditional home of the chief executive since Spanish times. Malacañang is historically important and a veritable museum of Philippine treasures and the excesses of the Marcos era. Aquino chose not to live there in such opulence but to make it a tourist attraction and a center for ceremonial functions.

As such, it has been an enormous touristic and political success. Where once only the elite of the world could enter, now long lines form daily for the five peso (US25 cents) tours through the mansion. Others can take more individualized tours for P200 (US$10.00) and on Sunday it is absolutely free. Over US$50,000 a week are collected.[99]

Beyond the badly needed money and the exployment it furnishes guides and staff within and the vendors outside serving the crowds, the tour itself is useful as political education. Since the Marcos family fled at night, one of the particular fascinations of the tour is the portrait of their greed and insecurity that emerges from the things they left behind. No amount of charges and countercharges by Aquino and Marcos has the impact of actually seeing Imelda Marcos' 3,000 pairs of shoes, the hundreds of ball gowns, the vault with hastily ransacked jewel boxes, the toy Rolls Royce, the drawers of imported chocolates, and amidst it all the remnants of fear.

The bulletproof glass that enclosed immense verandas, the miniature hospital for the president (who never admitted he was ill), and the mattresses laid on the floor where all the entourage slept the last few days reveal the Marcos family concerns. So fearful were they of the revenge of Filipinos that they all slept in the one room with a secret exit that could take them to the river and away from the palace if it came under seige. It was a lifestyle of the rich and infamous that has no peer.[100]

The Aquino government also conducts a "Freedom Tour" that goes to the major sites of the 1986 "People Power" revolution that unseated Marcos. A pictorial of events is another popular attraction at the Philippine International Convention Center, built by Imelda Marcos to showcase the arts and entertain "the beautiful people."[101]

The government initially decided to keep the *Balikbayan* program for both political and economic reasons. Like Marcos, Aquino wanted to encourage Filipinos living abroad and those of Filipino ancestry to visit. They represent a potentially influential constituency of nearly two million.[102] Economically, they are also needed. Beyond their normal tourist expenditures *Balikbayans* also are a source of remittances and gifts. In fact *Balikbayans* are now allowed to bring special "*Balikbayan* boxes" of goods when they enter. Gift-giving to relatives in large extended families actually constitutes in many cases the *Balikbayan*'s greatest travel-related expense. Currently, there is a campaign on to get *Balikbayans* to do their special gift-shopping in Manila so the economy can get the benefit of their largesse and they in turn are spared the hassle of transporting gifts.[103] Though still encouraged to return, *Balikbayans* found some special discounts stopped in 1988 as an economy move by the government.

Tourism policy under Aquino has also attempted to diffuse benefits more broadly than was true under Marcos. Three initiatives are worth noting. First, the government during its negotiating has found the Muslim insurgents interested in getting more tourism opportunities for their community. The government is receptive to encouraging more investment and doing more tourist promotion of Muslim areas, but it needs to be assured of tourist safety. It was insurgents in the past who by their kidnappings and terrorism of tourists destroyed earlier initiatives on Mindanao.[104]

A second program that is already being implemented is an effort to help families get involved in tourism, earn some money, and still provide basic accommodations for both domestic and international tourists. By early 1987 the homestay program, as it is called, was operating in several communities where tourist infrastructure is scarce and yet where local festivals attract both foreign and domestic visitors.

> The main idea behind the program is to make travel affordable to domestic tourists and give the foreigners the chance to experience Philippine culture among Filipino families. Participants in the program are families (in the festival areas) who can accommodate at least one paying guest . . . provided with . . . a guest room, clean toilet and bath, meals at reasonable prices, [and] clean surroundings.[105]

The only problem thus far is neither supply nor demand but over-generous hospitality: The host families are simply spending too much on their guests to make a profit! The DOT is now attempting to instruct host families in how to achieve a balance between their sociability and their need to develop a profitable clientele.[106]

A third initiative has been to set up in key cities several courtesy centers with clean restrooms and other basic facilities for the traveling public. Anyone familiar with touring in developing nations will realize that these are the kinds of no-frill amenities that demonstrate that the Aquino government's priorities are at least in good order.[107]

Whether the Philippines will be able to build a solid tourist record, however, is still open to question. The Aquino government has had to retrieve tourism policy from its disastrous and expensive excesses and recast it according to the needs and budget of the impoverished nation. This it has done with flair, taste, and imagination.

However, tourism remains ultimately dependent on political stability and peace for its successful development. To the extent tourism is no longer a source of instability and a focus of opposition, much progress has been made. Ultimately, however, Aquino must face the economic despair that has fed the insurgencies and encouraged widespread property crime or steady development of tourism is impossible.[108]

The Philippines has been the scene of many "miracles" since the 1986 presidential election provided the catalyst for a new political dynamic. If the past administration made "martial law, Filipino style" into a tourist attraction, then "People Power" and the reemergence of democracy should be at least as attractive.

4

Thailand: Where Tourism and Politics Make Strange Bedfellows

TOURISM in Thailand defies easy categorization because it flourishes at so many levels, from the most esoteric cultural pilgrimages to the most bawdy, degrading, and dangerous sex odysseys. Tourism politics ranges from the benign indifference of the monarchy to the elaborately woven economic and political intricacies that bind together such unlikely tourism sponsors as the military and the bureaucracy. Private sector giants such as the Oriental Hotel of Bangkok and the Grace Hotel, which operates a brothel, share kindred stakes on some issues like the hotel tax, but are light years from each other in demeanor, ambience, and clientele.

BACKGROUND

Thailand has 53 million people in a land area comparable to that of France. Thailand is distinct from most of its neighbors in that it was never colonized, a factor that has kept Thai culture evolving naturally without the sharp discontinuities that have affected most developing countries in Asia. Still, Thailand has not escaped the grinding poverty of the region. Nearly a third of the nation's population lives below the very austere Thai poverty line, and in some regions of the northeast, over one-half of the people are in desperate poverty.

Thailand's political structure is at once very complicated and yet remarkably consistent over the last generation. Thailand is a monarchy where the king has strong potential authority, but he seldom becomes involved in day-to-day politics. His immense personal popularity may be a reflection of his very selective participation, but other centers of power in the military and bureaucracy still behave as if he is a force with which to be reckoned.

The military has been the dominant de facto political force since Thailand began a process of democratization in 1932. Before that Thailand was an absolute monarchy. Although political parties do in fact exist from time to time and there have been periods of civilian rule, the military has been the major power broker on the scene. There have been, throughout the last 20 years, a series of coups; some victorious, some not; some against civilian leaders, others directed at ruling military leaders. And through it all, tourism has grown.

How can this be? When examples abound of political instability crippling tourism, why does Thailand remain impervious? One reason is that such coups are almost always "bloodless." In fact, it was a cause for great alarm in 1973 when some deaths actually occurred. As the governor of the Tourism Authority of Thailand (TAT) delicately put it, "Most tourists are quite familiar with Thailand's unique ability to solve its internal problems without any serious incident."[1]

Another factor encouraging an aura of political continuity has been the bureaucracy. It has provided stability, permanence, and cohesiveness at times of political change. The bureaucracy does not, however, have a reputation for initiative, innovation, or efficiency. Yet taken with the military, the bureaucracy has functioned to give Thailand a reputation for predictability and security that has enabled tourism to remain indifferent to political changes at the top.[2]

Power is dispersed in bureaucratic and military cliques within the Thai political system, which may be why the system is continually shifting as groups jockey for power.[3] In general, one can say that Thailand is a limited democracy in which the Parliament exerts only a modest influence over the actual functioning of the political system and even less over the economic system. The prime minister, often a military leader, does not fully control his own cabinet or the military. His powers are those of persuasion, with the cabinet the de facto authority unless the military intervenes.

The private sector, of which tourism is an important part, is similarly fragmented. In general, the government encourages a free enterprise system, relatively unregulated compared with countries like the Philippines or Singapore, which have similar economic philosophies. Although the laissez-faire attitude of the government is enjoyed by many touristic enterprises who fear government regulation of the industry, there is also an awareness that such freedom comes as a result of a general pattern of indifference to tourist interests, which is itself a product of reduced bureaucratic opportunities for patronage or influence peddling.

The government's past lack of urgency or active involvement with tourism may soon make industry leaders nostalgic, for as tourism's importance has grown, the government has reluctantly assumed a greater and greater role in its development. In 1985 the government increased government funding, especially for promotion, in response to a severe glut in luxury hotels in Bangkok. Despite steady growth and over 3.2 million tourists in 1987, past hotel building sprees threaten the current economic condition of the industry.[4]

Criticism of the industry has also grown as its reliance on sex tours and general prostitution has become more pronounced. Perhaps because Thailand was never colonized, and also because the nation has had a history of concubinage and prostitutes in its traditional culture, opposition was slow to recognize the difference in scale, violence, and social decay implied by sex tourism.

At this point sex tours and prostitution have merely been mentioned as external elements in the development of Thai tourism. As government tourism policy is explored it will be obvious that few sectors escape responsibility or credit for the social, economic, and political impact of that policy. Yet political and administrative options do exist for facilitating the integration of tourism into the nation's overall development scheme without all the heavy social costs now being endured.

TOURISM DEVELOPMENT IN THAILAND

The government of Thailand recognizes tourism's central place in the economy of Thailand. In 1982 tourism surpassed rice as the leading earner of foreign exchange. Tourism earned nearly a billion dollars in 1981 from slightly more than 2 million international tourists;[5] that revenue record changed to $1.8 billion in 1987.[6] Still, its salience to the politics of Thailand is only belatedly being recognized. "It is not automatically on the political agenda, as is defense, agriculture, or energy. It does not have the attraction and 'glamour' of a national airline, nor is it especially susceptible to influence, like Thai International, which is an integrated organization under one management."[7]

Even as a source of patronage, tourism is insignificant. In 1984, the Tourism Authority of Thailand (TAT) had only 496 employees, less than half the size of the Philippine Tourism Ministry or the bloated Bangladesh tourism corporation.[8] Ownership patterns in the industry are complicated as a result of mixed, Thai-foreign holdings, and even earnings in the fragmented private sector are not as lucrative as in many other sectors.[9]

Still the government, albeit hesitantly, has assumed a modest role in tourism development since 1960. Since that time tourism arrivals have mushroomed, with impressive gains and only two decreases in 24 years (see Table 4.1). During this same period, the number of hotel rooms in Bangkok alone went from 959 to 24,000.

The Tourism Organization of Thailand (TOT) began in 1960, and was

Table 4.1. Number of tourist arrivals in Thailand
and revenue received from the tourist industry
(1960–1985).

Year	Number of tourist arrivals in Thailand	Tourism revenue (million baht)
1960	81,340	196
1961	107,754	250
1962	160,809	310
1963	195,076	394
1964	211,924	430
1965	225,024	506
1966	285,117	754
1967	335,845	952
1968	377,262	1,220
1969	469,784	1,770
1970	628,671	2,175
1971	638,738	2,214
1972	820,758	2,718
1973	1,037,737	3,457
1974	1,107,392	3,852
1975	1,180,075	4,538
1976	1,098,442	3,990
1977	1,220,672	4,607
1978	1,453,839	8,894
1979	1,591,455	11,232
1980	1,858,801	17,763
1981	2,015,615	21,455
1982	2,218,429	23,879
1983	2,191,003	25,050
1984	2,346,709	27,317
1985	2,438,270	31,768
1986	2,818,292	n.a.

SOURCE: Tourism Authority of Thailand (TAT). *Annual Report,*
1987

charged primarily with promoting Thailand as a tourist destination. At
that time, Thailand was receiving less than 100,000 tourists. That would
soon change, however, as the Vietnam war escalated and Thailand
became a rest and recreation (R&R) base for war-weary soldiers. Those
without families meeting them found Thailand's burgeoning bars, cafes,
and nightclubs ready to receive them. Prostitution as an occupation grew
dramatically from its Thai-based, more or less stable clientele to an
increasingly large and fleeting dependence on foreigners.

By 1975, when American involvement in the Vietnam War ceased,
Thailand's tourist base was over a million and no longer dependent on
soldiers. Today in the late 1980s, tourism is based primarily on group
tours and business travel, though shore leave for sailors continues to fuel

tourism in resort areas like Pattaya. Sex, however, continues to be a major motivation for travel to Thailand for each of these groups.

Although the TOT and, since 1979, the Tourism Authority of Thailand do not emphasize such attractions, there is a heavy emphasis on the friendliness of the Thai people and it is women who are featured in the promotions. The governor of the TAT sees prostitution as more or less an inevitable side effect of tourism everywhere. His lack of zeal coupled with a laissez-faire attitude toward the less-inhibited marketing of the private sector has meant that even the more staid tourist guidebooks and trade magazines can scarcely ignore the manner in which Thai tourism has become infamous: "Witness the crude puns on the name of the capital and of the nation—Thighland."[10]

Perhaps in no other country in the world has tourist motivation been so obviously linked to sex. Consider just a few of the demographics. Estimates put the number of Thai prostitutes at one million, which would mean that at any given time almost 4 percent of Thailand's female population is involved.[11] That does not include all those women who have been prostitutes and have left this short-lived career, nor does it number all the men and boys now a part of the industry.

In Bangkok, there are 400,000 more female than male residents, yet 89 percent of all tourists are male.[12] Nor can business travel, which is male dominated, account for the male imbalance, for it declined in 1981, though overall tourism grew. (In any event many businessmen prefer not to choose between business and pleasure so there is considerable overlap between sex and business travel.) "The country's two largest sources of traffic—Japan and Malaysia, totalling a 29 percent share in 1981—account for a far greater proportion of male arrivals compared with the national average, than do other regional destinations. Only the Philippines had a higher male share than Thailand—and the Philippines has a similar reputation."[13]

With such striking private-sector success, it is easy to see why the government (1) is not obliged to mention women explicitly in its promotional narratives, (2) hesitates to intervene meaningfully in the selling of sex tours, and (3) in the case of the king has absolutely nothing to do with tourism.

What then does the government do with respect to tourism? The general answer is more and more. Since the Third National Social Development Plan (1972–1976), the Tourism Development Plan has been an internal component of government planning and has emerged as a major economic priority in the ambitious Fifth Plan (1982–1986). This has not translated into a corresponding political emphasis, however.

The primary objective of tourism development has always been to earn foreign exchange that will ease the onerous balance of payments

Table 4.2. Balance of international tourist trade, 1981–1985.

Balance of Tourism	1981	1982	1983	1984	1985
Tourism revenues	21,455	23,879	25,050	27,317	31,768
(millions)	$ 983	$ 1,038	$ 1,089	$ 1,156	$ 1,171
Tourism expenditures	6,027	6,151	7,896	7,208	7,587
(millions)	$ 276	$ 267	$ 343	$ 305	$ 280
Difference	15,428	17,728	17,154	20,109	24,181
(millions)	$ 707	$ 771	$ 746	$ 851	$ 891

NOTE: Exchange rate 1981   U.S.$1 = Bht. 21.82
              1982–1983 U.S.$1 = Bht. 23.00
              1984   U.S.$1 = Bht. 23.64
              1985   U.S.$1 = Bht. 27.13

SOURCE: Bank of Thailand

problem and so it did. A study done in 1982 discovered that of the entire trade deficit, 40 percent was reduced by tourism revenues. Because of the type of tourism development emphasized, which includes resorts and other forms of luxury tourism, the study went on to report that the country spent for tourism 34.76 percent of its total income from that sector.[14] The TAT assessment of tourist revenues to expenditures also does not attempt to cope with such indirect tourism cost in terms of such aspects as police, water, and health facilities. Nor does it measure tourism's ratio of revenues to costs compared with other sectors of government investment (see Table 4.2).[15]

A second goal is to stimulate regional economic development (see Fig. 4.1).

Running a distant third in terms of resources committed to it is tourism development's role in preserving natural resources, the environment, the culture, and historical sites. The government's evaluation of the tourist sector continues to be almost exclusively in economic terms with little concrete attention given to the distribution of income and the sociocultural impact of the rapid development of the tourist industry. Though lip service is paid to preservation, as in the Nature Protection Programme included in the Master Plan of each resort, actual effort is lacking not only in financial backing but also basic legislative authority.[16]

Although the TOT proved to be little more than a minor marketing arm of tourism, the TAT, established by Parliament in 1979, is a much more multifaceted body. The TAT also represents a political compromise. The government had wanted a Tourism Control Act that would have the tourism organization assume some regulatory functions vis-à-vis the tourist industry. This the industry was able to fend off, thanks to its close linkages in Parliament. Closer control continues to be an issue, and

Figure 4.1. Priority of tourist spots for development throughout the Fifth National Social Development Plan (1982–1986)

Priority	Tourist Spots
Step of upgrading to be a complete tourist spot	Chiangmai, Pattaya/Bangsaen, Karnchanaburi, and Phuket
Step of study program (rank from high step to low step)	
1. Feasibility study	Sukhothai, Phitsanuloke, Kampaengphet, Tak, Huahin/Chaam, Phetchaburi, Rajburi, Songkla/Haadyai, Samui/Surat Thani
2. Master plan	Chiangrai, Payao, Lampang, Lamphun, Ayutthya, Lopburi, Saraburi, Chantaburi, Rayong, Trad, Khon-Khaen, Nakorn-Ratchasima, Udorn Thani, Sakon Nakorn, Nakorn Phanom
3. Preliminary study	Phang-nga, Krabi, Nakorn-Srithammarat, Phattalung, Trang, Kalasin, Ubol Ratchathani
4. Preliminary survey	Phetchabun/Lomsak, Loei, Nakorn-Nayok

SOURCE: Tourism Authority of Thailand (TAT), *Annual Report, 1987.*

by early 1985 there were general expectations in the travel trade press that such an act would soon be passed. In 1979, however, the industry acquiesced to a stronger national tourism organization in the form of the TAT, for they felt that tourism promotion needed a more active advocate in government and better research and statistical studies.

Industry advocates also hoped that the TAT would protect the industry from further heavy taxes. Currently, there is a hotel room tax of 11 percent and a restaurant tax of 8 percent. Each of these represents close to if not the zenith of taxes on the tourist industry in any nation.[17] Some major tourist destinations, like Honolulu, have no hotel taxes. In Thailand, however, hotel taxes had been at 16.5 percent until overbuilding left many hotels in dire straits.[18] The taxes collected go not to the industry, but into the general revenue.

It is arguably better to make tourism support other sectors of the economy more central to national development. And unquestionably it is politically safer to tax tourists than residents. Still, the industry was annoyed that its overall economic contribution was largely unrecognized, while it remained a convenient source of general tax revenue.

The industry also hoped that a strong TAT would expedite the exquisitely slow and vacillating decision-making process. Specifically, the industry wanted affirmative decisions on a new international airport and a convention center for Bangkok. Neither have been forthcoming. But the TAT has moved to enlarge its role in the tourism development of Thailand with its change from an organization to a statutory-based authority.

Theoretically, TAT has at its disposal some impressive political clout. "Its board of 11 members includes some of the most important cabinet ministers and three non-government members. The chairman is an influential deputy prime minister who is a former director general of TOT and who has been concerned with the industry for many years."[19]

However, names on a board are not synonomous with commitment and political involvement. Membership on the board is chosen for political purposes (not necessarily related to tourism). Most have other primary responsibilities, and only one member is from the tourist industry, which limits the board's role as a communicator to or from the travel industry. Moreover the board tends to act more or less as a rubber stamp, ratifying the suggestions of the TAT governor, rather than initiating policies or serving as a channel for innovation and change. Thai administration in general is noteworthy for its heavy emphasis on hierarchy and relative indifference to productivity and achievement.[20] That hierarchy is evident at TAT, where even what are usually staff positions are arranged in a tight superior-subordinate pattern.

Currently, TAT spends 54 percent of its budget on administration, a figure that critics say prevents it from aggressively promoting Thailand. This figure probably reflects less of an interest in efficiency than a high tolerance for publicly supported entertainment and surplus staff.[21]

Tourist arrivals are not solely a matter of marketing, however, and as the TAT has stated, it has been powerless to deal with media reports of skirmishes on the Thai border, the strength of the Thai baht, or region-specific economic problems. In 1983, for example, Thailand's Asia and Pacific market, the most important source of tourists, was affected by the devaluation of the Indonesian rupiah and the repeated devaluation of the Philippine peso. Both countries also collected massive travel taxes on residents going abroad. In the case of the Philippines, those electing to pay the tax left, in many cases not on vacations but to relocate families abroad, to avoid the political insecurity.[22]

Domestic Tourist Promotion

Although it ranks a mere sixth in terms of TAT goals (see Fig. 4.2), domestic tourism has had some encouragement from the tourism organi-

Figure 4.2. Major policy of the Tourism Authority of Thailand

To achieve these objectives, TAT designates major policy according to the subsequent guidelines:

1. Promoting and inducing more international tourists to Thailand. The increase of revenue especially foreign currency from tourists helps the nation's economy in a short period.

2. Increasing tourist attractions in regional areas in order to distribute incomes from tourism to people of all regions.

3. Conserving natural resources and environment and reviving culture in order to retain Thai identity at its best.

4. Developing facilities and upgrading travel services to accepted standard to impress visitors in higher degree.

5. Promoting safety to both domestic and international tourists in order that they can reach their destinations with the confidence that their bodies and property are free from danger.

6. Encouraging domestic travel, especially in low-income and youth groups, in order to increase travel services for Thais.

7. Increasing manpower in tourist industry as far as possible.

8. Encouraging Thai people to participate in activities related to tourism development.

SOURCE: Tourism Authority of Thailand, *Annual Report, 1983,* p. 15.

zation.[23] The government sees domestic tourism as a means of diffusing tourism's economic impact beyond the major centers frequented by international tourists and keeping discretionary travel funds in the country. The goal is to stimulate more modest infrastructural development in the provinces, which will be affordable for Thais as well as less conventional foreigners. The TAT also hopes that domestic tourism will awaken more interest in Thai culture and its preservation, although recent studies of domestic tourists indicate a greater preference for the recreational travel to the south over the more cultural and historical landmarks of northern Thailand.[24]

In 1983 the TAT organized fifteen tours for a total of nearly 1,300 Thais, including some educational tours for the young. Its major role vis-à-vis domestic tourism was, however, promotional rather than implementational. Radio programs, posters, documentary films, television, and a monthly tourist magazine were all enlisted in selling Thailand to the Thais.[25] Apparently, it has worked, helped along perhaps by a tax on outbound travel.[26] Hotels are rapidly developing throughout the provinces and TAT is busy developing a series of tourist routes for the domestic tourist. In 1987 there were 8.7 million Thais traveling within the country.[27]

TAT Growth

Since 1979 the TAT has grown fairly rapidly, with projected growth between 1983 and 1986 to go from 496 to 715 employees.[28] Similarly the TAT has enlarged its share of the national budget. Immediately after the TAT was formed, its 1980 budget was increased 20 percent to $4.1 million.[29] The budget was $6,387,000 in 1983.[30]

It has also enlarged its primary promotional role. In 1983 TAT had nine offices overseas and was active in representing Thailand at international conventions, trade fairs, and through media activities. TAT also invited some 170 travel writers and industry entrepreneurs to visit Thailand. The TAT produced a travel magazine, developed brochures, and coordinated its publicity with provincial tourism efforts.[31]

TAT also encouraged convention travel, though it met with only limited success. Greater results came from its supervision of souvenir shops and tourism training, the simplification of immigration and customs procedures, and the formation of an expanded tourism police force.[32]

The latter became necessary as tourists increasingly became the targets of crime. Bangkok is one of the most violent cities in the world. In the first half of 1978, for example, 8,678 serious crimes took place.[33] The stepped-up implementation of such a force, however, was tied less to the number of crimes against tourists than the 1983 drop in tourist arrivals. The TAT speculated in its annual report that tourists from several major tourist-generating countries had been dissuaded by accounts of crime against international tourists reported in their local media.[34]

Thus in 1984, the TAT announced a tripling of the tourist police from 255 to 850 men, to be partially funded by the TAT although the men would remain formally part of the Thai national police.[35] Funding for the Tourist Police included US$13.6 million in 1984 with a proposed supplement of $820,000 for mobile units. This suggests that tourist security is a major concern. Another major deterrent to travel to Thailand, which is candidly acknowledged in the 1983 Annual Report, is supergonorrhea, an antibiotic-resistant strain infecting an estimated 70 percent of Thailand's prostitutes. Thus far, the TAT has been unable or unwilling to address this aspect of tourist concern.[36]

A major TAT effort has been directed at planning—a function that has thrown it unwillingly into the political fray. Environmentalists and church and women's groups have shown an increased inclination to criticize the laissez-faire development of tourism in the period from 1960 to 1980. They are particularly vocal in their complaints about Bangkok's congestion and ineffective administration and the haphazard growth of Pattaya. The latter developed totally without planning or regulation. It was only in 1979 that a fledgling municipal government was formed. Pattaya remains even today a wide open city, where crime and corruption are endemic. This tourist "paradise" had 298 violent crimes in 1982. Tourist police surveillance was accelerated and violent crime dropped nearly a third in 1983.[37]

Although regulation and the tourist police have brought some semblance of order to the boom town, it is the established large-scale enterprises that have benefited the most. Government subsidies, tax incentives, and opportunities to influence government come, as so often happens, to those already most advantaged. Small-scale operators, beach vendors, and the like with low and unpredictable incomes form what the International Labour Organisation calls the informal sector of the economy. They have lost as a result of the government's regularization of Pattaya's politics and economics. Shunted to unfrequented stretches of beach or subject to harassment for kickbacks to the police, these most vulnerable sectors of the tourist economy have done poorly as a consequence of government interest.[38]

Pattaya is often cited by Thai planners in and out of TAT with that chic sense of horror U.S. planners reserve for Waikiki. Both places, however, make money by the buckets—a result that scarcely augurs well for restrained and aesthetic development. Consequently, although the TAT has embarked on a variety of planning projects, including one for Pattaya, it has not been able to secure the necessary loans and privately has been opposed. Although the TAT continues to have its governor on the city council of Pattaya, the city resists further controls.

The international tourist industry, although sympathetic to critics of Pattaya, is seldom lacking in encouraging the government to open more and more areas to tourism. Phuket is another relatively new resort destination that wants to enjoy the same self-rule Pattaya has, a position in which the international industry and the developers are in general accord, and with which TAT appears to be in agreement. But not to worry, "Thailand has so many underdeveloped and unspoilt coastal resort areas that, while recognising the finite supply and desireability of keeping many of the beaches without major tourist developments, the Thai authorities are keen to appeal to as broad a spectrum of international tourists as possible."[39]

The clientele is not necessarily getting any broader with the development of more beach towns, but those now attracted by sex tours are certainly not limited to any particular geographic area. In that sense there is something (or at least someone) for everyone. Chiangmai in the north has its share of brothels, primarily catering to Westerners; Bangkok is international in its attractions, while some frontier towns such as Haad Yai cater to Malaysian males escaping a more spartan fate in Islamic

Table 4.3. International tourist arrivals to Thailand.

1. Number of tourists

Of the entire total 2,438,270 tourists to Thailand by country of residence, tourists from East Asia and the Pacific totaled 1,435,647. They possess a major market share of 58.88 percent. The minor market shares are tourists from Europe, totaling 455,329 with a share of 18.67 percent; tourists from South Asia, totaling 215,135 with a share of 8.82 percent; tourists from the Americas, totaling 192,965 with a share of 7.91 percent; tourists from the Middle East, totaling 127,441 with a share of 5.23 percent; and tourists from Africa, totaling 11,753 with a share of 0.49 percent.

2. Major markets	Total numbers	Percentage change
Malaysia	553,830	− 3.26
Japan	226,516	− 0.82
Singapore	189,861	+ 9.09
U.S.A.	150,765	+ 9.60
Hong Kong	131,853	+ 3.84
India	120,170	+ 2.21
Australia	98,742	+21.21
West Germany	96,473	+ 3.76
United Kingdom	81,635	+ 9.09
France	70,063	+18.76
Taiwan	68,890	+13.35
Saudi Arabia	57,594	+ 1.92
Italy	43,194	+10.66

3. Tourist profile

A. Repeat tourists made up 57.14 percent of the total. The other 42.86 percent were first-time tourists.

B. About 68.07 percent of the tourists came to Thailand independently, the rest (31.93 percent) by group tour.

C. Male tourists made up 71.66 percent of the total.

D. 22.73 percent of the tourists were administrative and managerial personnel, 15.30 percent were laborers, and production and service workers, and 14.97 percent were professionals.

E. 93.85 percent stayed in hotels and 6.15 percent stayed with friends or in other types of accommodations.

SOURCE: Tourism Authority of Thailand, *Annual Statistical Report on Tourism in Thailand, 1983,* pp. 10–11.

Malaysia. (Some contend that Malaysia has a well-developed prostitution industry, but is keeping a lower profile and depending on a domestic clientele. If so, it has not dampened international travel from Malaysia. Malaysia remains Thailand's number one market [see Table 4.3].)[40]

The TAT is currently planning tourist infrastructure in remote areas like Samui in the south of Thailand. Whether it will benefit from the mistakes made in Pattaya and Phuket remains to be seen.

In addition to international tourism promotion, planning, training programs, and statistical research, the TAT also manages a few tourist establishments, though it in no way parallels the levels of involvement of either the catalyst role of the Indian Tourism Development Corporation in India or even the infrastructural support position of the Philippine Tourism Authority. Nor does the TAT have the authority to monitor, regulate, or set standards for any segment of the tourist industry. In exchange for a high hotel and restaurant tax, the industry has virtual autonomy.

Nor is the industry willing to channel its political interests through the TAT, as the Tourism Organization of the Philippines did under President Marcos.[41] Each part of private sector tourism continues to bypass the TAT and make its case directly to government, a practice that TAT is powerless to stop and which lawmakers are quick to encourage, for it continues their traditional patron-client role. In this the system parallels interest-group politics in Pakistan.

The private sector did form a Tourism Awareness Committee to promote official and public understanding of tourism's economic impact even as it continued to oppose comprehensive tourism legislation that would set up a tourism minister and coordinate tourism planning and regulate tourist establishments.[42]

The one area in which the TAT and the private sector have been allied beyond general marketing has been in support of a new international airport and a convention center. When neither materialized, arrivals and lengths of stay declined, and when Bangkok hotels were, by the early 1980s, found to be overbuilt and underutilized, the atmosphere was right for cooperation. TAT and the nation's hoteliers formed the Convention Promotion Board in July 1983.[43]

The hotel industry went through a massive period of building, ostensibly for the 200th anniversary of the monarchy in 1982. Like the IMF–World Bank Conference in the Philippines and Asiad '82 in India, this building spree was financed in part by government concessions, in this case from the Board of Investments. In all three cases, some 6,000 rooms were added to existing stock in the respective capital cities, and in all three arrivals for the premier attraction were grossly overestimated and general demand has continued to fall short. The Bangkok case appears not to be quite as severe or as extravagant in supporting facilities, but that could be only the result of less scrutiny. Investigative reporting is not as finely honed an art in Thailand, and the language acts as a general barrier to outside researchers.

The nature of control over the major hotels is not quite clear. On the one hand, Robert Wood has argued that

> joint enterprises with multinationals may allow politically dominant classes without a strong economic base to circumvent their economically dominant

class (and ethnic competitors). This is likely to be a factor in countries like Malaysia, Indonesia, and Thailand, where alliance with the multinational avoids the necessity of doing business with the Chinese commercial classes. This ethnic-class competition may in fact bias tourist policy towards luxury tourism, since a tourism policy based on the expansion of the existing accommodation system would favor the Chinese already in control of it.[44]

Although that could in part explain the massive hotel building in Bangkok, it ignores the close working relationship between the Chinese commercial elite and the government. As Brewster Grace observed, "A highly successful accommodation has evolved. Government officials sit on the boards of directors of private enterprises and Chinese serve as management in the state enterprises and government monopolies originally established to keep some economic activity out of Chinese hands."[45]

Whether accommodation or competition is the practice followed, it is clear that participation by transnational corporations (TNCs) has not generally been in terms of equity or even medium- to long-term management contracts. Rather TNC involvement has tended toward ad hoc technical service agreements and associations with referral or reservation chains.[46]

SOCIAL AND POLITICAL IMPACT OF TOURISM IN THAILAND

The social and political impact of tourism may not be decidedly different in Thailand than in many other countries, but the type of information is. Thus, this chapter is, like the others, not exactly comparable in data and analysis.

Employment statistics are not, for example, readily available for the tourist industry. However, based on tourist arrivals, a conservative estimate is that there are probably one million or more individuals who are directly employed in legal occupations as a result of tourism. Further, over a million prostitutes are not included because prostitution is illegal. Another million people are indirectly employed as a result of tourism. The TAT also cooperates with several universities that either have tourism degrees, such as Payap College in Chiangmai, or tourist guide training programs, such as the one at Silpakorn University. The TAT also runs hotel training programs in several provinces as part of its efforts to encourage Thai upward mobility in the industry. In 1983 the hotel training program alone had 400 graduates.[47]

The specific impact of the tourist industry has been shown to vary markedly in its impact, depending on the region and the tourist clientele. Governments in Thailand and elsewhere have generally supported the diffusion of tourists (Bhutan and the Maldives being notable exceptions) if their security and comfort can be guaranteed. Few governments, however, have sought the low-budget tourists, perhaps because they offer less in economic and certainly in political terms to the ruling elite. Some governments have also feared that low-budget tourists might have a more pernicious effect on social values. Still they require much less in infrastructure. And so the debate persists.

Erik Cohen is perhaps the first to not take sides in this controversy and instead examine the low-budget visitor in Thailand, if not systematically, at least not ideologically. His studies show that budget tourists are neither cultural purists searching for the authentic travel experience nor degenerate beach bums looking for a cheap high, but that actually tourists in this expenditure category run the gamut of motivations. What Cohen did suggest is that, at least in Thailand, those who go to the north of Thailand are more apt to be interested in the culture, the tribal groups, and interaction with Thais. As such, they contributed more to the local economy and tended to be more considerate of local customs. Those heading for the beaches in the south, on the other hand, took little interest in the villages in which they stayed, spent very little, and generally were ignorant or indifferent to the mores of their chosen destination.[48]

In the north there have also been some mixed signals as to what kind of societies the visitor can expect. On the one hand, the government likes to promote an atmosphere of progress and increasing industrialization and modernity. The image is supposed to offset concerns of rebel strongholds in the poverty-stricken northeast. On the other hand, the TAT chooses to highlight "simple, unspoiled" tribal life and often shows pictures of tribal groups out working in their colorful poppy fields—a vision the government would just as soon ignore. U.S. pressure on Thailand to halt the opium traffic has been officially acknowledged in Bangkok, but has been erratically dealt with at the production site.

The suspicion of tribal peoples toward outsiders and government agents in particular has created a new cultural broker in the north, the jungle tour guide. Sometimes taking advantage of the lack of sophistication of various tribes, the guide may strike up gradual and apparently casual relationships with remote groups only to bring as "guests" at some later date the tourists who will pay him for a glimpse of a simpler way of life. Later he may need to develop new and more remote contacts to avoid arousing their curiosity. An alternative has been to routinize and regularize payments to the tribe that acknowledge, at least to the host, that the host-guest interaction is a commercial not a purely social transaction. Tourist demands for quick "authentic" experiences and tribal demands for respect and reciprocity keep the jungle tour guide juggling his escort roles.[49]

The recognition that tourists have money and an inclination to buy traditional goods like opium weights, or handicrafts like Hmong and Meo weaving, has encouraged many tribal people to produce for and market to the tourists. Some travel to Chiangmai with their wares; the trip alone is a profound excursion to new values, ideas, and products. Others find entrepreneurs ready to act as middlemen. Even the churches and social welfare organizations have become involved in the marketing of handicrafts to the tourist trade. Government and church organizations have hoped that making traditional crafts more profitable may dissuade northerners, especially the beautiful women, from migrating to Chiangmai, Bangkok, Pattaya, and Phuket to become prostitutes for the tourists.

Prostitution

The demand side of the market for sex tours and prostitution in general has already been discussed as a major feature of Thai tourism. At this point, it is important to examine the mix of motivations on the supply side and to look at the government dilemma in fashioning a successful policy to deal with it.

First, it is necessary to sketch a bit of background concerning prostitution in Thailand. Courtesans, concubines and prostitutes have been commonplace throughout the country's history. Each reflected a particular class accommodation to extramarital sex. Courtesans operated in monarchial circles, the number of concubines was a convenient measure of aristocratic power, and commoners patronized the local brothels. As in the West, women were divided into wives and whores. This pattern was common throughout Southeast Asia, and some consider it the dominant pattern in Asia.[50]

In 1935, the Thai government in a burst of moral zeal and a desire to be considered a modern society outlawed prostitution, but it has never proved to be an enforceable measure. Perhaps this is because, until recently, few have seen any value to its disappearance though many benefited from its being illegal. Prostitution is so widespread in Thailand that many have looked for ways to explain its domination of the tourist industry. Some see it as a reflection of Thai culture. They argue that Thailand has always had prostitution and that the new volume and depravity in form and effect are merely a response to a global demand. Thai women, however, are not raised to be promiscuous, despite articles like the one that begins with the claim that Thailand is "where they don't lock up their daughters."[51]

Although Thai women have always been involved in the market place, women are considered the moral authority in the home. Motherhood is considered the major role for women, particularly in the north. Women control the household spirits, who are believed to retaliate if unmarried women allow themselves to be touched by a man. Thai women, then, are acculturated to a strong taboo against prostitution.[52] Most women are expected to lead very chaste lives. In Thai culture women are generally reputed to consider being a woman a very powerful and important role. Most want, if reborn, to be reborn as women.[53]

Others have argued more compellingly that although Thai women are no more or less promiscuous than women anywhere, their poverty and their sense of familial obligation are sufficiently strong to encourage them to seek the most lucrative employment they can get. Unquestionably, even after all the middleman costs, prostitution pays better than anything else unskilled upcountry girls can get. Many, however, consider it a last resort after failing to make a living at more respectable trades. In the case of some, their parents sold them into prostitution at puberty after guaranteeing their virginity—an important comparative advantage in pricing. A smaller number have simply been abducted. The demand is sufficiently high and the turnover from age, disease, and emotional trauma so great that tourist prostitution constitutes a continual source of employment, albeit a short-lived one.

Migration to the cities also provides the necessary anonymity that makes prostitution bearable for many Thai women.[54] Parents are sent needed money without really having to know for certain if it is possible their daughter could make that much as a waitress or maid. The daughter can provide loyally for her family and perhaps prevent a similar fate for a younger sibling, without losing face in the village. The anonymity and transience of encounters with tourists are less a threat to her reputation than was the case in more stable town brothels in the pre-tourist era.

Even so, Erik Cohen found that many Thai women have developed coping strategies and euphemisms that allow them to hide their prostitution even from themselves. This applies particularly to the women who are not attached to brothels, sex shows, or tour agents. They prefer to refer to their jobs as "working with foreigners." They take solace from the ambiguity of their relationship. Striking up a friendship with a foreigner who then buys her things, gives her money, or takes her traveling with him can be described to others as a date because the transaction has no specific price. She controls her choice of customers and what she will and will not do. Though not answerable to a pimp, the ambiguity protects her self-image but not her emotions. She may try vainly to prolong the relationship and often suffers some emotional involvement. Many such girls also hope for marriage which seldom materializes and when it does seldom succeeds.[55]

Cohen's empathetic and empirical approach describes the lifestyle of only a tiny minority of female prostitutes. Most have no such protective ambiguity. Some have become as adept at exploitation as their exploiters. Some have become mail order brides, who take money from German, Dutch, and Australian pen pals for their legal expenses and travel to Europe and then promptly disappear. Others who have longed for marriage in the West discover they have been "married" to a slave trader. Thousands of Thai women are now in Europe as prostitutes, some voluntarily, some as virtual prisoners. One favorite ploy is to pay German homosexuals to travel to Thailand, bring back Thai "wives," and then leave them to German entrepreneurs. "So much can be earned with a Thai woman that the expenses are negligible."[56]

Prostitution in Thailand for the tourist industry has proved a real drawing card for a certain stratum (species?) of clientele. Not only sex but sex shows are part of the attraction. As in the Philippines not only so-called consenting adults but boys and young girls are involved. Shows purporting to demonstrate unique feats of "muscle control" are actually gynecological sideshows, threatening not only a woman's reproductive ability but her life.[57]

Europeans enjoyed erotic touring in Thailand until the late 1970s, when a Thai vacation became hazardous to one's health. Making up 25 percent of the Thai market and even more important in terms of expenditures, European tours began avoiding Thailand in the early 1980s. The big dip came in 1982. By 1983 European groups had restructured their clientele somewhat.[58] Whereas in the late 1970s Bangkok was selling 1,000 different package holidays, 1981 sales were less than a third of that. "This seems to have been due to publicity in the Scandinavian press about prostitution and venereal disease, coupled with public distaste about the number of men-only tours on the market."[59]

Ironically, the laissez-faire government approach to sex tourism has now left the government in a real quandary as to how to proceed. The king and others would just as soon not have Bangkok known as the "brothel of Asia." Church groups and women's organizations would prefer that outbound charters were not called the "gonorrhea express." The nickname is a reflection of the fact that 70 percent of the prostitutes (and many of their offspring) suffer from the disease and communicate it as an enduring souvenir to their visitors.[60]

The government attempted to crack down on prostitution and the infamous blue shows in 1981, but attempting an outright abolition of what is already theoretically illegal has been difficult to do. The attempt led to the cancellation of many Japanese tours and possibly some European ones, yet the continuation of them threatened to frustrate attempts to attract a more wholesome clientele.[61] The hotel overcapacity made hoteliers nervous about the outcome, and at least one mayor livid.

Mayor of raunchy Pattaya, Anusak Rocboormee "threatened to lead a demonstration of 50,000 industry men around the country if new curbs weren't relaxed."[62]

Police were selective in their enforcement because many were receiving kickbacks from everyone involved in the industry, from the nightclub owners to the girls. Even the *Bangkok Post* complained: "So we end up with hundreds of girls being arrested while pimps and brothel operators continue to rake in the flesh money."[63] Whatever the interim affect, it was clear that by 1986 tourist prostitution and sex shows were alive and thriving at least in all the major cities.

The government is unwilling to legalize prostitution for fear it will be unseemly for the monarchy after 50 years to appear to condone such behavior. Some also contend it will hurt the feelings of the women to have the ambiguity of their occupation resolved and to have to submit to licensing, inspection, and health checks.[64] Yet, if the government does not legalize prostitution after letting it become so enormous, the government cannot tax it and the corrupt and criminal elements will continue to tax it instead. A middle course is to cut out suggestive tours and advertising, penalize "freelancers," and require all related establishments, whatever their euphemism to require health checks of their employees. Although this is not a foolproof system, this has been done with fair success in the Philippines without formally legalizing prostitution.

In any case, Thailand is an excellent example of where allowing the consumer to dictate to the industry has been disastrous not only to national esteem, but also in terms of the very tourist industry that was supposed to flourish by such an approach. Today, Thailand is losing some sex tourists because of fears of disease or police crackdowns; but it loses untold others: couples, families, and culture-motivated travelers who reject this exquisite country because of the sleazy reputations of its cities. These groups are also the ones most likely to stay longer and have fewer negative social impacts. Thailand has learned the hard way how difficult it is to de-sleaze a destination once millions get a vested interest in its continuation.

> In the past Thailand has suffered from a much vaunted sex image—at least it has lost out in quality markets if gaining elsewhere. Ironically, just at a time when the TAT has been most successful at promoting more legitimate attractions, the question of AIDS is again highlighting the negative reputation.[65]

Space does not permit a thorough examination of all facets of socio-economic impacts tourism has had on Thailand. Obviously some are endemic to most developing countries, while others are more or less particular to certain societies. Thailand has neither a monopoly on tourist-related prostitution nor any lack of cultural, historical, recreational, or scenic attractions. The tragedy of Thai tourism is that one tawdry segment has been allowed to eclipse so much that is elegant, refined, and exquisite about Thailand.

5
Indian Tourism: Pluralist Policies in a Federal System

There is only one India. . . . The one sole country under the sun that is endowed with an imperishable interest for alien prince and alien peasant, for lettered and ignorant, the land that all men desire to see, having seen once, by even a glimpse, would not give that glimpse for the shows of all the rest of the globe combined.

—Mark Twain

THE POLITICS of Indian tourism policy are in striking contrast to that of the People's Republic of China. Unlike the PRC, which has not encouraged travelers until recently, India has lured travelers and inspired writers since the days of Alexander the Great. Indian scriptures encouraged travel. "There is no happiness for him who does not travel. Living in the society of men, the best man often becomes a sinner. . . . Indra is the friend of the traveler. Therefore wander."[1] Government support of travel was urged in scripture as early as 3,000 years ago in the Aitareya Brahmana when it enjoined the king to build inns to provide for the safe comfort of travelers. The Chhandogya Upanishad even notes with approval those leaders who built such inns in their kingdoms![2] During the nineteenth and twentieth centuries, as modern tourism expanded and developed, the romance of the British Indian Empire, of princes and palaces, elephants and tigers, helped to create an exotic image that has attracted generations of travelers.[3]

Tourism issues are all played out in the nation's press, with different papers—sometimes even the same paper—assuming intensely held and varied political positions. What tourism's goals should be—its pace, direction, and class clientele—are all argued in the public arena. The appropriate role of the national government (called the Centre in India), the states, the public corporations, and the private sector are debated almost ad nauseam.

No one is satisfied with Indian tourism policy, but ironically, of all the nations examined in this book, by many measures India is arguably the most successful of the developing nations in its gradual, often clumsy, use of tourism for national development. A combination of factors may be responsible: (1) an extensive colonial transport infrastructure on which to base further development; (2) a federal system that allowed states to pursue their own, often very innovative, approaches to tourism and remain somewhat apart from the vagaries of national politics; (3) an immense domestic tourism tradition that made tourism something more than a scheme to make foreign exchange from foreigners; (4) a public process that made tourism policy exquisitely slow at the Centre, but usually self-correcting (on those rare occasions where policy was allowed to swamp the process, costly public mistakes and private fortunes were made); and (5) policymakers who did not make the erroneous assumptions so often made elsewhere that the growth and needs of the tourist industry were the chief criteria by which tourism development should proceed.

In most countries, the tourist industry's health is assumed to be the best indicator of a successful policy. This is not so. A tourism policy in a developing nation, particularly, should be judged by its net impact on the economic, social, and political life of the people. Since net economic benefits, as opposed to overall receipts, and social and political factors are seldom considered quantifiable, in many countries they are simply left out of the policy equation.

This has happened on occasion in India, too, and it is always a danger when people urge greater centralization, consistency, and reliance on tourism experts and insulation from political considerations. Politicians are not saints, but experts on developing tourism per se are not experts on integrated national development either, and this writer has a bias for their confronting each other rather than being separated. "Maximum feasible participation" as it came to be known in the United States is not a panacea, but India's messy policy-making style, which is part planned economy and part private enterprise, does surprisingly well in a democratic mode.

THE GEOPOLITICAL CONTEXT

Regional Context

Indian tourism policy, like its politics in general, is shaped by India's geopolitical setting as the dominant country on the South Asian subcontinent. Until 1947 India included Pakistan and what is now Bangladesh. The countries of Sri Lanka, Nepal, Bhutan, and the Maldives were peripheral in both a geographical and political sense. Taken as a whole those nations contain nearly a quarter of the world's people and form a microcosm of the issues, interests, and dynamics of international tourism.

Despite this tradition, and despite the richness and diversity of its cultures and scenic attractions, the levels of international tourism are not exceptionally high on the subcontinent. For example, twice as many tourists visited Honolulu in 1984 (over 4 million) than all of the South Asian countries combined.[4] With 25 percent of the world's population, the region has a share of less than 2 percent of world tourist arrivals and receipts. The global context is a bit misleading, however, because 90 percent of all tourist traffic is still confined to 16 developed countries. In varying degrees, some of the difficulties in expanding tourism in South Asia are attributable to global and Third World economic factors, some to conscious policy choices, and some to cultural, political, or other factors.

Although this chapter makes no attempt to weigh tourism's value vis-à-vis other national development sectors, this clearly should be a major factor in the type of tourism encouraged or the decision to pursue tourism at all. These are not easy calculations to make. The economic, social, and political benefits of tourism are often not susceptible to quantification any more than the costs. For example, nations with tourist arrivals seem to receive more foreign aid than comparable countries.[5] The aid is not a part of the tourist contribution but it may in fact have been stimulated by tourism. Should such revenues be credited to tourism or not?

In many respects, the countries of South Asia share with the rest of the Third World some of the same motivations toward tourism development and some of the same problems and doubts concerning the cultural impact of foreign guests. The earning of foreign exchange is most frequently cited as a justification for investment in tourism, or for selecting one strategy of tourism development over another. The desperate need to find some 20 million jobs a year for the region's unemployed also encourages South Asian governments to consider tourism development, a reputedly labor-intensive sector.[6]

In many respects, South Asian tourism differs significantly from that found in other developing nations. Most notably, despite the relatively low levels of international tourist arrivals already noted, the region displays high levels of domestic and intraregional tourist travel.

Domestic Travel

Although it is often more difficult to document than international tourism, the domestic component is often an important economic, political, and cultural element in the country's overall tourist trade. It tends to be neglected by policymakers because it does not generate foreign exchange and is not perceived to be as glamorous as international tourism. Nor do governments seem to find domestic tourism as much of an indicator of the nation's intrinsic attractiveness. This is particularly true in developing nations because the governments often limit international travel to curb foreign exchange losses. Thus, there is no way of knowing whether the domestic tourist chose to be one or simply was unable to travel elsewhere.

There is also the heightened sensitivity of developing nations to Western approval, perhaps a holdover of a colonial mentality, that ascribes more importance to the wishes and tastes of outsiders than to the desires of their own people. This is particularly apparent in the way the international travel industry's pronouncements or the visits of its representatives are received, as opposed to the way the local travel industry is regarded.

On the other hand, as case studies of tourism in developing countries repeatedly demonstrate the fickleness and political vulnerability of international tourism, domestic tourism looks better than ever. For example, it does not require as much foreign exchange to develop and its cultural effects are generally less disruptive. Another advantage of domestic tourism is that it cushions the often precarious dependence on foreign airlines, marketing, reservation schedules, and the capriciousness of international travel tastes. It also mitigates the seasonality of foreign arrivals and departures.

Domestic tourism in South Asia has developed along two lines. The older pattern, still very important today, centers around the traditions of festivals and of religious pilgrimages to the numerous Hindu, Buddhist, Sikh, and Muslim holy places. A second pattern of domestic tourism, which developed during the colonial era in those countries ruled by the British, was the retreat to the hills during the hot season. Dozens of hill stations, such as Simla, Darjeeling, Mussoorie, Dalhousie, and Ootacamund (Ooti), and cooler inland cities such as Poona and Bangalore became the destinations of choice for the English, the princes, and, increasingly, a wide range of upper-class Indians. Simla, the inspiration for many of Kipling's poems and short stories, was the seat of the imperial government during the pre-monsoon months, when the heat made Delhi unbearable.

Colonial rule contributed to later tourism development in other ways as well. Railway and highway systems extending throughout much of present-day India and Pakistan provided an infrastructure for inexpensive surface travel. In addition to the privately owned hotels in the hill stations and major cities, government rest houses and *dak* (post) bungalows built during the colonial period continue to provide tourist accommodations that are particularly appropriate for middle- and lower-income tourists.[7]

For at least India and Pakistan, size and diversity are additional factors that help to encourage domestic tourism. With a population second only to the People's Republic of China and a land area approximately one-third that of the United States, India has more languages and cultural regions than all of Europe. Although considerably smaller, Pakistan is also sufficiently large and diverse enough to provide a variety of cultural experiences and scenic attractions for its own citizens.

In addition to its potential for fostering national integration, domestic tourism helps to temper and dissipate some of the more egregious consequences of international tourism. In most developing nations, however carefully the tourism policy is designed and regardless of how meticulous the nation is in distributing the profits of the tourist trade, facilities and infrastructure tend to be created essentially for the comfort and pleasure of foreigners. Because this has been less true in South Asia, particularly India and Pakistan, tourism has had less of a colonial character. A wealthy national elite can enjoy luxury accommodations alongside foreigners so that white enclave tourism does not develop (of course, the hill stations, gymkhana clubs, and other facilities were white enclaves earlier in this century, before Indian independence). Moreover, more modest accommodations attract a mix of domestic population and a potpourri of other nationalities. This in turn reduces the potential for backlash or outright sabotage that has accompanied luxury tourism in such varied societies as Jamaica and the Philippines.[8]

Tourism is a vulnerable industry, which is why India is extremely fortunate in having such a huge domestic base. Over 12 million alone visit the Ganges River each year to bathe and pray.[9] Domestic tourism has, however, moved beyond religious pilgrimage. Holiday travel is becoming increasingly important among the middle and upper classes. Though these groups are small percentage-wise, 10 to 15 percent of over 800 million people constitutes an enormous market target. Further, what many tourism specialists overlook is that India is the tenth largest industrial power in the world. With its industrial and service sectors has emerged a significant stratum of business travelers whose journeys and conventions across the vast subcontinent mean a market for affluent and moderate accommodations, which in most developing countries are occupied only by foreign tourists.

Intraregional Tourism

The numerous instances of international conflict within the region have taken their toll on the tourist industries of each country. For example, the travel of Pakistanis to India was well over 30,000 in 1963, but miniscule 12 years later.[10] Still, intraregional travel, often buttressed by religious or familial ties, is far more resilient in the face of political conflict than that from beyond the region. There is today a significant tourist flow among the nations of South Asia. India, of course, is by far the most active tourist-generating nation in the region. Its size and location alone would dictate that. Pakistan, Sri Lanka, and Nepal, for instance, receive more tourists from India than from any other nation.

Getting the data about such travel flow is difficult because figures are often designed to blur or dilute the effect of political controversy rather than to document its social and economic impact. Pakistan, for instance reports no figures on Indian arrivals, not because they are not terribly important but because they fluctuate dramatically and generally do not have a major impact on foreign exchange. Similarly, Indian figures often exclude Pakistan and Bangladesh. Nepali figures often omit Indian visitors.

Religious travel is a major impetus to intraregional as well as to strictly domestic tourism. When political conditions permit, Indian Sikhs visit *gurdwaras,* the tomb of Ranjit Singh and other sites in Pakistani Punjab. Muslims from India, Pakistan, and Bangladesh visit mosques and tombs in one another's countries. Buddhists in the subcontinent journey to the Temple of the Tooth in Sri Lanka, or to Bodhnath or Lumbini in Nepal, or even to the giant Buddha statues at Bamian in Afghanistan. Hindus from India, Nepal, Bangladesh, and Sri Lanka travel to sites throughout the subcontinent.

The economic implications of intraregional tourism are somewhat unclear. On the one hand, there may be more net gain to host economies from Indian tourists in Sri Lanka than from Westerners or Japanese where travel and lodging profits may be channeled through several multinational sieves before ending up in the national economy. On the other hand, visitors from neighboring countries may often stay with relatives or friends or in low-cost accommodations, thereby decreasing the economic benefit of their presence.

In many respects, the political and cultural consequences of intraregional tourist travel will be no more disruptive than those of domestic tourism. The cross-cultural sharing of languages, cultures, and some dietary habits should make South Asian visitors less prominent than Europeans or Japanese. On the other hand, the central position of India within the context of intraregional tourism has potential for exacerbating the often considerable resentment that may exist among India's neighbors concerning that country's dominant political and military role in the subcontinent.

Extra-regional Tourism

The relatively low numbers of international tourists in South Asia compared to other parts of the world are, in part, a result of the distance of this region from the major tourist-generating parts of the globe—North

America, Western Europe, and Japan. Still, distance is only a partial explanation. Only 1 percent of all Americans traveling abroad in 1982 visited India,[11] but in 1984 over twice as many visited the People's Republic of China as India.[12]

One positive consequence of distance is a broad clientele. No single nation constitutes a critical source of tourists, as is often the case in many developing areas. Even Britain, as the formerly dominant colonial power in this region, at 13 percent does not have an exceptionally large share of tourist arrivals. In this respect South Asia is less prone to develop the sort of center-periphery dependency relationship that affects many other Third-World countries.[13] Another consequence of the effort and expense of coming to the subcontinent is that those who have come tend to do so more for its cultural attractions, its trekking possibilities, and its exotic birds and other wildlife than for the more conventional pursuits of sun, sea, sand, and sex. This may be changing, however, as we shall see.

It is common for political scientists interested in the way nations perceive each other to observe the frequently unflattering and hostile images countries in conflict have of each other, for example, India and Pakistan, or the United States and the Soviet Union. This is not well understood when it comes to countries about which more neutral, less salient reporting is done.[14]

Interestingly, the exotic character of the subcontinent, which serves to attract many, may also repel others because of fear of the unknown and the unfamiliar. Moreover, India and other South Asian countries also suffer from what might be called the "begging-bowl" stereotype—an exaggerated image of mass poverty, squalor, and disease that continues to be perpetuated in political cartoons and other mass media in the West, particularly in the United States.

Two studies done nearly ten years apart document the persistence of images of India that work to the disadvantage of tourism development. The first measured the attitudes of prospective American visitors in the mid-1970s. Overwhelmingly their dominant assumptions were negative (see Table 5.1).[15] A decade later Sudhir H. Kale and Katherine M. Weir found similar impressions among the 90 business students they questioned (see Tables 5.2 and 5.3), plus a tendency to assume that very few people speak English—an added deterrent to the traveling public.[16]

In the earlier study, 88 percent of North American visitors sampled said that before they came to India they felt their health would be endangered. In fact only three percent had any ailments. Many had envisaged a lot of red tape, a difficult climate, much dirt and poverty, poor food, lack of personal security, and problems with the language. Respondents from the United Kingdom were the most negative. Most who came were therefore pleasantly surprised. The fact, however, that they came with such

Table 5.1. How did prospective American visitors rank India?

Factor	Ranking	Percentage of tourists associating factor with destination
Warm and friendly people	18	22
Comfortable accommodation	10	18
Beautiful natural scenery	23	20
Reasonable prices	7	20
Attractive customs, way of life	15	18
Good climate	24	10
Beautiful creations of man	4	54
Outstanding food	18	4
Good shopping	6	23
Exotic environment	9	27
Historical or family ties	5	7
Exceptional recreation facilities	22	1
Would visit or recommend	20	51
Would like to visit	9	31
Too commercial	11	2
Dirt and poverty	1	67
High cost of getting there	3	18
High prices for food and lodging	10	7
Lack of personal security	4	6
Not enough to do here	19	41
Poor food	1	17
Problem with language	4	14
Red tape, visas, etc.	1	19
Rude unfriendly people	3	7
Unsanitary conditions	1	53
Unpleasant climate	1	27
Would not visit or recommend	7	49
Would not like to visit	18	69

SOURCE: M. M. Anand, *Tourism and the Hotel Industry in India: A Study in Management.*
New Delhi: Prentice Hall of India, 1976, p. 52.

expectations illustrates a certain temerity on their part. Many more were probably discouraged from coming by their fears.[17]

Respondents from Eastern Europe had a different set of expectations. They regarded India as a "land of Gandhi, Nehru, and Tagore, a democratic, socialist country." Once they arrived they were shocked by the level of economic inequality. Those from Afro-Asian countries, perhaps reflecting a more realistic understanding of conditions in developing countries had the greatest congruence between their expectations and what they discovered.[18]

Because of cross pressures both attracting and discouraging tourism, dramatic fluctuations in tourist arrivals generally have not occurred. For India, the exceptions were in 1962 when there were frontier battles

Table 5.2. Perceptions of India ranked by tendency to agree ($n = 90$).[a]

Rank	Item	Mean
1	There is a lot of poverty in India.	2.02
2	India is an exotic travel destination.	2.06
3	The standard of cleanliness is lower than in the United States.	2.10
4	There are opportunities to observe local customs.	2.19
5	India has many historical monuments.	2.64
6	There is a lot of political instability and turmoil.	2.81
7	India offers many opportunities to sample local cuisine.	2.83
8	The climate is hot and uncomfortable.	2.84
9	Tours and guides are available in India.	2.91
10	There are many reasonably priced handicrafts.	2.96
11	India has many architectural landmarks.	3.00
12	There are many beggars in India.	3.11
13	The cities are very crowded.	3.13
14	There are many opportunities for shopping.	3.22
15	India offers a variety of music and dance.	3.44
16	India offers a lot in terms of natural scenic beauty.	3.43
17	There are many museums to visit.	3.56
18	Boat rides and cruises are available in India.	3.58
19	Vacations in India are much less expensive than elsewhere.	3.74
20	There are national parks to tour.	3.87
21	There are many first class hotels in India.	4.19
22	Nightlife and entertainment are available in most cities.	4.33
23	There are many opportunities to engage in sports activities.	4.44
24	Many people in India speak English.	4.47
25	Local transportation in India is convenient.	4.83
26	Travel between cities is comfortable and convenient.	4.96

a. All items were measured on a seven-point scale, with a value of 1 indicating "strongly agree" and 7 indicating "strongly disagree."

Table 5.3. Major reasons cited by our respondents for not visiting India.

Reason	Number mentioning	Percent
Poverty/beggars	37	41.6
Politically unstable	25	28.1
Not clean	24	27.0
Climate	21	23.6
Fear of the unknown	19	21.3
Prefer to go elsewhere	17	19.1
Crowded/overpopulated	17	19.1
Nothing to "see or do"	12	13.5
Expensive	9	10.1
Not safe	9	10.1
Poor accommodations	8	9.0
Language barriers	7	7.9

SOURCE: Kale and Weir, "Marketing Third World Countries to the Western Traveler: The Case of India." *Journal of Travel Research* 25 (no. 2): 4 (Fall 1986).

between India and the PRC and in 1965 when there was a short but bloody war with Pakistan.

Impact of Regional Politics on Tourism

To a large extent, India's international tourism fortunes are out of the hands of its promoters, the Indian Tourism Development Corporation (ITDC), Air India, the State TDCs, and the Tourism Ministry. As W. D. Patterson aptly observed, "War, politics, public opinion, and civil unrest can be the greatest enemy of tourism."[19] Politics and public opinion *need not* be enemies of tourism if the policy has considered them in its formation and execution, but war and civil unrest are certainly detrimental. Expansion of tourism in India has suffered from unrest such as wars with Pakistan in 1965 and 1971 and quarrels with Sri Lanka over the latter's treatment of Tamils of Indian descent. Violence in Delhi, the Punjab, and Assam and religious strife in Hyderabad are considered far more newsworthy in the Western press than India's many places of scenic beauty, ancient treasures, or areas of multi-cultural harmony.[20] Following the assassination of Prime Minister Indira Gandhi on October 31, 1984, 70 percent of all tour bookings for November were cancelled, an immediate U.S. 100 million dollar loss to the struggling industry.[21]

But even more than India's own political fortunes, Indian tourism continues to be the victim of the political problems of other countries in the region, factors that interrupt air travel, make overland travel impossible, or lead to the cancellation of multi-country tours of the region. Turmoil in Iraq and Iran led to the cancellation of Pan Am's round-the-world service, which had a stopover in Delhi. The same conflict, along with the war in Afghanistan, effectively sealed off all overland tourist travel from Europe and the Middle East. Martial law in Pakistan and Bangladesh discouraged travel to those nations. Since July 1983 sporadic communal violence in Sri Lanka has discouraged travel there and to nearby South India.

Thus, India's steady development of international tourism in the face of such political strife is an encouraging sign rather than an indicator of policy failure. Popular movies, books, and television mini-series will probably do more to encourage travel to India than anything Indian tourism officials can do.

Actually, the pace of Indian tourism development is not all that slow nor are absolute figures terribly low. In 1951, India had 20,000 international tourists, in 1978, 748,000,[22] and in 1986, over 1 million.[23] The enormous domestic base is scarcely measured. Moreover, Pakistan, Bangladesh, and Nepali tourists are not explicitly counted. These number several hundred thousand in any given year, though exact components differ according to the degree of political warmth existing among the nations. Further, India has one of the highest average lengths of stay of any country in the world, nearly 26 days. This means that they get the value from one tourist that a country like Jamaica may get from five.[24]

Tourism's Economic Effects

India's gross receipts from international tourism (Rs. 18 billion in 1986), substantial though they are, cannot be compared directly to similar receipts from other developing nations such as the Philippines. The latter tragically mortgaged its revenues to its scandalous and showy infrastructure development. India, on the other hand, not only underestimates its receipts via its peculiar accounting procedures (and unfortunately, a flourishing black market); it retains more of its tourism income (94 percent) and generates far greater economic activity from tourism receipts.[25]

It does this two ways. First, it imports almost nothing for the tourist industry. This means that relatively little foreign exchange leaks out in contrast to so many destinations, which often lose between 40 and 80 percent of their foreign exchange. Secondly, tourism revenue has a multiplier effect as it gets spent and respent throughout the economy. India has a multiplier estimated at 3.2 to 3.6. This means that every dollar of tourism revenue generates US$3.20 to $3.60 of economic activity before its impact fades. This, some feel, is also understated because India's own industrial sector benefits so handsomely from tourist-related infrastructure, designs, and furnishings, as well as the actual expenditures of the tourists.

Although figures differ dramatically, between 4.5 and 10.5 million people are estimated to have jobs as the direct or indirect consequence of tourism. Of this figure, over three-fourths are attributable to domestic tourism. In general, foreign tourists create more accommodation and food-related employment, while domestic tourists create more jobs in transportation. Within the transport sector, domestic tourists choose bus and rail services, which are less costly and more labor intensive. Foreign tourists utilize the more capital-intensive and expensive airlines. Within the accommodation area, domestic tourists tend to stay at smaller, less capital-intensive establishments. Domestic tourism in general creates more varied but generally less-skilled employment.[26] These employment patterns are important not only for measuring the impact of tourism on economic development, but are also critical for the political support tourism must have to flourish.

They also illustrate how essential it is to disaggregate tourism statistics. It is not enough to say that tourism is labor intensive—sometimes it is; sometimes it is not. To plan for tourism one must understand its differential impact. For example, a Tata Economic Consultancy Services study in 1981, commissioned by the Indian Department of Tourism, found that foreign tourism would have to increase 400 percent to be as important in terms of employment as domestic tourism. Moreover, because of the different levels of accommodations and transport, such growth in international-level infrastructure would be extremely costly.[27]

INDIAN TOURISM POLICY

Tourism Organization

The organization of tourism in a country reflects the government's general orientation toward such issues as centralized versus decentralized administration and public versus private ownership, operation, and promotion of tourism. In most socialist states, the government not only organizes the entire industry but owns and operates all facilities, including transport, accommodations, tour services, restaurants, and shops. All promotion is government sponsored. Foreign involvement is restricted to consulting and sometimes construction services and limited imports for the industry. At the other extreme is the laissez-faire government attitude of the United States, which operates only a very modest U.S. Travel and Tourism Administration that each year has been targeted for extinction by the Reagan administration.[28] All U.S. travel facilities, including airlines, are privately owned. States usually have some type of visitors' center, but differ widely in their commitment to the promotion of tourism.[29]

All of the countries of South Asia fall between these two extremes. Airlines, the railway system, and some hotel facilities are government owned and operated, but most of the tourist industry is in the private sphere. In all of the countries of the region, however, the government has taken a significant role in tourism development.

Despite many common features of South Asian tourism, there is considerable variation among the countries of the region in terms of their values, priorities, resources, tourism organizations, and policies. Although the four chapters dealing with South Asia are uneven in their treatment of each country due to the greater availability of data for India, the other seven countries of the region are also examined because they illustrate a variety of political objectives and policy responses that have planning implications for many other developing nations.

The Evolution of Indian Tourism Policy

Of all the nations in the subcontinent, India has by far the longest experience with tourism planning, the most fully developed organization, and the most extensive and diverse array of tourist attractions. The first governmental effort to promote tourism was the formation of the Sargent Committee in 1945, well before independence and the partition of the subcontinent. The Committee's interim report, submitted in October 1946, recommended among other things the creation of a national organization to coordinate publicity, training, liaison, and the collection of statistics.[30] As noted, India already had a large tourist infrastructure in both Indian and foreign hands, extensive transportation links throughout the country, and facilities at all class levels.

Essentially, there have been five main policy phases in Indian tourism development. From 1949 to 1966 tourism gradually grew with limited involvement from the government. Most states were not very active and, since tourism is primarily a state subject, the Centre had only a minor role. Most of the accommodations and transport were built before independence. The first move in independent India to create a central tourism body was the formation of the Tourist Traffic Branch in the Ministry of Transport in 1949. During the 1950s the scope and functions of this agency were expanded, tourist information offices were opened throughout India and abroad and, in 1958, a separate Tourism Department was created within the Ministry of Transport.[31]

The second policy phase marked the beginning of major changes in both the administrative and operational development of tourism. In 1966, the Indian Tourism Development Corporation was created, and it has become a model for tourism promotion throughout South Asia. In 1967 the Ministry of Tourism and Civil Aviation was established. This ministry coordinates civil aviation and tourist issues, handles technical information, and provides planning and financial assistance. As the main policy-making body for tourism at the central level, the Union (another term for national government) Ministry also coordinates basic tourist programs with the states. It is currently intensifying its campaign to develop incentives for national and foreign investors.[32]

Tourism policy in India is a combination of both national and state policies and in many instances specific urban policies, like that of Delhi. Tourism organization very clearly reflects the federal character of the country. As a concurrent subject in the Indian Constitution, tourism is the responsibility of both the Union and the states. "The Ministry of Tourism, Central or State, is the ultimate authority responsible for the development and promotion of tourism and tourist services operating within its jurisdiction and has powers to lay down and enforce minimum standards of tourist services."[33] To a large extent, the Centre concentrates on promotion and facilities for foreign tourists, both the Centre and the states have programs for encouraging domestic tourism, and the states develop local programs and activities for local recreation. Such an arrangement has provided great scope for local initiative and innovation. The state of Haryana, for example, surrounding the Union territory of Delhi on the west, "with no hill station, and with practically no places of historical or archeological interest," began its tourism program in 1971. Haryana has become a real success story by its development of highway tourism: the creation of more than two dozen tourist complexes on the well-traveled roads leading from Delhi to Agra, Jaipur, Chandigarh, and other destinations beyond the state. By 1984 the Haryana government was serving as a consultant to other states in India. [34]

At both the central and state levels, tourism organization has been augmented by the creation of public corporations. Since 1966, with the creation of ITDC and the future delineation of responsibilities between the states and Centre, targeted funding in the various Five Year Plans has allowed for rather rapid infrastructure development. Air India and the government tourism offices have greatly expanded tourism promotion while the states have instituted their own programs for developing domestic tourism and preserving or enhancing touristic sites. Where possible, the states have been alert to the integration and multipurpose uses of sites. For example, in Lucknow electricity generators have turned dams and power stations into parks and recreation areas. [35]

From 1966 to 1977 one could characterize the overall policy as one of limited but thoughtfully considered incentives for Indian tourism, as opposed to tourism development of both domestic and international tourism. Indian tourism development was characterized by balanced growth, the stimulation of indigenous industry control and an emphasis upon the social diffusion of the economic benefits of tourism.

As in most popularly controlled governments, the patronage interest in tourism development has undoubtedly been a strong motivator. The attempts to spread tourism development are also rooted in good planning. Early programs sought to diffuse tourism's economic benefits by fostering its development in the South. Madras and Tiruchirappalli (Trichi) were expanded into international ports of entry and ITDC hotels and resorts were established at Madurai, Kovalam Beach, and other points of tourist interest. The government also attempted to respond to the needs of both domestic and international tourists. The popular *son et lumière* at the Red Fort in Delhi is given in both Hindi and English. ITDC and city bus tours are provided both in more expensive air-conditioned luxury buses and in more modestly priced non-airconditioned transport.

Phase three was marked by the defeat of Indira Gandhi's government. The ascendancy of Morarji Desai's much more puritanical *Janata* (People's) Party had a major impact on the direction of tourism policy between 1977 and 1979. In early 1978 the *Janata* Party Minister for

Tourism and Civil Aviation, Purushottam Kaushik, announced that the Indian government would no longer assist in the construction of four-star and five-star hotels. "The limited resources available for tourism would be used entirely for the creation of facilities for domestic and foreign tourists in the middle and low income groups."[36] New, simple, clean hotels for people of modest means were to be built and called—what else —*Janata* hotels. The cornerstone for the first, a 20-story, 1,250-bed *Janata* hotel, was laid in the spring of 1978. At the time the government claimed a new set of priorities. "The foreign exchange earned through tourism is not to be the only aim in expanding this industry. The modest budget tourists from universities and other enlightened groups help to project a good image of this country abroad which is also an important outcome of tourism."[37]

The *Janata* concept never had much chance to get off the ground, though a prototype was built in the state of Gujarat, a *Janata* stronghold. The party lost control of the central government in 1979. In general, during the first three phases of Indian tourism development the government sought to make tourism pay its own way. It resisted the temptation to entice large multi-national investments in India, and instead structured incentives more to support the Indian tourist industry.[38]

The fourth policy phase was ushered in with the return of Indira Gandhi's government in 1980. By this time it was apparent that India would not have one million arrivals for its 1980 Year of the Tourist. Arrivals increased by only 2 percent in 1979, less than one-seventh of that of previous years. The short-lived Charan Singh government cancelled the bid secured in 1978 for India to host the Ninth Asiad Games in 1982, and there was a general aura of gloom and doom in the press and among those in the domestic and international travel industry. Mrs. Gandhi proceeded to dust off the Asiad '82 plans and began the first "crash" tourism development in Indian history. The Asiad case will be discussed at length later in this chapter.

The fifth phase in tourism policy began in 1984 with the tragic assassination of Indira Gandhi and the assumption of the post of prime minister by her son, Rajiv Gandhi. The Bhopal gas tragedy, Indira Gandhi's death, and the subsequent tour cancellations plus the hotel overbuilding in 1982 that had preceded her death combined to put the industry in desperate shape.

Initially, Rajiv Gandhi personally took charge of the nation's tourism and civil aviation ministry. Gandhi's own background as a former commercial pilot gave him perhaps more empathy with the beleaguered industry.[39] In any event, his interest in tourism has been reflected in unprecedented commitments to the industry. He established a separate tourism ministry and appointed Mufti Mohammed Syed as Minister of Tourism. The Planning Commission has tripled its previous commitment to tourism spending and the National Development Council has accorded tourism official status as an industry.[40]

After its stagnation in the early 1980s, tourist growth is now once more significant. In 1986, for the first time, over one million international tourists visited, earning India about Rs. 18 billion, nearly 40 percent more than that earned in 1985.[41] Impressive as the growth and revenue figures are, the actual amounts are modest. In dollar terms this country of almost 800 million earned about one-third of what the U.S. state of Kansas earned, itself a state not noted for its tourism.

New estimates project 2.5 million arrivals by 1990 with anticipated receipts at Rs. 50 billion. This fifth phase growth is a reflection of several factors. Political stability has been reassuring, but major tourist-generating markets have also been stimulated by exposing India's numerous attractions through several outstanding and popular films, television series, and exhibits. *Gandhi, A Passage to India, Heat and Dust, The Jewel in the Crown* and *The Far Pavillions* have exposed tens of millions to the lure of India. In addition, the Festival of India exhibits that have toured Britain and the United States have attracted widespread attention to a country that too often gets publicity only for disasters.

The government reaction to all these fortuitous events has been not only to increase spending and authorize more hotel building, but also—more troubling in my view—to initiate several government-sponsored beach and ski resorts.[42] This may reflect a reasonable effort to diversify the tourism "product." Such resorts seem to be irresistible to planners as we have seen even in the People's Republic of China, but economically and socially such oases of play make little sense. More to the government's credit is its announced intention to shift its hotel building support from the deluxe to the three-star market. Plans are to have state governments furnish the land for the modest accommodations and have the central government contribute development costs. The private sector will be encouraged to participate with incentives as long as it builds one- to three-star hotels. Immigration procedures and health checks are being simplified, and plans to develop a government agency for handling tourist complaints are being considered. Training centers for hotel industry staff are being planned and increased government tourism funds are going into research and statistics.[43]

What has been illustrated in this brief chronology is that as tourism has grown in size and complexity, so too has the struggle to develop an administrative structure and a tourism policy, which reflects the political goals and priorities of India's leadership.

Components and Features of Indian Tourism Policy

The ITDC and State TDCs. The ITDC has evolved into one of the most elaborate and successful government tourism enterprises anywhere in the world. The Indian Tourism Development Corporation (ITDC), created in 1966, was expanded in 1968 and again in 1970. The ITDC's mandate was to stimulate tourist facilities in areas not yet commercially developed but having tourism potential. The ITDC's hotels, tourist bungalows, airport shops, and rest houses set a standard and provided alternatives for the rest of the industry. To do this, the ITDC gets loan capital at a concessionary rate from the Planning Commission which allocates funds on a five year basis. The loans are to be repaid over the next ten years. All personnel must be Indian and the hotels must "blend into the local environment and promote local industry and handicrafts."[44]

Performance has been impressive. From 129 rooms and a transport fleet of 50 cars and coaches in 1969, the ITDC in 1982 was India's largest accommodation chain with over 2,700 hotel rooms in 22 hotels and 14 travel lodges and a transport fleet of over 200 vehicles.[45] The ITDC also operates duty-free shops, restaurants, and tours, and publishes promotional materials. The latter have been of such fine quality that three ITDC posters won gold medals at the International Tourist Posters Exhibition in Milan.[46] The ITDC has also won high praise for its hotels, tours, and other facilities. This may help to explain the significant growth rates in international tourist arrivals and the unusually large proportion of tourists (39.3 percent) who return to India for second or third visits.[47]

The ITDC has a formidable reputation for tourism expertise in contrast to public tourism undertakings in most countries. Its profit-making zeal is blunted only when it is forced to take over marginal properties in remote areas, but even there it has often been able to make those facilities productive once more.

It has also had its share of mistakes, and can perhaps be faulted for being overzealous. For example, at the Pacific Area Travel Association Conference in 1978 the ITDC rented, at prohibitive prices, exhibit space in the ITDC-owned Ashoka Hotel to the less affluent state TDCs. Some state TDCs simply could not afford the rates, denying PATA delegates a marvelous opportunity to make contacts with regional Indian tourism programs.[48]

State TDCs, which have sprung up in recent years with the Centre's encouragement, perform functions similar to those of the ITDC. Many operate their own guest houses, gift shops, restaurants, and tour facilities. Gujarat TDC, for example, built a modest hotel in Ahmedabad, administers several tourist bungalows, and operates a central reservation service. This TDC format has much to recommend it. The government corporation retains a flexibility of operations that allows it to respond in innovative ways that encourage future private investments.

The advantages of state programs in promoting diversity and a certain amount of flexibility are considerable. Moreover, by allowing the state autonomy to plan, implement, promote, and market their own attractions and infrastructure, the states have become a breeding ground for tourism expertise. Again, Haryana serves as an example. S. K. Mitra, the former chief of Haryana's tourism program, became the managing director of the ITDC, where he has supervised the unusual expansion of ITDC beyond Indian borders. Today the ITDC earns foreign exchange not only by serving tourists in India, but also by acting as a consultant and manager of tourist-related establishments abroad. "The move to overseas operations reflects India's expertise, its ability to provide a total turnkey project (including all the furnishings but the dishwasher) and the fact that for the first time, the outside world is accepting Indian designs."[49]

By 1981, ITDC had a hotel in Cyprus and restaurants in Moscow and Czechoslovakia and was bidding on projects throughout the Middle East and Africa. It had also become involved in organizing conventions and was starting an airline catering service. ITDC is one of the best examples of indigenous tourism development where government seed capital and corporate management have combined for beneficial results.

Federalism. Indian Federalism, although generally judged a success in terms of general policy-making, has been criticized sharply in terms of tourism development. Some charge that it leaves the nation as a whole without an overall national tourism policy.[50] Whereas in a unitary system all policies can be consistent nationwide, this is not the case in federal India. For example, in some states prohibition is still in force. Although foreigners are generally exempted and allowed to drink in their rooms, such a restriction does have implications for convention and restaurant development. In the United States, Kansas, which until 1987 did not allow sale of liquor by the drink, and Missouri, which does, offer similar contrasts with similar tourist ramifications. It is even more complicated in India because in some states there are "dry" days, or "non-cereal grain" days and these may differ from state to state.[51]

Although it may be possible to achieve better coordination on this and other issues, many of the complaints about the federal nature of Indian tourism policy reflect the fact that such variety is inconvenient to the tourist industry and sometimes the tourist. But is that really an important criterion for national or regional policy-making? Providing for local and regional autonomy has been one of the important ways in which multiethnic, linguistically diverse India has avoided the Balkanization of the country which so many predicted.[52] India's relative political stability and democratic society have been envied by her politically unstable neighbors. Federalism's role has been important in keeping a semblance of political stability. It has also probably stimulated more creativity and variety in Indian tourism than it has caused lapses of coordination.

Certainly industry critics have felt that the national government has not given sufficient attention to the industry (what industry in any country does not feel this way?), yet tourism has been in the national budget since the Second Five Year Plan (see Table 5.4). These sums are low relative to return on investment, but one could argue that perhaps they should be. At any rate, they have grown appreciably from the nil allocation in the First Five Year Plan to a total of Rs 63 crores of planned central investments for tourism in the Sixth Five Year Plan.[53] This represents, however, no more than 0.2 percent of planned investments. This is despite the fact that tourism employs 0.66 percent of the labor force, contributes 1.5 percent of the gross national product (GNP), and is a leading source of foreign exchange.[54]

In 1985, the government reacted again to the slow growth in tourism by announcing it would triple its support for tourism from US$200 million in the Sixth Five Year Plan (1979–1984) to $600 million for the years 1984 to 1989.[55] This dramatic increase in support reflected concern that began in 1979 when the increase in tourist arrivals began to drop sharply.[56] Although the new sums may be entirely appropriate, there is a danger in expecting tourism investments by either government or the private sector to be at a fixed percent of anticipated return as the travel industry might wish.

Indian Tourism Administration. "Why do we believe that speaking about tourism is a substitute for developing it?"[57] Depending on one's point of view, the Indian Government has a reputation for being (1) wary of international tourism,[58] (2) unhelpful or even hostile to private sector tourism development,[59] (3) a positive model of government intervention as a countervailing power in tourism development,[60] and (4) generally in pursuit of a cautious, balanced approach to integrating tourism development into the total development plan.[61]

Let us look at the record. Until 1984, India's tourism development could certainly be accused of lacking a sense of urgency. The changes in organizational development tend to mask the fact that the enlargement of jurisdictional turf was not matched by any sense of priority status for the tourist sector. As one critic put it when speaking of the GOI Tourist Department: "With the passing of time it has grown from a small tourist traffic cell in the Ministry of Transport in 1949 to the full-fledged Minis-

Table 5.4. Allocations for tourism development in India's five year plans.

Years	Outlay (Rs. in crores)	Remarks
1949–1951		Initial organization problems.
I. Five Year Plan 1951–1956	——	No amount was allocated for tourism, either by state or by central government.
II. Five Year Plan 1956–1961	3.33	In which Rs.110 lakhs was the Centre's share and the rest that of the states.
III. Five Year Plan 1961–1966	8	Rs. 3.5 crores was the Centre's share, and the rest the states. Out of the Centre's share Rs. 2.92 crores were earmarked for foreign tourism and Rs. 0.58 crores were given to states to develop domestic tourism.
IV. Five Year Plan 1969–1974	40.34	In which Rs. 14.50 crores were earmarked for ITDC and Rs. 2.81 crores for integrated development scheme.
V. Five Year Plan 1974–1980	113	Rs. 7.50 crores for hotel industry; Rs. 2.50 crores for transportation loan fund. Rs. 78.00 crores for central plan; Rs. 32.00 crores for state plan; Rs. 3.00 crores for Union Territories.

SOURCE: K. Thangamani, *Studies in Tourism Development Planning.* Mysore: University of Mysore, Institute of Development Studies, 1981, p. 45.

Note that the value of the rupee fluctuates greatly, but as of 1988 12 rupees = US$1.00. A crore = US$833,000. A lakh = US$8,330.

try of Tourism and Civil Aviation of today. In the process relevant and irrelevant additions have been made to the organization. No part of it can be discarded simply because it has become established."[62]

The Indian Tourist Department has grown rapidly—regionalizing, localizing, and moving overseas. The structure of the tourism organization, even in its simplest form, also works to blur responsibilities, set up overlapping jurisdictions, and provide a system that is distinctly different from any of the other political systems this book examines. The political characteristic of federalism divides the tourism responsibilities among levels of government; the economic system of a mixed economy with central planning divides the implementation of tourism policies between the government and the private sector.

As M. M. Anand describes it,

> Government plays a crucial role and organizationally has a preeminent place. But being at the same time a mixed economy, it has to reckon with the number of public and private autonomous organizations that are free to perceive the policy as they like and execute it as they wish. It is as if policy-making and goal-laying is in the Russian type of central planning and execution is in the American style via private autonomous bodies.[63]

Policy-making regarding tourism depends on the political machine in power and tends to be less flexible and responsive than in an open economy. Chief among the government organizations charged with policy formation is the National Development Council, which formulates broad goals "largely conditioned by the political values of its members."[64] The body that makes these goals operational, sets up targets, and develops specific policies for particular sectors is the Planning Commission. Through the Commission's subcommittee on tourism, these policies are more precisely coordinated with the targets for the economy and society as a whole. Below this is the Tourism Development Council, which is charged with coordinating the activities of various private and governmental interests.

Most of these bodies are dependent on information supplied by the Tourist Department. They could but do not collect independent data on tourism. This means that those supplying the information have a vested interest in how it is perceived. The Tourist Department appears to be in a position rather like U.S. federal agencies before the former Bureau of the Budget was created to gather and monitor and screen agency data.

Other organizational problems are connected with the overseas offices that are directly responsible to the Director General. They are the government's direct link with potential visitors. Generally they act as little more than distribution centers for literature on India. They have no input into development plans because they have no real information to convey and consequently feel little responsibility for tourism targets and goals.[65] Moreover, India has an inordinately large number of such offices for a country with such a small international tourism return.[66] Fully 25 percent of the tourism budget went simply for salaries.[67] Officials enjoy the prestige of their offices and many look forward to serving abroad, but this author knows of few if any places where their current functions could not be more efficiently performed by consular or embassy staff.

Setting up separate tourism offices abroad is an enormous investment of foreign exchange that rarely facilitates tourist inquiries. In fact, a good deal of correspondence gets shuffled back and forth between the embassy and tourism offices.

The Cabinet Sub-committee on Tourism consists of the Minister of Tourism and Civil Aviation, the Minister of Education, the Minister of Works, Housing, and Urban Development, the Minister of Information and Broadcasting, and the Minister of External Affairs. Although in theory it should provide coordination on tourism matters at the very highest level, it has not been judged successful and coordination problems continue.

The Tourism Development Council is another good idea that has bad problems because its recommendations are often ignored at higher levels and neither the states nor the private sector trusts it really to represent their views. Rather, it tends to function as a mistrusted conduit of Centre views to the few states and private enterprises that attend.

ITDC and the Tourism Department have also blurred responsibilities for integrated infrastructure development, and friction often exists between them. M. M. Anand's excellent management study of the Ministry of Tourism and Civil Aviation documents repeated problems of coordination, duplication, lack of evaluation, and difficulties associated with administrators who have generalist rather than technical backgrounds. Although his research gives us an excellent picture of legitimate organizational conflicts, it is "all trees and no forest." Few organizations can withstand intense scrutiny in isolation from other agencies. Their record must be compared with others operating under similar cultural, economic, and political constraints.

One could take each of Anand's criticisms and illustrate how under some conditions such characteristics could be examples of strengths. For example, U.S. President Franklin Roosevelt regularly gave individuals and committees overlapping jurisdiction in order to maximize information perspectives and preclude premature narrowing of options. In some sectors redundancy or duplication is an absolute safeguard. Extra personnel, planes, hotel rooms, back-up generators, and cooling systems are not necessarily wasteful. Often they are essential. Even the generalist administrators, the bane of Anand's tourism development critique, can often provide for a broader national perspective than the so-called tourism expert. Admittedly, that is not always the case and generalists can become totally dependent on more permanent and possibly more parochial expertise. Still, it should be some comfort to those in Indian public administration chaffing at the problems of British-style administrative strategies to learn that those working within the American pattern of technocrat-specialists are not wholly sanguine either.

Given the clumsy, uncoordinated fashion in which tourism policy appears to be determined, what can we say about the macro-level policy that has emerged? A general consensus in the travel industry would probably be that India has not done a very good job because it just does not take tourism seriously. Every tourism minister—and there has been a parade of them—announces that the government is getting serious about tourism (after all, if it is not, the minister's job looks rather petty) and every year or so industry analysts insist that the government is not responding to its needs, that is, tourism is not being taken seriously.[68]

The press will confirm that the government is botching the tourism development effort. On that they can agree. Except when space is devoted to special tourism supplements with speeches by tourism officials reprinted, one sees little of the official enthusiasm for government's noble development efforts that are the norm in Chinese accounts. The press, however, cannot decide if the government is doing too much or not enough, encouraging the wrong kind of development, going after the wrong tourists, putting visitors in the wrong places, or charging tourists too much or too little. Sometimes the same editorial staff will criticize the government's tourism program for doing too little and too much. For example, here are three samples from the *Indian Express:*

> Like an elaborately planned sumptuous dinner going to waste for want of guests, India's ambitious "get-a-million tourists" program for 1980 might come a cropper. . . . India's new target . . . is the "so-called high spending" group. . . . India's tourism organizers . . . understand the requirements of those who come to India to relax and spend generously to get their money's worth. But those in power in New Delhi are exasperatingly slow in responding to such needs. Aged politicians who run the government give tourism promotion a low priority.[69]

> There has never been greater depression in the tourist trade as today. Nothing seems to be moving in tourism. The tourism scene is dark. At the same time, the Department of Tourism paints a rosy picture.[70]

> Hypocrisy and cynicism are even more evident than usual in New Delhi. The crores being spent on Asiad [The Asian Games of 1982] stand out in sharp relief against the real requirements of the people. . . . The twisted values involved in advertising the luxuries and choice of expensive dishes available in five star hotels when millions are in search of food . . . descriptions of spacious air-conditioned suites each fitted with colour television sets . . . and other luxuries, appear side by side in the newspapers with grim reports of near famine conditions in large parts of the country.[71]

In spite of being damned if it does and damned if it does not show dramatic initiatives toward tourism, on balance and in toto, India has done a good job of promoting international tourism cautiously, prudently, with substantially good results and with minimum disruption of the citizenry. It has taken tourism seriously, so much so that it has not, with few exceptions, allowed the dynamics of the international travel industry to dictate the terms by which tourism growth is determined. Would that all nations had the political and economic clout plus the balance to do likewise. Where the government has not been so calculating, slow and careful, as with Asiad '82, it has made costly social, economic, and political mistakes.[72]

The Asiad Stumble

The decision to reverse an earlier administration and hold the Ninth Asian Games (called Asiad '82 in India) in New Delhi was a political decision that went beyond tourism considerations, though it was defended in such terms. India is a major world power often treated with condescension and annoyance by the West. High profile sports events, international forums, and the like produce marginal doses of prestige intently sought by governments that feel neglected or underrated by world opinion. Moreover, Prime Minister Indira Gandhi badly wanted the publicity and attention of such an event to focus world attention on her triumphal return to national power and domestic attention to focus on her ability to get things done and to attract massive world interest. By the time she was finished in November 1982, 22 months later, 12 five-star hotels with a total of over 3,284 rooms had been built or were under construction.[73] Five giant stadia had been erected, seven highway overpasses built, an electrified ring railway completed, bus services expanded, an athletic village developed, and well over US$5 billion dollars spent —all in New Delhi for a 15-day sports event. Additionally, an advanced hotel management institute was set up to begin a crash program to train personnel for the games.[74]

How one stood regarding this mega-development was a classic case of where one sat: Govind Hari Singhania, Chairman of the Federation of Indian Chambers of Commerce and Industry, observed a year earlier in the midst of the hotel-building that over 1,000 groups had cancelled their winter trips to India during the previous two years because of a lack of hotel accommodations. Expansion of hotel facilities generally was acutely needed.[75] *Travel Age West,* an international travel magazine, was enthusiastic: "The government is spending vast sums of dollars. . . . The new infrastructure will become a permanent asset to help the country bid for hosting future sports events such as the Commonwealth Games or even the regular Olympics."[76]

The travel press was glowing and the Western press generally was upbeat. An exception was the *Bulletin of Concerned Asian Scholars,* which did a scathing feature on inhumane labor conditions endured by 150,000 construction workers at the Asiad sites. After detailing the labor law violations, which included not paying the US$1.00 a day minimum wage, not observing basic safety and health precautions, and employing children as young as 10, the article concluded that guests at the new hotels built for Asiad would spend more in one day than those who built the hotels earned in three months.[77]

The hard-to-please Indian press was livid over the excessive hotel construction. One of India's better known commentators, Ajit Bhattacharjea, put it this way,

> As for the Asiad, its relevance can best be judged by the "talisman" Gandhiji left to test measures claiming to be undertaken for the public good: "Recall the face of the poorest and most helpless man you have seen and ask yourself if the step you contemplate is going to be of any use to him. Will he gain anything by it? Will it restore him to a control over his own life and destiny?"
> The answer is obvious.[78]

At least two tourism consultants were also appalled. Although India needed hotel rooms, it did not need virtually 100 percent of them to be luxury class and all in the capital city. As they pointed out, analysis of visitor arrivals showed that the largest group of tourists was in the 17-to 30-year-old age range with over 60 percent under 40 years old. "In other words, most of our tourists are young enough to rough it out in fairly cheap accommodations: they don't need to cosset themselves in high-priced cocoons in the capital."[79]

Even more ironic, the government has for years struggled to diffuse tourism development, to break the hold that Delhi-Agra-Jaipur ("The Golden Triangle") has had on tourists. It had been announced that travel circuits would be created as a means to create new tourist centers in the country. Because Asiad money absorbed most of the hotel infrastructure funds, there may be neither money nor the political will for development at other locations. Until 1988, Delhi was seriously overbuilt. During that time the taxpayers of India helped to finance a buyer's market for the international tourist.

> Competition is creating bargains among the best of New Delhi's hotels. Excess room capacity built for 1982 Asian Games remains largely unused because of poor tourist traffic in 1983. India's capital had 1,600 top-rank hotel rooms before the games. It has 3,536 now, with more to come.
> New Delhi hands say tourists need only walk in and start bargaining.

Most prestigious inns will discount 30 to 50 percent of normal rate. In newer hotels geared to average $100 rate, single rooms are being offered at $40 to $50 a day. Some will do even better—and add meals. Critics say faulty planning assumed that all foreigners could afford five-star luxury and the government neglected low-budget hotels.[80]

The bubble has burst and as the Gantzers predicted, hotel investment may dry up as investors decide that tourism is simply too risky.

Why did the Asiad '82 hotel fiasco occur? Why did the government predictions of 50,000 visitors fall so far short of the mark? Planning was not the problem any more than it was in the cases of the hotel-building sprees in Seoul and Manila. The government's own research showed that as early as 1977 single, inexpensive accommodations were the greatest infrastructure need, not luxury hotels. To diagnose the problem as planning is to suggest that better economic analysis could have avoided it. That is nonsense. The same political dynamics were present in all three countries: authoritarian leadership wanted to showcase a veneer of development at a high-profile international function to boost its political status.[81] This strategy has been used since the days of Franco in the 1930s. The old constraints are relaxed so that the extravaganza may proceed and the government underwrites massive infrastructure costs. "Of the 3000 additional rooms envisaged for meeting the Games rush, no more than 1200 may in fact be ready. But this does not seem to bother anyone . . . because everyone knows the Asiad was merely an excuse to expedite clearance of building plans, etc. in many cases in direct contravention of rules and regulations."[82]

And the whole scenario works, at least in terms of international politics. High praises, for the smooth-functioning games, the incredible security, and the beautiful buildings were common in the international press. Few seemed to question why such elaborate security was necessary or how appropriate such herculean efforts were on behalf of a sports spectacular. The Indian press took a more jaundiced view of the entire effort. "The speed with which the massive new stadia, the Olympic village, the numerous fly overs and new street lighting has been accomplished for Asiad shows what the administration can achieve if the government is serious. The tragedy is that this urgency is exhibited for projects that bring no benefit to the common people."[83]

Local politicians and entrepreneurs are quick to take advantage of leadership objectives even when the initial results are underutilized, because the government's generally slow response and lack of concessions on material, that is, imported items or scarce local products like cement, may mean that another opportunity will not come soon.[84]

The Asiad '82 Aftermath

The international travel industry, frustrated by India's past unwillingness to allow charters, sharpen tourism training, curtail prohibition, and develop what it perceives as the essential infrastructure, is quick to exploit Delhi's post-Asiad dilemma. It can now advertise bargain luxury accommodations. It has also convinced the government to abandon its concern about Air India's competition and proceed to allow charters. This comes as a big blow to the government's international airline, which has just committed itself to a massive expansion. It had expected to have until 1990 before it would face foreign charters.

Now the pressure is also on to expand Indian Airlines (IA). One of the world's largest domestic airlines, IA has long been the butt of travel industry complaints. No one would argue that it has first-rate service, but it does have a good safety record and for most of the Indian travelers fortunate enough to be traveling by air, it has proved more than adequate. But for international travel agents the hassles of booking a ticket on an airline without a computerized reservation system had bordered on hellish. In late 1984, however, IA did complete computerization of its system.[85]

As charters deliver more and more tourists to India, the pressure will build for more funds to be approved for expansion of Indian Airlines. Of course, theoretically, each of these steps will garner foreign exchange, but each also deflects important investments away from sectors of primary domestic importance and serves to isolate international from domestic tourism. Each step also furthers dependence on an external market whose most affluent personnel are especially fickle even without the question of political turmoil. It would be naive to assume that after 30 years either India as a country or South Asia as a region should build its development program too heavily on nonregional patronage and political serenity.

Consider the difference between the advice heeded by the post-1980 Gandhi administration and that of some development analysts that has been overturned. The latter advocated establishing charters, providing hotel incentives, relaxing prohibition, developing night life, and catering to the more affluent traveler, especially the high spending, oil rich West Asians, in order for India to maximize tourist arrivals. Much of their advice, however, was based on an ignorance of Indian culture and a total blindspot when it came to empirical evidence regarding cost-benefit analysis. One article presumed to maximize foreign exchange earnings by concentrating on the affluent, but it did not offer data concerning foreign exchange leakage, the less labor intensive nature of luxury establishments, or the fact that the affluent need a different transport and infrastructure base with disproportionate capital, energy, and water needs—all elements in drastically short supply. Amazingly, the article contended that West Asians should be the target of marketing, because they currently cannot tour Lebanon and other West Asian countries because of political chaos there.

> The type of holiday West Asians prefer needs to be emphasized. Travel packages, hotels and restaurants, excursions and tours, shops and merchandise, airline flights, car rental agencies and other intra-country travel facilities, cultural programmes, sight-seeing, and entertainment should be oriented toward these high spenders.[86]

So Gibbons and Fish recommended that India should base its tourism not only on political peace at home, foreign tourism, and luxury tourism, but also on political instability in countries whose closer proximity and luxury facilities have historically been provided for the West Asian traveler.

For a moment, let us ignore the whole issue of building a market around such an ephemeral base. Let us consider what has happened to those entrepreneurs who have followed the Gibbons and Fish recommendation and have attempted to target a West Asian clientele.

> Though India has never encouraged such satiation seekers, it is now mounting barriers against those Arab tourists who, denied the fleshpots of Lebanon, now jet into India seeking similar diversions. Hotels which once welcomed the flood of petro-dollars now discourage all but the most urbane Arabian Gulf customer: establishments which have earned an unsavory "Arab Hotel" reputation have registered an unhealthy fall in occupancy rates as their more regular clients moved away.[87]

Currently West Asia does provide an area of significant growth in tourism arrivals, but the surest way to attract those West Asians appropriate to Indian culture is to maintain a balanced product.

Moreover, there are other potential sources of international tourism growth premised on genuine ties to India—thereby providing a more stable growth market without elaborate capital inputs. Those inputs needed would support both domestic and international tourism, and in contrast to West Asian nightlife would not add to the over concentration of tourists in the major cities. Such tourists are those from countries in ASEAN. Sixty-five percent of those ASEAN travelers are expatriate Indians. The other growth groups are also from Asia—those coming from Japan, the Republic of China, and elsewhere who are interested either in trekking or visiting Buddhist pilgrimage shrines and historical places. To them India is a destination, not just a stopover. Because they stay longer, they provide as much or more foreign exchange than those who may spend more and stay briefly in accommodations that are costly in capital, energy, and symbolic consumption.

Hopefully, one aberration, the Asian Games, despite its long-term impact, will not turn Indian tourism policy in absurd directions. There are positive signs that India's general good sense and conservative policies toward tourism will continue to avoid "the sort of tourism overkill . . . often complained about in Bangkok and occasionally in Sri Lanka."[88]

THE POLICY DIRECTIONS OF FUTURE INDIAN TOURISM

India's tourism base is sound. The core of domestic tourists is profitable enough to encourage entrepreneurs to expand. There are few restrictions on the movements of tourists, and the economic and political climate has provided both public corporations and private entrepreneurs a generally successful return on their investments. In fact, India is cited as an excellent example of government's forming a positive countervailing force to the private sector instead of, as is frequently the case, the government's merely becoming involved in rescuing sick and dying enterprises. Indian tourism is basically Indian-owned, managed, and directed. Although occasional franchising and market agreements have been allowed, the Indian government has usually prohibited management contracts. As mentioned earlier, imports for the industry are extremely low compared to those of most third world destinations.[89]

Major problems remain, which are not naturally the ones most salient to the travel industry. First, as noted earlier, too much investment of scarce foreign exchange has been spent on overseas travel offices. Although many tourism authorities urge India to do more marketing, it could not do better than to let film crews do the promotional work. Given very limited resources, Air India and the consulates and embassies need to handle whatever overseas government role is envisaged.

Second, there is a serious problem of providing stable electrical and water supplies for tourist and nontourist needs. The over-concentration of mammoth luxury hotels in Delhi only aggravates this problem. Ironically, the more deluxe the accommodations, the more inappropriate and uncomfortable such facilities become when air conditioning, lighting, elevators and water supply fail. At such times, people can cope better in low-rise, more modest facilities that are open to the outside air.

Third, pollution is another serious policy question of touristic import. Although more of a political issue in the cities, some of the worst damage occurs to the fragile ecosystems of the hill areas. Sometimes the very effort to disperse trekkers and other tourists seems only to spread the damage to more vulnerable areas. To keep tourism development and mountain ecosystems from working at cross purposes, better exchange of recreation management research is critical. A positive step in this direction is the Institute of Himalayan Studies and Regional Development at Srinagar. Integrated development in which tourism is a planned component can be successful.[90]

The government, the Pacific Area Travel Association, and organizations like the Indian Heritage Association, sponsored by the Indian tourist industry, have worked to associate tourism with the preservation rather than the desecration of the environment. The Indian Heritage Association's work to save the Taj Mahal from sulfurous wastes and industrial vibration has particularly highlighted the positive force tourism can be.[91] Wildlife protection policies have encouraged the development of much special-interest tourism. Though both the state and local governments have been encouraged by Kenya's ability to make safari tourism lucrative, India, like Kenya, is discovering that human needs for space and agriculture and animal protection often force the government to make hard decisions about the relative developmental importance of tourism and agricultural sectors.

Despite the hotel building, despite the Asian Games, in 1982 Indian tourism recorded a growth rate of only 0.8 percent, the lowest since the government began keeping such statistics in 1970. Three years of lackluster growth led to a Tourism Policy Statement made in Parliament, November 3, 1982. It called for a "well-planned, well-defined and fully-integrated programme of tourism development."[92] A component of that approach will be the Star Tourist Circuits proposed by Hugh and Colleen Gantzer as a means of diffusing tourism's impact and correcting the lopsided growth in tourism now concentrated in Delhi, Jaipur, and Agra and farther south in Bombay and Goa.

Initially, the Ministry of Tourism and Civil Aviation had planned to link clusters of potential tourist sites by circular coach tours, with an overnight stop at each destination on the circuit. This plan was abandoned when it was pointed out that the accommodation inputs would be tremendous. The Star Circuit approach limits start-up costs and holds promise for gradual development.

Tourists will now be accommodated at the focal points in the Star Circuits. From such points, they will be taken out on day-long excursions to the various points of tourist interest, returning to the focal points every night. . . . In the course of time, the more popular excursion spots will, by a normal process of supply and demand, develop into overnight stopovers. These in turn, could well grow into independent focal points serving their own Star Circuits.[93]

The integration of this tourist diffusion scheme is a particularly exciting approach, which if it works well could be a model for the political
and economic acceptability of tourism in the Third World. At the focal
points, tourist needs and non-urban technology and heritage must be
made compatible.

> These constraints have led to the concept of the condominium hotels, or
> contels: a joint venture of the government and private industry. . . . Briefly
> it is the responsibility of state governments, with their concern for economic
> development, to identify the points on the Star Circuit and to develop its
> communications and basic facilities. . . . The state government then lays
> down the infrastructure . . . roads, power, sanitation, water, landscaping.
> It then auctions plots by function: here a hairdresser, there a health club, a
> restaurant around that corner, a grocer, drugstore, etc. . . . The logic is that
> no single entrepreneur should have a major say in how the contel is run: it
> should be a cooperative endeavor . . . a living community built around
> local tradesmen and entrepreneurs who do not individually have to invest
> very much. . . . And because the buildings use local materials, building
> techniques and skills, they too can be largely maintained by the locals.[94]

Although the premise of integrating tourism into the economy is excellent, it will take a rather scaled down version of this approach to be successful. As the World Bank noted in 1972, the political decision of which
"non-urban hamlet or village" gets costly infrastructure will have a great
impact on surrounding land values. That may be inevitable—a make or
break situation analogous to the issue of which American town had a
railroad in the nineteenth century or which in the twentieth century is
near the turnpike. Another problem is local skills: hairdressers and
health club entrepreneurs do not reside in most Indian villages, nor do
they want to. Although this writer thinks the need for either is scarcely
basic to touring India, if they are deemed essential they will need to be
persuaded to migrate to a contel.

Finally, although there are obviously some excellent features in this
concept, a major stumbling block is that countries and regions react differently to cooperatives. Though in India they have generally been
accepted, elsewhere in Asia they have often been a failure. It seems more
likely that the use of ITDC hotels or state TDC lodges at the sites would
introduce more auspicious expertise while still assuring local employment and a market for building materials and food. ITDC facilities have
already established their acceptability with foreign and domestic tourists.
As of 1982, nearly 50 percent of the ITDC clientele were foreign tourists.[95] Probably in no other facilities are foreign and domestic tourists so
evenly represented. What better mechanism for integrating the two markets and avoiding neo-colonial enclaves of Westerners.

In conclusion, India offers many examples of good, solid tourism development. The many initiatives, the federal structure, and the division of responsibility for different aspects of tourism among many specialized units make it difficult to summarize tourism policy for the entire country. Many policies co-exist, but most of those this writer has examined reveal thoughtful development. Some of the exceptions have also been noted.

Perhaps the best thing about Indian tourism policy and the element that poses the sharpest contrast with Chinese policy is that much of it is policy made in public, debated in public, and subject to accountable political control. Tourism consultants may carp that "decisions have been too long dominated by politicians who too often express views on tourism developments, not on the basis of the development's *true* [emphasis is mine] merits, but on the basis of what they anticipate their audience would like to hear."[96] But what makes the world's largest free society an irritant to the tourist "experts" is what also keeps it from going on Asiad adventures very often: an imperfect, clumsy, but still functioning democracy.

6

Creating Tourist "Meccas" in Praetorian States: Case Studies of Pakistan and Bangladesh

PAKISTAN

A craze for secrecy and an invitation to tourists will be like a three-legged race.[1]

The Holy Koran repeatedly speaks of gardens with canals and trees . . . as a reward for those who do good deeds in this life . . . it is our religious duty to establish more parks and playgrounds. . . . It is now for us to gear up our loins and get "heaps" of wealth from such peace-loving Ambassadors, namely the tourists.

—K. A. Hussain[2]

PAKISTAN is an enigma. There are countries that fail to succeed in using tourism for development because they adopt it too quickly, too massively, or too uncritically, for example, the Philippines. There are countries that do not use tourism for development because they do not want tourists and so do not issue tourist visas, for example Saudi Arabia. And there are many countries in between that use tourism with varying degrees of success or failure. But perhaps no country—Uganda might be an exception —has managed to avoid tourism success more consistently than Pakistan. When it has not suffered from external political and economic problems affecting tourism, the country's internal political administrative machinery has managed to sabotage its program.

This is surprising. Superficially one might expect Pakistan to have a political tourism history rather like India, of which it was a part until 1947. Pakistan was created in August of that year out of the predominantly Muslim portions of British India and adjacent princely states. Because it was created to conform with concentrations of Muslims, it was a bizarre polity that was hard to govern and even harder to defend. Essentially, Pakistan was composed of two large chunks of land separated by 1,000 miles of Indian territory. And thus it uneasily existed until 1971 when the cement of an Islamic raison d'être proved insufficient to

134

Table 6.1. Foreign tourist arrivals in Pakistan.

	(West) Pakistan	East Pakistan (Bangladesh)	Total
1965	71,691	1,900	73,691
1966	74,243	3,239	77,482
1967	84,942	4,499	89,441
1968	89,670	7,722	97,392
1969	103,829	7,328	111,153
1970	122,097		
1975	178,000	n.a.	178,000
1980	292,000	n.a.	292,000
1982	313,700		313,700

SOURCES: Pakistan Department of Tourism *Annual Report, 1969; Pakistan Affairs* 34 (no. 9): 2 (May 1, 1981); *Asia Travel Trade* (February 1984): 48.

hold the two linguistically, culturally, economically, and politically distinct parts together. In a savage civil war in 1971, East Pakistan seceded to become the Republic of Bangladesh. Naturally, that year tourism did rather poorly, but what of the more than 40 years since independence?

Pakistan inherited a much more limited tourist infrastructure at the time of independence than India. Colonial rule, though of shorter duration in West Pakistan than in most of the rest of the subcontinent, provided roads, railroads, and the most extensive system of canal irrigation in the world, but development in general was more limited: major cities and scenic areas were fewer and the entire bureaucracy and political system was much more fragile and ill-equipped than in India.

Pakistan's tourism potential is enormous. The ethnic diversity of its 100 million people; the archeological importance of Mohenjo-Daro, Harappa, Taxila, and lesser-known sites throughout the country; the religious shrines; the wide variety of terrain; and the dramatic scenic beauty far outshine in touristic value many of the globe's most popular destinations. Despite all this, growth in tourism has not been impressive and has been in spite of, more than because of, government effort. In 1980, 292,000 tourists visited Pakistan, one-tenth the number visiting Honolulu and considerably short of what was described only three years earlier as "the Prime Minister's target of One Million Tourist Arrivals to Pakistan each year by 1980."[3] As Table 6.1 illustrates, this is still a gradual growth over earlier levels. It also shows that East Pakistan's share of pre-1971 tourist arrivals was miniscule. Beyond sheer total and a pattern of increase or decrease, government figures tend to be distrusted by industry sources because of distortions in the way they are gathered. In 1988, arrival figures were scarcely higher than a decade earlier.

The organization of tourism in Pakistan superficially parallels that of

India but, as we shall see later, performance tends to be greatly divergent. Official interest in tourism in Pakistan began in the early 1960s under the leadership of President Mohammad Ayub Khan. Small tourist information centers were set up around the country and, in 1965, a twenty-year Master Plan for the Development of Tourism in Pakistan (1965–1985) was prepared by a team of French consultants, with United Nations Development Project (UNDP) financing.[4]

When Yahya Khan took over in 1969 as president, he proceeded to dismantle the fledgling government department of tourism, although tourism development was permitted to be refashioned into a public corporation. After a series of what would become endemic delays in tourism development, the Pakistan Tourism Development Corporation (PTDC) was created in 1970, on the model of India's ITDC, with offices in both East and West Pakistan. As such, it was partially funded by the government, partially by private enterprise, and is theoretically accountable to the Secretary of Tourism. The PTDC was charged with promotional responsibilities abroad, some limited infrastructure management and with encouraging travel and information between the two parts of Pakistan.[5]

The major impetus for tourism development came under Zulfikar Ali Bhutto, who was placed in power in Pakistan in the wake of the 1971 Civil War. Bhutto decided to make tourism a priority policy, apparently on the basis of a variety of considerations. Perhaps the most crucial factor at that time was Pakistan's need for a positive identity at home and abroad.[6] Pakistan has historically had a dual identity problem. First, foreigners lack a clear image of the nation or tend to think of it as a part of India. A group of British tour operators told the Pakistani press in 1977, that "Pakistan is not yet known to the outside world as a tourist destination, mainly because the foreign tourist is not aware of the attractions that the country has to offer, and he does not know what specific places to visit in case he does arrive in Pakistan."[7] Second, Pakistanis, too, think less in terms of *Pakistan* and have tended to identify more with their locality or region. This became tragically clear in the 1971 Civil War, and separatism continues to be a major problem today. Tourism thus was perceived as a potential instrument for forging both a stronger national identity and a more positive image abroad.

Tourism also fit well with Bhutto's design to reorient Pakistan westward following the 1971 war. Without East Pakistan, the nation more than ever looked to the Middle East for trade, aid, and cultural identity.[8] Tourism would not only garner much-needed foreign exchange but would also enhance Pakistan's chances for direct aid by becoming a recreational oasis for Middle Eastern elites. Bhutto accordingly promoted plans to build a casino in Karachi and other facilities to entice visitors.

Several important foreign interests reinforced these directions in policy. The Japanese sent reconnaissance groups to Pakistan to survey tour opportunities and the United Nations Development Project (UNDP) and Pacific Area Travel Association (PATA) offered assistance. Middle Eastern rulers did indeed respond by vacationing in Pakistan and giving sizeable grants. In fact, the Cholistan Desert of the former princely state of Bahawalpur became a popular destination for such visitors because of the opportunities there for falconry.

Bhutto also saw in tourism development a way to make the society more modern and less parochial in its politics and social views.[9] Traditional barriers to the emancipation of women might erode if the country were subject to the presence of large numbers of tourists. Ironically, most third world countries are concerned with how to keep tourists from "polluting" the national culture. Bhutto, more aware of the pressures from fundamentalist clergy, saw tourists as allies in exposing Pakistan to more modern Islamic and non-Islamic views. Bhutto also felt that women could have a conspicuous employment role in such a service industry. Stereotypes favor the female as the more hospitable and gracious sex, qualities appropriate in many of the new positions in the tourist sector. His political and social vision of what tourism might have become was never given the time to be tested.

Paradoxically, it was his personal interest in tourism and other issues that tended to prevent Bhutto from protecting the decision-making apparatus essential for its continuity. His intervention in locating a motel in his home community of Larkhana diverted the building from being built at a more appropriate location, near the 3,000-year-old ruins of Mohenjo-Daro. His private PTDC villa was reported after his arrest in 1977. It had been bought by the PTDC from one of the parade of PTDC Managing Directors who had briefly held the post.[10] One of Bhutto's most serious mistakes was the appointment of Riaz Agha as Managing Director of the PTDC. Most appointments to the post have been undistinguished, but Riaz Agha was a reputed scoundrel who had been sacked from Caltex for forgery and who had had a succession of unsavory business deals.

But Agha had contacts and, as most people in the public and private tourism sectors affirmed, it is who you know, not what you know. So Bhutto reportedly ignored his own instincts and ordered him hired. "Let Riaz Agha get the post of Managing Director of PTDC. In my opinion he is a big badmash (scoundrel) but the Chief Minister of Sind is sold on him and I do not think it fair to refuse his persistent requests."[11]

It was a huge mistake. Agha lived and traveled lavishly at government expense, made numerous appointments of friends to high offices, and awarded contracts to associates and relatives for tourism infrastructure.[12] Even so, some foreign consultants who conceded he was a crook rather hated to see him flee to the United States because he was one of the few in that position who could make things happen—albeit only when his needs and tourism's intersected.[13]

For all of Bhutto's political instincts of modernization, he neither allowed the technocrats discretion nor allowed a free political process truly to function. Securing the spoils of position dominated over any attempt to make the bureaucracy function.

Like India, Pakistan is also supposed to have additional tourism programs in each of its four provinces, but it was apparent as late as 1980 that most of these existed only on paper. During the Bhutto era (1972–1977) the personalistic rule of Bhutto tended to override constitutional allocations of authority. Most of the tourism planners and authorities within the tourist infrastructure knew nothing about provincial tourism responsibilities.[14]

Yet as a result of the failure to institutionalize tourism in Pakistan while it was considered a priority policy, the industry has been especially defenseless since the July 1977 coup that replaced Bhutto with General Zia ul Huq. Although, like Bhutto, Zia is interested in forging closer ties with his middle eastern neighbors, he is considerably more fundamentalist in his religious and social views than any of his predecessors, with deleterious consequences for tourism. Islamic injunctions against the social mingling of the sexes, the consumption of alcohol and gambling militate against certain types of convention and resort development, as well as against common types of individual and group travel.

General Zia, called President Zia since 1978, has always had a certain ambivalence about tourism, and those close to Zia were hostile to foreign tourism long before Zia came to power. Many of the conservative mullahs (priests) consider any facility with a swimming pool as condoning nude bathing, and western dancing is railed against as striptease.[15] The fits and starts that have characterized Pakistani tourism reflect the genuine ambivalence of both the society and the government towards tourism. The wariness about tourism is healthy, but alternately attempting policies that invite and then discourage tourism is a tragic waste of scarce resources and demoralizes public and private tourism sectors.

Social Factors Affecting Tourism Policy

Historically, there appears to be a much weaker tradition of domestic tourism in Pakistan than in neighboring India. Though like India, much of the domestic travel is based on religious pilgrimages, many of the most important historical sites are Sikh, Hindu, or Buddhist, which are ignored by most domestic tourists. In India all of these faiths, including

Islam, have millions of adherents (India's 10 percent Muslim population is nearly the size of Pakistan's population). Since the loss of East Pakistan with its 25 percent Hindu population, however, Pakistan is 97.3 percent Muslim.[16] For such believers, the most important travel is to Mecca, a trip meaning tremendous foreign exchange leakage from Pakistan, and yet one that no Islamic government can restrict. In fact, the Haj (pilgrimage to Mecca) has been given high priority in the tourism planning of the government. Assuring comfortable, safe travel out of the country for Haj participants has involved President Zia's personal attention. Haj travel is directed by the Ministry of Religious Affairs rather than the Tourism Division.

Other forms of travel by Pakistani tourists involve, as they do in India, summer trips to the hills. Here again, the shorter colonial experience in this area meant that there were fewer hotels, roads, and other tourist infrastructure to inherit and little has been added. Maintenance of areas of touristic importance have been neglected. Also, Pakistan's population, like India's, has very little money for discretionary spending. In 1974 only 44,000 of the 11 million households in Pakistan had more than Rs. 300 (about $30) per year to spend on reading and recreation.[17] Pakistan's impressive growth (6 percent per annum) since 1977 has probably changed this, especially since remittances from Pakistanis working abroad have brought changes in distribution. Though the remittances from the Middle East have declined with falling oil prices, Pakistan is still considered to be on the verge of becoming a middle income nation.

Complicating the decision to travel are the restrictions imposed by Islam on the public role of women and on certain forms of tourist behavior. For example, restaurants are much less common at the middle and lower income hotels because families tend to eat in their rooms rather than subject their women to the gazes of strangers. As a consequence of the general seclusion of women in touring, public restrooms for women are extremely rare compared with even the scarce facilities for men. The dearth of such facilities is an indication of the typical absence of women from the public scene and a barrier that the more intrepid must somehow surmount.

Moreover, women and children usually travel in separate railway accommodations, which like facilities for women in all other aspects of the society, tend to be less abundant, more crowded, and generally inferior to those provided for men. The continual efforts of President Zia to further Islamicize the society according to the most conservative Islamic interpretations reinforce the isolation of women from men and women from recreational and touristic opportunities.[18] Women are strongly encouraged to be veiled, to dress so as to be covered from head to toe, or to wear the cumbersome *burkha* (ten yards of usually black covering with mesh peepholes). The reinstatement of such dress in Pakistan after its general obsolescence for two generations is seen as a particularly inhibiting garb by most women, who are unaccustomed to its use.

The dress code has several implications for tourism. Such garb, discarded in most Islamic societies over 50 years ago, is not conducive to touring. Such clothing is hot and uncomfortable in a climate that, except for the very northern parts, is tropical or semi-tropical and where air conditioning is rare.

Because dress codes now exist for even young girls, opportunities for sports such as swimming, riding, or running, are not well developed. Also, because girls are segregated from boys, girls lose again, as limited school facilities are disproportionately built for males—a disastrous consequence confirmed by the dramatically lower literacy rates for women.

Those few women who do have both sports talent and opportunity may only compete with women, before female audiences, and may not travel abroad for meets since the Zia government seized power. Thus, one does not find the sports-related tourism among women in Pakistan that exists in other societies. They rarely swim at public beaches or avail themselves of other recreational pursuits that require interaction with the public.

Consider the implications of government policy on the hapless non-Pakistani female tourist, who even if modestly garbed may still want to travel, eat in restaurants, swim at the seashore, or just walk the streets unmolested. Since the advent of the Zia regime those activities are not easy.

Islamicization, or *Nizam-i-Mustafa* (Rule of the Prophet) as President Zia calls his crusade, is not conducive to domestic or international tourism. President Zia was concerned that place names in Pakistan did not project an Islamic image or extol great men in Islam, so the names of some cities were changed (e.g., Lyallpur became Shah Faisalabad), confusing directories, rendering maps obsolete, and destroying any familiarity between historical references, pre-1977 publicity, or other markers that the tourist may have had. Admittedly not all names changed, some are just written in Urdu instead of English. Only a minority of the population reads Urdu and most domestic and foreign tourists read English, so this step, too, may hurt tourism marginally.

President Zia then became annoyed that some Pakistanis were not observing the Ramadan month of fasting for Eid, so he had all restaurants, soft drink establishments, and all catering facilities, including those for railroads and airlines, closed between dawn and dusk during the month. One headline read "10 Held for Eating in Public."[19] Although in some places western tourists who knew to plan ahead could get box lunches to eat in private, others went hungry. Hungry tourists do not write euphoric post cards home! Hungry tourists do tell their travel agents!

Even after dusk and before dawn, facilities for tourists continue to be spartan. All night clubs have been closed, strict prohibition is enforced (unless the non-Pakistani tourists want liquor in their room or in rooms designed for hotel guests who declare themselves "habitual users!"). Most stocks of liquor in hotels and restaurants were initially destroyed. Reports differ on whether the government is now allowing liquor importation by hotels for nonpublic use by foreign guests. Prohibition of liquor for private foreign use also depends on the hotel. Large hotels with good connections have been the only ones allowed the exemption.[20] Folk dances as well as belly-dancing have been axed. Muzak is gone. In its place are Muslim calls to prayer over the hotel's intercom and convenient instructions in each room as to which direction faces Mecca![21]

Obviously, none of these remarks is meant as a criticism of Islam. What is implied is that the interpretation of the Koran President Zia has chosen to promote is particularly atypical of most Muslim adherents and is at variance with the expectations of much of the traveling public.

One splinter Muslim group, the Ismailis, has the majority of its followers in Hunza, Gilgit, and Chitral in the mountainous north. In 1975, the Aga Khan Tourism organization, with Bhutto's encouragement, had planned to develop hotels in the area with the help of Pakistan International Airlines.[22] This has been an area of major tourism potential. But it is also one plagued by tricky weather and similarly capricious political fortune that have kept groups stranded in the mountains or denied access.[23] Either way it has stymied attempts at economic and tourism development of the region. Zia has closed this northern region to foreigners periodically perhaps fearing foreign contact with a particularly disenchanted minority. More recently there are indications that the PTDC is once again actively developing the region. That could mean that once again tourism promotion is not synchronized with government political policies; it could mean that PTDC is planning—many times projects get labeled as accomplished once the blueprints are complete—or it could mean that the government and the PTDC are, in fact, using the beautiful north for tourism development.

Once one accepts the Zia government as legitimate (not everyone does since it seized power in a coup d'etat, hanged the previous chief executive, Prime Minister Bhutto, and did not hold elections for years), the policy decisions it has taken with regard to tourism can be weighed on two scales. By one measure, the health of the tourist industry, the policy has been a disaster, alienating the international industry, persecuting the domestic industry, intimidating all attempts at collective lobbying on behalf of travel organizations, and unknowingly discouraging domestic and international tourism. By the second criterion of whether the policy helps national development, the impact would on balance probably still be negative, but the appraisal would be mixed.

The most zealous tourism development since 1977 probably could not have succeeded, given the external political problems on Pakistan's borders. Revolution in Iran, the Iran-Iraq War, and the Soviet invasion of Afghanistan have effectively sealed off overland travel to Pakistan from Europe. This is a serious blow, for nearly 20 percent of Pakistan's tourist arrivals came by land. Although travel within South Asia continues, it operates erratically and is always an early casualty of the chronic tension.

A nation in uneasy peace with its neighbors and suffering from a veritable tradition of "persistent praetorianism" is also not many's idea of a vacation idyll.[24] Executive support for tourism has also been erratic and characteristically half-hearted, premised often it would seem on aping India rather than on internal political and economic goals.

Some Pakistani observers, and even government officials lamenting the malaise of tourism in their country, have exhorted private industry to take more leadership in tourism development.[25] But the private sector is not much more effective than the government. There is a hotel and restaurant association, but it is rendered impotent by its membership's mistrust of any collective approach to problem solving. The habits of pursuing political and economic advantages on an individual basis according to whom one knows with influence, has meant that no significant funds, discretion, or authority undergird the Pakistan tourism association.[26]

Implementation of Tourism Policy

To this point, a sketch has been drawn of the evolution of Pakistan tourism policy and the way it was designed at each stage to assist domestic or international political objectives. We have also looked at the cultural, religious, and foreign policy dimensions that have affected tourism developments. At this juncture it is appropriate to consider the public administration of tourism policy, for it too is illustrative of more general administrative characteristics that can explain much of the character of Pakistan's politics and public institutions.

Pakistani public administration did not inherit as secure or well developed an administrative corps as India at the time of partition. Traditionally, there were far fewer Muslims in the government than their numbers in the population warranted. Historically, much of the best Muslim talent went to Muslim schools with more classical religious and philosophical training, rejecting the English education the upper class Hindu would get. That changed in the two decades before independence, but not before the Muslims had lost the edge in government service competition.

There was a hasty division of the Indian public sector down to pencils and glue. Then followed the bloody agony of partition as some 10 million moved either to Pakistan or India, under the most terrifying communal conditions, with perhaps a million slaughtered enroute.[27] The public sector was overwhelmed.

In the 1950s, as the weakness of political and administrative institutions became apparent in Pakistan, a favorite type of U.S. technical assistance focused on public administration. Institutes for the training of individuals for the public sector were formed. Unfortunately institution building and political development never turned out to be the simple technical tasks so many assumed they were in those days.

Pakistan's failure to overcome "persistent praetorianism" and the country's inability to preserve human rights or political freedoms has taken its toll on the administrative system even as it has on the civic life of the society. If the administration had been well developed and in place before Pakistan had lost Mohammed Ali Jinnah and Liaquat Ali Khan, the founders and leaders of Pakistan, either the political life of the country might have been more stable or the administration might have had the esprit de corps and respect it needed to function in the face of political instability. That was not to be. Both Pakistani leaders died very early in the beginnings of independent Pakistan and the administrative structure has, for the most part, performed poorly ever since. There are, of course, some sectors that do better than others, but most have very low levels of efficiency or honesty and tourism is no exception.

The conclusions of the French consulting firm charged by the United Nations Development Project with developing a Master Plan for Tourism for 1975–1980 put it this way: "Any recommendations . . . must bear in mind the very mediocre standard of business and public service morality which unfortunately still exists in Pakistan today. . . . Without an improvement, the efficacy of most of the other recommendations will be greatly moderated."[28] What are the chronic problems facing Pakistan's efforts to utilize tourism for national development? They are not the country's intrinsic attractions. As mentioned before, Pakistan is richer in sites of potential touristic appeal than the vast majority of currently more popular nations. Essentially the problems fall into two categories: (1) those that are external to the nation or at least tourism policy and cannot be easily changed and (2) those that are internal and subject to improvement.

In the first category is luck. Pakistan has had very bad timing when it comes to tourism. In 1965 when the first major effort was made to launch a 20-year master plan for tourism, war broke out between India and Pakistan; in 1971 all the plans for East Pakistan tourism development were aborted when it seceded. The next big push came with UN consultant financing and its elaborate report, which was to provide a program for tourism from 1975 (the South Asia Tourism Year) to 1980. We will never know how that might have worked, for the country was racked with demonstrations following the 1977 elections, and in July 1977 General Zia seized power in a military coup, setting up a "90 day caretaker regime" that lasted over eleven years. *Nizam-i-Mustafa* had never been imagined in the plans. The entire Islamicization program has given mixed signals to the foreign tourist.

No sooner did the dust settle from that episode than the Iranian Revolution began and only one week before the beginning of Pakistan's push to get a million tourists in 1980, the Soviet Union invaded Afghanistan. Even one of the small tourism projects that the government attempted, a *son et lumière* show at the Lahore Fort, had its gala opening rained out![29]

Pakistan is caught in a catch-22 situation when it comes to luring tourists even in good times. Despite being in the same general region as India, air fares are higher because fewer customers mean that volume discounts are harder to negotiate and higher air fares keep the tourists away. Poor relations with India have also made regional cooperation on tourism more difficult.

The foregoing should help the reader understand why, even without administrative problems, civil servants are reluctant to become overly involved in the execution of tourism policy. It also helps one understand why Muslims in Pakistan often follow any statement of intent with *Insha' Allah* (God-Willing).

There is only one thing that can be done with relative security: plans. Much has been planned. A ski resort to be financed in part with Austrian aid has been on the drawing board for at least 23 years.[30] On several occasions over the period it has been pronounced near completion. Yet during this writer's 1977 visit it had not even been started. Although funding for tourism has never been bountiful, the 40 lakhs (about $400,000) budgeted in 1962 were 27 times that of 1958 and funding has increased substantially since then.[31] Still, the editorial comment made on January 31, 1964, is still accurate today: "The development of the tourist industry in Pakistan has yet to pass through its many initial stages."[32]

A specific assessment of the lack of implementation of the 1965 Plan highlighted development problems that are chronic in the development of tourism to this day. Yet these problems can be improved, should the government consider them important:

1. a failure to integrate tourism planning with the total planning process;
2. a refusal on the part of other government departments (particularly the planning division) to take tourism seriously;

3. lack of clear guidelines and an outdated Master Plan;
4. lack of credibility of PTDC because of poor performance and management changes;
5. lack of finance;
6. a complicated, time-consuming mechanism for getting projects reviewed requiring foreign exchange;
7. poor quality feasibility studies that ignored the market until after the project was planned; and
8. total lack of data on markets and on existing services.[33]

Most of these problems still exist.

For all the foreign interest and Bhutto's concern, the momentum for major tourism development has not been sustained. Implementation has bogged down for several reasons, some organizational, some political, and some cultural. The Department of Tourism, resurrected to provide overall guidance, has been shuffled from ministry to ministry and eventually relegated to the status of a minor portfolio in the Ministry of Culture, Archeology, Sports, and Tourism. With a small budget, even less status, a crippling turnover of top-level personnel, and lower-ranking officers who often have not traveled abroad or even visited the project sites they help plan, the program is anything but a demonstration of efficient administration.[34] Though there are mid-level officials with some expertise and background in the initiation of projects, the rigid administrative system and the unpredictable political climate tend to make subordinates timid in the face of the virtual parade of political superiors that the department has seen.[35]

At one point Islamabad was to have been the venue for the 1978 Asian Games, but as of 1977, there were no hotels in the city. Many were planned, but even as late as 1987 few had been built.[36] This is characteristic. A project on schedule is virtually nonexistent. Even maintenance of existing infrastructure is a disgrace. For example, the PTDC took over four of the leading hotels in the country at the time of the 1965 war with India because they were owned by an Indian national (Oberoi). In contrast to its Indian counterpart, ITDC, PTDC management allowed the hotels to deteriorate until in the 1980s they are attempting to sell them to the private sector.[37] In one of the few cases where promotional materials attracted international interest, a Japanese tour agency investigated tourism facilities in the highly promoted north, but pronounced them too dirty and inadequate for Japanese tastes.

The lack of continuity of leadership is particularly critical in the PTDC, where a succession of temporary and incompetent heads has averaged an eight-month tenure over the course of the corporation's turbulent history.[38] PTDC has been in turbulence and scandal for much of its existence. Far too much of its limited resources have gone to salaries and the junkets of its leadership. "Leadership" may be too classy a label. At least one major travel operator claimed that the transient managing directors seldom even attended the tourism marketing functions for which they were sent abroad, being too busy shopping and relaxing.[39] One managing director interviewed by this writer during his three months tenure told me his chief accomplishment was that he had managed to see all the tourist sites and sights of Pakistan. Not a bad first step, but now he was leaving. He said three months was too short a time but he was overqualified for PTDC so it had really been a post between real positions.[40]

In the weeks immediately after the 1977 coup, *Viewpoint,* an outspoken publication, now more politically subdued, felt free to discuss the problem frankly.

> The Pakistan Tourism Development Corporation, the dumping ground of unwanted Government officials, and an attractive pasture for all manner of men who know the ropes, has just changed its 9th managing director in 8 years. Mr. Riaz Agha, a veteran of the oil industry has been removed and succeeded by Mr. Saeed Ahmad Qureshi, until recently Chief Secretary to the Sind Government. No official explanation is available at the time of writing, but according to newspaper reports, Mr. Agha has been charged with grave irregularities in management and administration.
>
> What ever the case against Mr. Agha, there is no doubt that the organization is plagued by some grave and chronic disorders. The frequent change of the chief executive is one of the symptoms of its sickness. No government in the past has taken tourism seriously, and while one has heard now and then of reorganization and streamlining, the body has continued to grow flabby and rot. It is now beginning to reek, and must be seriously examined by a committee of independent men who know what it is all about. Tourism is now a specialised business and in all the countries where it has developed, it is handled with professional care. We may have to learn from these examples.[41]

It is ironic that PTDC was set up in the first place to correct problems like the overplanning, under executing, and personnel failures that now plague it.[42] Equally troubled by mismanagement and inexperience is PSL (Pakistan Services Limited), which owns the only chain of five-star hotels in Pakistan.[43]

More recently (1979–1982), the PTDC has suffered from declining and flat rates of foreign arrivals to Pakistan.[44] It has therefore decided, with much prompting from the press, to reorganize its structure to place greater emphasis on domestic tourism.[45] Fortunately, such an emphasis is consistent with President Zia's penchant for declaring national holidays and encourages the preservation and maintenance of Muslim monuments.[46] It is also reasonable in view of the fact that the famed attraction of the Khyber Pass or the gun-making villages, like Darra on the Afghan border, are now off-limits to foreigners.

The government continues to talk of expanding tourism and it was the seventh largest earner of foreign exchange in 1982 despite the low arrival figures.[47] To expand will be difficult, however. Pakistan did not opt for import-substitution as India did when each fashioned its development strategy. Therefore, Pakistan must import far more to sustain and expand its tourist infrastructure even when not building five-star facilities. Although the Pakistan government announces numerous concessions for those interested in developing the nation's tourist infrastructure, it may be too little, too late.[48] The private sector has been badly burned by the erratic government policies toward tourism over the past two decades and by the political instability of Pakistan and neighboring countries. The domestic tourist associations have failed to work collectively and have sabotaged cohesion by each entrepreneur attempting to work out private favors from the government. The international hotels continue to find that struggles with the bureaucracy take years, leaving half-finished capital investments floundering.[49] Moreover, staffing of tourist establishments once completed has been complicated by the heavy exodus of ambitious service personnel to the Middle East. The government badly needs their remittances but their abrupt departures often play havoc with hotel and transport needs.

The tax structure both supports and inhibits tourism: given the scarce supply, profitability of hotels is generally high but the delays in opening are formidable. The political climate is simply too capricious for consistent planning and successful implementation.[50] The new intention of the PTDC to play more of a coordinating role between the central government (called the Centre in Pakistan) and the provinces, and the public and the private sector may mean a new era in tourism development. But cynicism runs deep in the government, the public, the private sector, and the international industry.

In sum, the problems of tourism policy in Pakistan are, in large part, the problems of the society and the political system per se. Tourism policy cannot serve national goals until there is a clearer and firmer consensus on what those goals are. Tourism development is likely to continue to be held back until some form of stable and effective political order is established. As even some Pakistani writers wryly observe, all the tourist potential in the world will not make Pakistan a mecca for tourists unless the government and the culture are supportive. As Niaz Mir argues:

Expert opinion apart, what is the actual prevailing situation in the context of tourism promotion? Singularly dismal, to say the least. Of course we have every right to follow any course we choose to in accordance with our whims or convictions. We are thus most welcome to forego all those pleasant pursuits which in the eyes of the rest of mankind improve the quality of life. In other words if in the absence of any decent cinemas, theatres, opera-houses, museums, libraries etc., we also are hell-bent on leading highly self-denying . . . though certainly not spartan . . . dull and lack-lustre lives, who is there to stop us.

But let's not kid ourselves for a second that others will be flocking to our shores at great expense and even greater discomfort just to share, experience and even enjoy our prohibited and provocation-free way of life. No, like it or not, they will go where there is fun and facilities, be they in Nairobi, Bombay, Colombo or Singapore.

The honest truth, however is that Pakistan with its present totally inadequate facilities and even worse managerial inefficiency, is no tourists' paradise.[51]

If Pakistan has done few things very well in terms of tourism development, it at least has not done much damage. Social costs have been minimal. The tourist who comes to Pakistan comes on Pakistan's terms. Tourists to date have included all socioeconomic classes and all are encouraged. Camping sites are going up at the equally leisurely rate at which five-star accommodations are being completed. Moreover, Pakistan is not overly dependent on any single foreign market. Even neighboring India accounts for less than one-third of arrivals, with England providing 22 percent and the United States about 7 percent.[52]

If tourist arrivals have not kept pace with projections it may be just as well. Rapid tourism influx could threaten the security of cultural treasures and incur severe social and environmental costs. Pakistan today lacks the political and administrative organization to successfully monitor tourism development. The country should move slowly towards development. It does so, but generally for the wrong reasons—the timidity of subordinate bureaucrats, the transience of political leadership, the unwillingness of private industry to cooperate collectively, and the failure of the executive to support his political rhetoric with substantive decisions to buttress the implementation of tourism development.

Much of what has happened or not happened to accelerate Pakistani tourism is not unique to tourism as a policy area, but reflects features of policy implementation in other sectors of the political system. But the impact on tourism has been more telling than within some other policy sectors because of tourism's relative newness and vulnerability. Tourism needed greater attention for it to be a viable ally for Bhutto's modernization objectives. The sector did not get that attention, not because Bhutto backed away from tourism as a policy but because his support was not sustained by substantive actions. He appeared to forget that though tourism had few opponents, it also had few supporters. President Zia attempted to undo Bhutto's secularizing influence and yet maintain and expand tourism development for empathetic Muslims from the Middle East and for domestic tourists. He only managed, however, to deepen the distrust of the domestic travel industry, make future investors more wary, and reinforce the general timidity and apathy of the public tourism bureaucracy. For the time being those tourists who do discover Pakistan will enjoy a more authentic experience than one finds in destinations more experienced with marketing and packaging. There is no staged authenticity there.[53]

As a frequent critic of the tourism excesses of many third world countries, I am rather grieved to see that a country that has avoided most of the pitfalls of luxury tourism and mass charters still has so little to show for its tourism policy in terms of employment, foreign exchange, or even pride. Articles like Niaz Mir's point to the fact that not being a tourist destination can contribute to a sense of relative deprivation. Everywhere in Pakistan one finds a sort of inferiority complex about a country that by so many standards is immensely rich in culture and tradition. Unlike the Chinese, who assumed that the rest of the world would be awed by their country, Pakistan tourism specialists are much more defensive and apologetic—a trait one finds in other sectors as well. It may come from having split from India, that Pakistan must always unhappily compare itself with its giant neighbor. One gets a sense of this attitude in the remarks of tourism advisor Begum Viqar-un-Nisa Noon when she states, "Let us become in spite of our shortcomings, our obvious, natural difficulties of harsh variety of climate and stark contrast between national beauty and desolation, the most friendly, hospitable country in the world in consonance with our culture and the tenets of Islam, the religion we follow."[54]

In the decades ahead Pakistan must resolve its internal conflict as to whether it wants to become an essentially conservative Islamic state or a more pluralistic society. Until 1977, the leadership of Pakistan appeared to be moving toward the latter goal. Under President Zia a completely different and much less liberal political agenda has emerged. His death in 1988 may signal a change in tourism policy but in what direction remains unclear. Tourism, if thoughtfully planned and monitored, can be designed to complement either set of national goals. What it cannot do very well is to continue to market to a clientele with secular, Western values while instituting a series of what to Western eyes appear to be Draconian social standards. Pakistan has always lacked a basic consensus on national values that has prevented political stability. It still does. Pakistani tourism policy is but one of the many casualties of Pakistan's ideo-logical debate.

BANGLADESH

Visit Bangladesh Before the Tourists Come
—Tourist Poster

There is still some time. Bangladesh shares many of the cultural and political problems that have crippled Pakistan's tourism effort. Until 1971 Bangladesh was a part of Pakistan (East Pakistan). All sectors of Bangladesh society were politically and economically neglected by the central government despite the fact that East Pakistan was the more pop-ulous half of the country. Elections in 1970—the first free national elec-tions since independence—were won by the Awami League, based in East Pakistan, but economic power and the military remained based in West Pakistan, which refused to accept the election outcome. East Pakistan threatened secession, and the military began a brutal crackdown. India joined the political struggle on the side of Bangladesh, which won the war in 1971.

The upheaval, poverty, and population density all contributed to Bangladesh's image of being, as Henry Kissinger put it, "the basketcase of the world." Today, in fact, after neighboring Indians, most foreign arrivals and visitors to Bangladesh are people from dozens of aid mis-sions, technical assistance teams, and United Nations personnel.[55] Development specialists have become a growth industry in Bangladesh. The government estimates that in 1983 only 22 percent of its foreign arrivals were tourists. Forty-two percent came on business and the rest in official or advisory capacities.[56]

Bangladesh inherited almost no tourist infrastructure either at the time of the formation of Pakistan or at the time of its establishment as the Republic of Bangladesh. Unlike West Pakistan, the East had no mountain scenery to lure the British to establish hill stations. Bangladesh is mostly delta; although it does have a cooler climate in the Chittagong Hills. Although Pakistan had established some information centers in East Pa-kistan shortly before the civil war, most of the staff was drawn from the West and all the power rested at the center. East Pakistan tourist centers were treated as "merely post offices," without much public information or a promotional budget.[57]

Since the establishment of Bangladesh, tourism growth has continued to be stunted. The travel magazines see it as a chicken and egg dilemma. "No one will promote it (tourism) until it is there; and it will not be there until it is promoted."[58] Since the national tourist organization, the Bangladesh Parjatan Corporation (BPC), was formed in 1973 only 5 percent of its tiny budget has been spent on marketing. More pressing needs have been establishing local offices and refurbishing the existing infrastructure. Promotion has been left to Bangladesh Biman, the national carrier.

Biman is notoriously inefficient, frequently overbooked, and running (not necessarily flying) at a staggering loss. The carrier did not start off under auspicious conditions. It, too, was a product of civil war. Biman began in 1972—without any aircraft—but with 2,500 employees. The former Pakistan International Airlines (PIA) employees were there but the planes that had survived the war were in Pakistan. These handicaps were exacerbated by the government's decision to massively subsidize domestic air travel. Since only 0.01 percent of even the traveling public were domestic air travelers, this was a decision that obviously reflected the interests of a tiny political elite and made no sense in economic development terms.[59]

Because of Biman's financial woes, it has had little incentive or time to promote tourism. It, like Indian Airlines or PIA in Pakistan, finds that business and other domestic travel keep it relatively full. Similarly, travel agents in Bangladesh (many inexperienced and not too scrupulous anyway), who have increased from 15 to over 400, do almost nothing but ticketing, with business, government officials, and international development personnel their chief clients.[60]

The political dimensions of tourism in Bangladesh are based on the country's underdevelopment. For example, most tourists are also development or business personnel temporarily residing in Bangladesh. They desire a level of tourist infrastructure that is extremely expensive for a country like Bangladesh to provide.[61] Since the country must import virtually everything for its luxury hotels, it is a real irony that the capital that could be used for providing desperately needed public housing is used for housing those studying poverty or implementing aid programs. Ross Coggins satirizes the all too common development assistance milieu in this poem:

THE DEVELOPMENT SET

Excuse me, friends, I must catch my jet
I'm off to join the Development Set;
My bags are packed, and I've had all my shots
I have traveller's checks and pills for the trots!

The Development Set is bright and noble,
Our thoughts are deep and our vision global;

Although we move with the better classes,
Our thoughts are always with the masses.

In Sheraton hotels in scattered nations
We damn multi-national corporations;
Injustice seems easy to protest
In such seething hotbeds of social rest.

We discuss malnutrition over steaks
And plan hunger talks during the coffee breaks.
Whether Asian floods or African drought,
We face each issue with an open mouth.

We bring in consultants whose circumlocution
Raises difficulties for every solution—
Thus guaranteeing continued good eating
By showing the need for another meeting.

The language of the Development Set
Stretches the English alphabet;
We use swell words like "epigenetic"
"Micro," "Macro," and "logorithmetic."

It pleasures us to be esoteric—
It's so intellectually atmospheric!
And though establishments may be unmoved,
Our vocabularies are much improved.

When the talk gets deep and you're feeling dumb
You can keep your shame to a minimum:
To show that you, too, are intelligent
Smugly ask, "Is it really development?"

Or say, "That's fine in practice, but don't you see:
It doesn't work out in theory!"
A few may find this incomprehensible,
But most will admire you as deep and sensible.

Development Set homes are extremely chic,
Full of carvings, curios, and draped with batik
Eye-level photographs subtly assure
That your host is at home with the great and the poor.

Enough of these verses—on with the mission!
Our task is as broad as the human condition!
Just pray God the biblical promise is true:
The poor ye shall always have with you.

—Ross Coggins[62]

Even the usually pro-resort, pro-luxury international tourist industry
was concerned that the priorities of Bangladesh's tourism program were

unrealistically skewed to an affluent clientele that was unlikely to become very numerous:

> It would be a pity if Bangladesh were over-influenced by advisors who believe only an injection of millions of dollars for white elephant resorts will produce tourism growth at a rate deemed satisfactory. . . .
>
> A U.S.$8 million mini-village for Kaptai Lake is impractical; the money would be better spent on upgrading the existing facilities. . . . Adding speedboats is foolhardy; few will go to Bangladesh to ride in speedboats and anyway, they will be unrealistically costly to maintain. . . . Bangladesh is also very proud of its Cox's Bazaar (beach resort). But this pride has manifested itself into a decision to expand the resort; its beauty lies in its present serenity and solitude. . . . The travel industry does not need another Pattaya.[63]

One segment of the tourist market that does not require much in the way of infrastructure is the American and Canadian backpackers—a group government officials feel ambivalent about. Although they need tourist arrivals, they fear Bangladesh will be labeled a hippy country. Sometimes, however, hippy tourism introduces and promotes a destination, as with Goa in India and Kuta Beach in Bali.[64] Although some countries like Singapore have viewed young, casual travelers like the plague, net economic gains are often higher from tourism pegged at these groups with their longer stays and simpler lifestyles than those requiring capital intensive facilities. This writer would argue that the social and political costs, although harder to measure, are likely to be less in terms of relative deprivation, conspicuous consumption, political payoffs, kickbacks, and political grandstanding. Consider Asiad '82 in India or the International Monetary Fund–World Bank Conference in Manila in 1976.

There is little information available on domestic tourism and no indication that the government has encouraged it; but the religious impetus for pilgrimage should be a natural one to develop, because Bangladesh, like India and Pakistan, has numerous Buddhist, Islamic, and even Hindu shrines, mosques, and temples. Religious and ethnic bases of tourism are not the only potential drawing cards. Tourism, theoretically, could some day be a way of ameliorating the communal tensions that threaten the country's cohesiveness. Hill tribes have felt particularly left out of the political and economic planning for development. There are also fine examples of colonial architecture, plus some unusually long and magnificent beaches. Infrastructure improvements at these sites are on the drawing board and some are in progress.[65]

What appears to be happening in Bangladesh is that the development programs for tourism bear little or no relationship to either the international or domestic tourist market and show no signs of being integrated into the country's overall development strategy. There are reasons for this and they are political, not economic.

First of all, Bangladesh is almost totally dependent on outside advisors and aid. When it comes to a relative afterthought like tourism policy, their tastes—not market information—have prevailed. Tourism policy is shaped to the pattern that a narrow international and domestic elite prefer. Thus, the mini-village and its speedboats and attendant foreign exchange leakage are not designed to lure people to Bangladesh but are for the entertainment of an affluent strata that for one reason or another perceive themselves as being stuck in Bangladesh. Depending on the concessions the government may provide contractors and others, there could be domestic economic and political benefits or cronyism involved.[66] It would not be unique to the tourism sector if such proved to be the case. There is already considerable evidence of overstaffing in the BPC. With 1,000 employees the ratio of permanent employees to annual tourists is running at 1:53, probably the highest in the world![67]

Public administration in Bangladesh works no better and in many cases a lot worse than it does in Pakistan. Aid programs, part of the problem, are also trying to be part of the solution. If tourism is not closely integrated with national development, it is not too much of an overstatement to say that is true of most sectors. Some countries and relief organizations, operating on several different fiscal timetables, are attempting to achieve their separate goals and implement their projects. In the process, national planning in Bangladesh becomes rather an exercise in creative writing. One needs a plan to appeal for aid, but because the aid component is so large and unpredictable, the formal plan is continually amended.[68]

In addition to its chaotic beginnings in civil strife, its economic woes, administrative deficiencies, and enormous social problems, the country has suffered from chronic and bloody political instability. Martial law and political assassinations have made capital investment in Bangladesh unlikely. Even multinationals like Intercontinental have withdrawn their management contracts in some instances. The political instability has dramatically affected tourist arrivals. Despite the overwhelming odds, some tourism infrastructure has been built, a Tourism Training Institute is in place, and tourism has found a niche—albeit marginal—in the two five-year plans the country has had. A tourism master plan was also developed, though critics contend it was, like the budget, rather a paper exercise because "no feasibility study was carried out and source of finance was found."[69] Presumably, however, some priorities were identified.

A more important question than whether tourism is doing well— which it is not but it yet might—is whether it is at all relevant or appropriate for tourism to be utilizing development resources. The airline cannot cope yet; tourism has been capital intensive thus far; even the international travel industry says its priorities are bizarre. And of the 16 BPC projects underway in 1983, only four—all Duty Free Shops—were earning profits.[70] This suggests that Bangladesh is a classic case of putting the cart before the horse or the hotel before the house. The most reasonable "tourism" policy is minimalist. Build small comfortable guest houses, if one must, for aid personnel, for example, like the one that U.N. personnel have been staying in at Cox's Bazaar. Put up a hotel for business types in the capital. Keep the Duty Free Shops since they earn foreign exchange painlessly and without being obvious to the poor. Then operate a holding action for security around archaeological sites, and coordinate environmental protection of beaches and lakes for domestic public health and future tourism. Protect, preserve, and get on with basic needs development.

But it will not happen—for political reasons. It is ironic that one of the only countries without tourists is Saudi Arabia: it does not need the marginal international prestige tourism could mean. Nothing is too marginal for Bangladesh. The incredible public employment in the BPC—with more people employed than in the U.S. Travel and Tourism Administration or in three-fifths of the American state tourism programs put together—is further indication that tourism development will continue.[71] Patronage and underemployment plus elite perceptions of how to acquire international prestige are powerful political rationales that defy econometric analyses.

7

Sri Lanka and the Maldives: Islands in Transition

THE SMALLER countries in South Asia can be divided neatly into two categories: one made up of islands in the Indian Ocean (Sri Lanka and the Maldives) and one including landlocked and mountainous countries (Nepal and Bhutan). Yet as with India, Pakistan, and Bangladesh, commonalities of geography, culture, and in some cases colonial rule, have not obscured significant differences in timing, style, and administration of development. In the next two chapters the variations in political, environmental, and policy features of these four tourism programs will be examined.

SRI LANKA

Sri Lanka is often referred to as the "Resplendent Isle" and that it is in terms of culture, scenic beauty, and climate, though its chronic political violence and ethnic tensions have exposed a darker side to this "tourist paradise." The country known to the Arabs as Serendib, from which our word *serendipity* comes, was well labeled by them, for it is a country of contrasts, of sudden discoveries and pleasures but one that continually surprises not only visitors, but also its own planners and politicians.

With a population of over 15 million, Sri Lanka is dwarfed by her massive neighbors, but is still larger than over half the world's nations. Sri Lanka was called Ceylon by the British, who ruled it as a crown colony for about 150 years. It became a fully independent dominion within the British Commonwealth in 1948. With the ratification of a new constitution in 1972, it became a republic and adopted its present name. As in India, the experience of colonial rule provided Sri Lanka with a good infrastructural base of railroads, guest houses, and administrative experience upon which to build its tourism program.

156

Background and Organization of Sri Lankan Tourism

From 1948 to 1966, international tourism was quite small and what promotion was done at all was done by the central government's Tourist Bureau, "an obscure government department under the Ministry of Commerce."[1] A hotel school was inaugurated in the early 1960s and tourists could stay in the training hotel, which was one of the few hotels in Colombo at that time.

In 1966 Sri Lanka's real policy-making interest in tourism began. An Act of Parliament established a Ceylon Tourist Board as the chief policy-making body for tourism. It had statutory authority with legal powers, a large degree of financial independence and jurisdiction over tourism matters throughout the island. Even today it is the promotion, development, control, and regulatory authority for all aspects of tourism. Established almost at the same time was a Hotel Corporation, which like India's ITDC, and to a lesser extent Pakistan's PTDC and Bangladesh's BPC, operates and regulates hotels.[2]

Sri Lankan development allows for public and private sector involvement in the entire gamut of tourist services. At the same time the government committed itself to developing the supplemental infrastructure of power, water, roads, and airport facilities in a Ten Year Tourism Development Plan.[3] The Ten Year Plan was drawn up by a United States firm and feasibility studies were financed by the U.S. Agency for International Development (USAID). The entire plan was adopted by the government without discussion.[4]

The government also introduced fiscal incentives to get local capital involved. It encouraged the arts and the use of indigenous materials in the construction and decoration of tourist facilities. It restructured its national carrier, opened the country to international charters (primarily from Europe), introduced five-star accommodations and convention facilities and even began some research and monitoring of tourism. In short, Sri Lanka's development of tourism has been a model how-to-do-it case study.[5]

The Tourism Record

The record of what happened to tourism between 1970 and 1980 is impressive. Tourist arrivals increased at 21 percent annually throughout the decade.[6] A Six Year Tourism Plan (1978–1984) was adopted to sustain the momentum though the government had hoped that tourism growth would increase at about 17 percent growth—a figure that could be more easily absorbed.[7] The industry's reaction was predictable.

The government's approach to tourism has been cautious. The last thing wanted is monolithic beach resorts or rows of shops selling cheap thrills.

. . . Already the country voices that somewhat jaded talk about quality visitors . . . as opposed to quantity. Such talk is premature . . . until the country is able to diversify its source of visitors away from Europe, it shouldn't be so choosy about who should come.[8]

Seven years later, travel industry magazines would complain, however, that spoiled, prostitute-filled resorts like the once simple fishing town of Hikkaduwa "lacked style."[9]

Gross earnings from tourists, the other easily quantifiable measure of tourism success, are also impressive. In 1967, 19,000 tourists visited Sri Lanka and spent US$1.3 million. In 1982, tourist arrivals were 407,230 and tourism had become the fifth largest source of foreign exchange with receipts of US$146.6 million.[10] With a length of stay of nine to ten days, the tourist in Sri Lanka stays nearly twice as long as the average, minimizing entry and exit costs per visitor.

What a success story—but is it? By conventional measures, tourism has been a tremendous development success, but those measures only calculate the most superficial data and that only for the industry itself. True cost-benefit analysis must measure net costs and benefits against alternative uses of those development funds. This research only suggests a more complex assessment of Sri Lankan tourism. Such studies have not been done.

Clearly, the government has shown unusual sensitivity to tourism development. Like India, Sri Lanka attempted to regulate tourism in order to reap its benefits without incurring its ills. Building restrictions have been imposed, "so as to prevent the proliferation of box-like monoliths on the beach as in some other Asia/Pacific destinations," and the government has "stood firmly against the development of any of the easy money-spinners of tourism such as gambling, sleazy night-clubs, etc."[11] The country attempted to reduce the leakage of foreign exchange by utilizing indigenous materials in construction and furnishings. "Even in the big hotels sometimes as much as 85 percent of the materials used are locally produced. Only electrical equipment, central air-conditioning units and sophisticated kitchen and 'lift' equipment are allowed to be imported."[12] Nonetheless, this policy has not been without implementation difficulties. Until July 1977, liberal import concessions were given to hotel builders and operators, with the consequence that at least one higher-class hotel imported even its doors, door-frames, and pillows.[13]

Social Impact of Tourism

Let us first consider the multiplier effect, which is usually cited as a positive example of how a tourist dollar is respent over and over in the local economy. But, as one author observed, the multiplier works both ways.

Economic activities generated by the so-called "multiplier effect" are also to be considered as multipliers of a triangle of resources away from the population to the guests. Thus, economic activities associated with the production of food (lobsters and other fish, meat products, vegetable growing), accommodations . . . recreation . . . are to be seen in this light.[14]

As Goonatilake noted, prices for protein soar and shortages are created for the local population—a complaint also voiced in Nepal.

There are other diversion of resources problems. The cost of building a room in the Hotel Oberoi is Rs. 300,000—equivalent to the cost of 100 worker cottages. To the extent that the government subsidizes loans or provides tax breaks for hotels it cannot provide the capital for general housing. "By diverting the resources that Sri Lanka already has and which could provide the essentials for its people, provisions of these facilities is being postponed."[15] There is also a diversion of water resources. Tourists use ten times as much water as residents and pools for visitors remain open even in times of scarcity.

In fact, one of the real ironies seen by Sri Lanka's critics is that tourism is much like the colonial plantation economy that Sri Lanka took pains to dismantle. Both required a special infrastructure for a non-Sri Lankan elite. With both, police and security forces kept locals away from places of privilege. The tea plantations were enclaves nationalized as a result of independence, but now new tourist enclaves are being created. There is one difference, however. The tea plantations used to be justified as deserving of special treatment because those on them produced, and their work was highly important to the economy. The tourist's role as tourist is not a productive role model.[16]

Although the argument is frequently made that tourism is an important export because tourism earns foreign exchange, it is politically worth noting that many do not perceive it that way.

> But the tourist industry is not like other economic activities in agriculture or industry which produces goods for export, such as tea. . . . Rather it entails the production of food, shelter, and recreation for the visitors. In short, the tourism industry is providing for visitors those items of consumption which are needed in this country and which in fact are the end products of its development efforts.
>
> Tourism can be justified only if this diversion is small in proportion to the requirements of the country and if the foreign exchange components provide sufficient inputs to compensate for this diversion of resources.[17]

Tourism is not justified by such criteria, critics feel, although by now the major infrastructure costs are in place.

As early as 1975 it was apparent that as a strategy for accelerating employment, tourism was costly. Rs. 36,231 were calculated as the cost of creating each tourism job, making tourism jobs comparable to the most capital-intensive employment in the country.[18] The demand for middle-class English speakers in traditional low status jobs means that most are educated beyond what the job entails. Although the relatively high salaries undermine the old class hierarchy, the glamour of the job quickly ends and a sense of relative deprivation develops from being surrounded by the conspicuous consumption of leisured foreigners. Moreover, the employees, while developing over time a certain contempt for the foreigners, nevertheless tend to give better service and deference to foreigners than to the local clientele.

The government has made several other decisions that have affected tourism development. The Ceylon Tourist Board, following the advice of the westernized international tourist industry, switched its early emphasis on the magnificent Buddhist sites and mountain tea estates to an emphasis on Sri Lanka's lovely beaches. The latter were expected (and this was confirmed) to be a real drawing card for tourists from Northern Europe. First hippies and then charter tourists have flocked to Sri Lanka as a result of beach development. Each group has brought social problems. Sri Lankans are extremely offended by nude bathing and the casual dress and perceived promiscuity of the tourists. The rapid influx coming as it does into what were once sleepy fishing villages further disorients the society.[19]

Although the hippies have been a well-publicized problem in Sri Lanka as well as in India and Nepal, other problems are to be encountered with the higher-income traveler. It is the higher-income tourist who attracts prostitution and who, "with his camera, cassette recorder and binoculars and a preference for luxury living, creates a preference for foreign goods, which are not accessible to the majority of poor people."[20] Although Sri Lanka has not done so yet, it appears quite possible that it may move in the direction of enclave tourism. Over 93 percent of the tourists arriving in 1977 indicated sun, sand, and sea as their primary motivation and the government has since attempted to develop beachfront areas on the more sparsely populated eastern coast of the island.

Other problems are emerging from the juxtaposition of villagers and tourists, including a disruption in norms of behavior and family control. Children start skipping school to beg on the beach, and may in the process earn more than their parents do at fishing or in other jobs. This makes it difficult for parents to persuade children to stay in school or to accept parental authority.[21] Daughters and, increasingly, sons are being drawn into prostitution as tourists in anonymous settings and local inhabitants tempted by the sight of unusual wealth and promise of a tiny share each shed restraints that might have controlled them under other circumstances.[22] Not all encounters are negative. Some achieve an independence and security that they have never known before, from selling handicrafts, renting out rooms, or cooking for tourists; but this is most apt to be true in areas where tourism is small-scale and the clientele middle income.[23]

Actually, the more modest hotels have also enjoyed commercial success. Non-air-conditioned, but designed to catch the breeze, "they allow the visitor to feel close, rather than separated from the natural environment."[24] They also allow Sri Lanka not to become separated from the tourist dollars, which so often happens in the larger, more capital-intensive establishments. The only independent study of tourism done of Sri Lankan tourism before 1978 was that of West German D. Radke. He determined that even as early as 1972, only 46 percent of the money spent by tourists in Sri Lanka remained there.[25] Given the greater emphasis on attracting more and more affluent travelers and the infrastructure being designed for them, it is doubtful whether Sri Lanka's share has remained even this high.

In 1983, the Sri Lankan government—to the chagrin of the tourist industry—dropped its tax-benefit incentives for hotels. Previously, developers were given 5 to 10 years of tax-free profits from hotel operations, and those whose building plans had already been approved continue to have the concession.[26] That means that since most large hotels were built in the late 1970s and early 1980s most will not be paying taxes until 1990! One major impetus for hotel building had been the 1984 PATA conference, which would have been a major marketing opportunity for Sri Lanka. As it turned out, delegates were more concerned about the law and order situation in the face of communal violence than in the hotel accoutrements.

The Impact of Political Turmoil on Tourism

Sri Lanka has discovered painfully what Lebanon, Northern Ireland, Jamaica, and the Philippines also learned, that no matter what has been done right in tourism, it all amounts to very little if the country's image of vacation bliss is defaced by headlines or evening news footage showing political violence even if no tourists are involved. Unfortunately, in recent years as tourism has become controversial, tourists have been the targets of violence, for instance in Hawaii and the Philippines.[27]

The accommodations buildup, which had occasioned fears of overcapacity before, looks even more desperate as strife continues between the nation's Sinhalese majority and its Tamil minority. Reporting on the impact of the violence, *International Tourism Quarterly* observed that 75 percent of all tours were cancelled in July and August 1983. All charters

were suspended and the average occupancy rate in the hotels plummeted
to 15 percent.[28]

> The tourist industry, which was facing difficulties even before July mainly
> because of the recession in the west and competition from the tourist desti-
> nations in the Asian region, suffered a major setback on account of that
> month's events. Although tourist arrivals steadily increased after August,
> the November arrivals were still only 61 % of the total for the same period in
> 1982.[29]

Although few tourists have been hurt by the current violence, there is
some ethnic conflict associated with the tourist industry.[30] The northern
part of Sri Lanka, which is Tamil-dominated, has received very little promotion. *The Far Eastern Economic Review* saw that as healthy. "Sri
Lanka's explosive and potentially ruinous tourist invasion has not
reached Jaffna."[31] Whether one considers Jaffna spared or neglected,
there has been friction when Tamil entrepreneurs have been unable to get
power or water for guests because of Sinhalese jealousy.

The government has launched costly multi-million dollar campaigns
since 1983 to counter all the negative publicity. Its slogan, however, has
been in the flavor of the classic double speak of Orwell's *1984*, "Sri
Lanka, The Land of Smiling People." Violence has greatly accelerated,
however, and tourism has been a major casualty. The toll on the industry
has not been tallied, but just eight days of ethnic violence in July 1983
were computed to have cost the industry US$7 million a month from
August to November. Twenty thousand of the 100,000 employed in the
tourist industry lost their jobs, together with 30,000 out of 150,000
employed in the supporting service and supply sectors.[32]

Could Sri Lanka have foreseen such violence or the social problems of
Hikkaduwa? Did it have an alternative use for development funds that
could have done as well? Hindsight often is unrealistic. Sri Lanka was,
after all, more cautious than the travel industry advised, though in most
respects it followed the industry's assumptions about tourism development. And it did succeed in developing tourism.

But given the other more complex political problems the country
faces, it has not, thus far, succeeded in protecting tourism against the
negative publicity the riots have generated. Law and order is a highly
salient issue to tourists. Although tourism can be used successfully to jus-
tify repression in authoritarian societies, it is futile to try to persuade
tourists to come to places where security is an issue. They have too many
other competitive destinations from which to choose—a factor that also
keeps countries from challenging travel industry dictates.

Sri Lanka is deeply committed to tourism, but tourism may or may not deliver for Sri Lanka. The odds are against it. First of all, for the foreseeable future the threat of ethnic violence is likely to dissuade tourists and those with tourism capital from investing in Sri Lanka. Second, Sri Lanka's foreign exchange return, now low, will go lower. Charters from Europe, on which Sri Lanka is very dependent, increasingly demand greater concessions because of the political problems. And because of the problems they will probably get their bargains. Although Sri Lanka is not as vulnerable to tour operators as small South Pacific destinations like Fiji, which may suffer for years because of its ethnic strife, the case of Tunisia is instructive. Neckerman, one of Europe's largest tour operators and one of Sri Lanka's major tourist suppliers, wanted to raise its profit margin in Tunisia. Tunisia objected, and Neckerman, which had brought 60,000 tourists in 1972, responded by booking only 12,000 in 1973.[33]

Sri Lanka may yet recapture its lure for tourists and its reputation as "Pearl of the Orient," but it has discovered that tourism's image of glamour and easy money understates its unreliability and fickleness, its expensive promotion, and its foreign exchange leakage. To its credit, the Sri Lankan government has tried mightily to reconcile the interests of developers and the Sri Lankan people. They have put out tasteful brochures advising tourists on customs and appropriate dress.[34] They have monitored the social impact of tourism. They have encouraged experiments in alternative tourism, and they have attempted to reduce environmental damage from tourism. But the best land is still going for tourism. The promotional advertising still plays on almost colonial fantasies of ease and service supplying every whim, and women are still displayed as ornaments in the advertising.

Although on balance, Sri Lanka represents one of the clearest examples of using government policy to develop tourism skillfully, it also illustrates the hazards that remain. Assuming all goes well with the industry, the market, and the domestic and international scene—major assumptions every one—there still remains the question of whether tourism is an appropriate sector on which to base national development.

THE MALDIVES

The Maldives has the distinction of being by far the tiniest country in South Asia and one of the smallest in the United Nations. Until the 1970s it was also one of the most isolated. With a population of only about 150,000 on a string of islands off the southwest coasts of India and Sri Lanka, the Maldives subsisted for years on fishing. In fact, until the mid-1960s the Maldives continued to pay tribute to Sri Lanka with baskets of fish! Until the 1970s few travelers were even aware of the tiny nation, though the Maldivian word "atoll" had become basic to any discussions of Pacific islands.

The tourism program was initiated in 1972, but until the 1980s it was handicapped by being dependent for air services on Sri Lanka, a nation with its own tourism agenda. Their conflicting interests over tourism have caused some friction between the countries. In 1977, with the Maldives holding 20,000 advance bookings and another 10,000 expected, Sri Lanka held up landing rights until after the peak season, thereby crippling the smaller neighbor's program. To establish greater autonomy, the Republic of Maldives built an airport at Gan. Even with poor air services before, the Maldives earned over US$2 million in receipts from tourism in 1977.[35] By 1986, tourism had become the largest earner of foreign exchange, thanks to over 100,000 arrivals bringing $5.8 million to the tiny country.[36]

As an Islamic nation with almost no tourism potential other than recreation, the Maldives was faced with a potential culture clash between the conservative dictates of Islam and the hedonism of sun, sea, sand, and sex tourism.

The Maldives government has sought to contain "tourist pollution," which it fears will contaminate its Islamic culture. It has targeted its promotions and facilities toward sports fishermen, snorkelers, and scuba divers. Sunken ships in the waters around the archipelago add to the interest in underwater exploration.[37] Not only has the clientele been preselected, but the pattern of development has kept cultural clash to a minimum.

The country has an abundance of tiny islands (1,187) most of which are uninhabited. In fact, the Maldives has not even bothered to build jails. Most offenders are put under house arrest and more serious crimes are punished by banishment to a remote atoll.[38] The government owns all land in the Maldives, so it was a simple legal matter to lease an island to each resort developer. By 1984, over 40 resorts had opened in the Maldives, most with islands to themselves. This is not as extravagant as it sounds since the largest island is 4.5 miles long and most are less than six feet above sea level.[39]

By setting aside previously uninhabited islands for resort island tourism there has been no displacement of local population and in fact very little contact at all. Tourism employs only about 5 percent of the total work force, but it has had an impact on the larger fishing and shipping sectors by luring away some workers to the better-paying tourist jobs.[40] Nearly all of the 22,155 tourism employees are local male Maldivians. Maldivians not employed by the resort are not encouraged to visit and few of the chiefly European clientele visit the tiny (population 35,000) capital of Male. Although the government generally adheres to Islamic injunctions against alcohol, pork, and graven images, such restrictions do not apply on the resort islands. So far, there has not been a problem of conspicuous consumption seducing poor Maldivian males. In fact, despite fairly good wages, the resorts are finding it hard to retain their staffs because of their loneliness for families on other islands.

Though the government has taken an active interest in tourism development, most tourist facilities are owned by Maldivians, a factor that minimizes foreign intervention. Moreover, they are locally designed and built. Still, the resorts are dependent on foreign management and the import bill for the resorts is quite high. In addition, the government has become more receptive to foreign investment and has angered local developers by offering some concessions to outsiders, like the Taj Group from India, that it has not given local capital. Also, resorts have become more lavish in recent years, requiring more costly imports.[41] These are worrisome trends that can only compromise tourism's ability to provide stable resources for national development.

Because of its isolation, the Maldives remains quite vulnerable to the strength of the world economy. In the early years of tourism development the oil crisis and the difficult transportation links nearly killed the industry. In 1986 an explosion in Colombo and a fine summer in Europe caused a drop in arrivals. The Maldives is also very dependent on West Germany and Italy (see Table 7.1). Tourism, although lucrative by Maldivian standards, is therefore still rather chancy. There is no domestic base or alternative use for the widely scattered resorts should tourism decline.

Because the culture dictated a "quarantine" of the tourist and also because the tourist relished the isolation and serenity of the resort island, none of the infrastructure developed for the tourist has meant any benefit to most Maldivians. "Each resort is a self-contained island unit with its own boats, generator, restaurant and bar, staff living quarters, sports facilities, sewage and refuse disposal systems, etc."[42] It is as if the whole nation were composed of Club Meds!

The Maldives government understands its predicament, however, and is actively attempting to diversify its economy to avoid being permanently dependent on a sector like tourism, which it knows from its neighbors has significant downside risks.[43] It has also set a maximum goal of 160,000 tourists, has restricted development on several main atolls, has prohibited spear fishing, and is now trying to cope with the litter created by modern tourism. In short, on many tourism development fronts the mini-country appears to be developing its tourism industry with care and concern. It is hoped that it can avoid losing control of this volatile industry by allowing foreign investment concessions and luxury imports to erode its base for building a sound tourism industry.[44]

Table 7.1. Arrivals to the Maldives from the top ten source countries, by nationality, 1980–1986.

Market	1980	1981	1982	1983	1984	1985	1986	% change 1985–1986
West Germany	11,085	15,352	19,226	21,307	22,101	29,101	30,820	5.9
Italy	7,359	9,963	12,863	14,181	17,026	17,525	19,049	8.7
Japan	595	1,165	1,380	1,844	7,264	14,117	9,422	-33.3
France	4,776	6,126	6,839	4,935	6,476	7,826	7,327	-6.4
Switzerland	2,332	3,690	4,512	4,412	4,990	6,337	6,793	7.2
Australia	261	413	638	1,022	2,937	5,833	—	—
UK	1,217	2,323	3,117	2,934	3,732	4,840	—	—
Austria	1,397	1,811	2,138	2,265	2,884	4,634	—	—
Sweden	2,323	2,314	1,566	1,214	1,564	3,029	—	—
Netherlands	160	476	509	704	1,530	1,859	—	—
Other	10,502	16,725	21,623	19,345	13,278	19,453	34,589	—
Total	42,077	60,358	74,411	74,163	83,814	114,554	108,000[a]	-5.3

a. Estimate.

Still, outside of a bit of friction with Sri Lanka over air transport, the Maldives is blessed with a heritage of independence for most of its existence, a homogeneous population, and no external enemies—rather an idyllic situation by South Asian standards. It remains to be seen whether tourism can appreciably ease the poverty of the island, but the country has approached tourism development with considerable intelligence.

8

Nepal and Bhutan:
Two Approaches to Shangri-La

THE HIMALAYAN kingdoms of Nepal and Bhutan are distinguished by their spectacular mountain scenery, their ancient religious culture, and their monarchies, but their approach toward outside visitors has differed markedly in recent years.

NEPAL

The wildest dreams of Kew are the facts of Kathmandu.
—Rudyard Kipling

Nepal remained quite isolated until the 1950s when a motorable road was constructed from the Indian border to the capital city of Kathmandu. Bhutan has still more recently emerged from isolation. Prime Minister Nehru of India rode donkey-back into Thimphu, the capital, in 1958. Today there is a motorable road into the capital and even regular flights.

Nepal was sealed off from all but a few by a succession of hereditary *Ranas* (Prime Ministers) who kept the country off limits to overseas visitors for over a century. Although never deposing the monarchy, like the shoguns of Japan, the *Ranas* usurped de facto power. The Chinese invasion of Tibet signaled a change from business as usual in Nepal. The Nepali-Tibetan border was sealed and the remnants of an ancient and lucrative trade between the two countries ended. New sources of income were needed, particularly as thousands of Tibetans fled Tibet and became refugees in Nepal. In 1951, the *Ranas* were overthrown and the monarchy took de facto as well as de jure control.[1] In 1952 the nation tentatively opened its borders. At the time of the 1956 coronation of King Mahendra cars for the event were carried in over the mountains on cables to Kathmandu. Following the development of the airport in 1954, Thomas Cook organized the first tour in 1955.[2] As late as 1965, how-

168

ever, there were only 125 miles of paved road in the entire country, and 90 percent of the pavement was the road between Raxaul on the Indian border and Kathmandu.[3]

Initial tourist traffic was primarily composed of mountaineers attracted to the unmatchable climbing opportunities and later low-budget youth who were looking for a different kind of high from cheap drugs and an inexpensive life-style. Although Nepal's clientele has diversified greatly since the mid-1960s, when the only hotel of any star was the old Royal, Nepal continues to be heavily dependent on tourist conditions in India and the rest of South Asia. In most cases Nepal is part of a much larger regional or international tour rather than *the* destination. Sixty-two percent of international tourists stay fewer than seven days.[4] Although Nepal has good relationships with all its neighbors, its heavy dependence on air connections means that it tends to be affected by the pronounced seasonality of tourist arrivals in adjacent countries like Pakistan, India, and Bangladesh. Although the annual monsoons do curb trekking, for many international visitors Nepal could be a year-round destination. The government is currently attempting to make that point with travel operators.[5]

The only country with which there is much land traffic is India. Indians also constitute Nepal's largest tourist clientele, but usually Indians are not figured into the international tourist figures, because Indian tourists are generally not a source of foreign exchange. The Indian rupee is accepted as local currency in much of Nepal. Political conditions in all surrounding countries affect landlocked Nepal, but so far tourist arrivals have kept pace or exceeded tourist infrastructure so that Nepal has not been much affected by erratic conditions elsewhere.

Today, tourism is Nepal's largest source of foreign exchange, bringing in over 50 million dollars to the struggling economy in 1983.[6] But that often seems to give little satisfaction to either the travel industry or the government for neither has found that Nepali tourism has met their objectives.

The industry, which has a vested interest in expansion and, unfortunately to a certain extent, overcapacity, has found Nepal's tourism development too episodic and its infrastructure too limited, incentives too irregular, and government concerns about the industry too petty. For example, the industry is frustrated that the country has not implemented a ten year tourism master plan developed by German advisors in 1968.[7]

What it does not recognize is the fact that Nepal is beseiged with master plans that do not bear any relationship to revenue. Nepal is like Bangladesh in the sense of being heavily dependent on foreign aid. As a consequence, its plans are designed to apply for aid, not to spend it. Budgeting in Nepal is not an activity that occurs once a decade, once every five years, or once a year. It is continuous, unpredictable, and as a matter of survival is highly conservative and contingent in nature.[8]

The tourist industry's complaint is that Royal Nepal Airlines Corporation (RNAC) is often short of planes, though it is acknowledged that landing strips and airport facilities in general have been significantly improved in the last ten years. The Asian Development Bank (ADB) has extended several loans for such development because air travel is of central importance in a country like Nepal. Not only do 85 percent of all tourists come by air, but the economy as well as health of the country as a whole depends on air connections to remote areas.

Particularly annoying to the travel industry is the fact that it is so dependent on an airline that clearly has tourism as only one of its priorities. As its name implies, the RNAC is available to the ruling family, which has on occasion disrupted schedules by using previously committed planes. This is obviously an enormous irritant to tour operators who are also faced with problematical flying weather during part of the year. The industry's solution would be to allow charters access to Nepal, but the RNAC is opposed. We have already seen that the injection of charters greatly weakens the leverage a government or a national carrier has over the tourist industry, though it generally assists expansion of tourist arrivals. Charters also reduce net foreign exchange receipts because of the deals struck and increased competition for the national carriers. Although the RNAC's domestic flights are heavily subsidized, much of its profit is generated by its international flights, which might be diminished with charters. The industry is not persuaded. "In monetary terms RNAC only makes 40% (US $11 million) of its revenues in foreign exchange, but it is subsidizing air transportation for locals in the kingdom."[9]

Is the RNAC really doing anything so bizarre? Most developing countries underwrite or defray some of the costs of essential services. Actually, in many cases, it is the local population that should feel aggrieved because tourists are frequently given priority on flights, especially to the more remote areas, and Nepalese citizens are prevented from using the few flights available.[10]

The industry, which is quick to complain about import duties on transport vehicles and the like, is also rather breezy in sweeping away complaints of foreign exchange leakage, which by their own estimates runs between 45 and 75 percent of all foreign exchange earned by tourism. "But as Nepal has few manufactured goods, the anxiety appears to be superficial. The country can earn enough revenue on the labour employed and on retailing in the service industry."[11]

But can it? Does tourism have a comparative advantage over other development options when such costs are computed? The government has not been able to do such calculations with much precision and the industry quite naturally is not eager to develop data that questions tourism's development role. In fact, the industry is annoyed that although there are no foreign exchange limitations for tourism imports, the industry's receipts are credited at a slightly lower rate of exchange than that at which it is permitted to withdraw them.

In general, the government has pursued tourism because it sensed it had few alternatives. For the same reason, the World Bank assisted Nepali tourism until the Bank's general retreat from tourism projects. In 1977 the World Bank financed a major tourism feasibility study; 2,200 pages later it was completed, but by that time the World Bank had decided not to finance any new projects.[12] Government tourism policy has, like its overall planning, been subject to fits and starts, but it has never approached tourism as anything more than a necessary evil.

In contrast to the other South Asian countries we have considered, the Tourist Department of Nepal is not a corporation. It does almost no overseas promotion, instead relying on the RNAC and the private sector for most publicity.[13] Recently, the government has set up a joint venture with the private sector and the Nepal Tourism Promotion Board with a fund of US$500,000. Half of the funds were provided by Royal Nepal Airlines, 25 percent by the Ministry of Tourism, and the rest by various private tourist-related businesses.[14]

The government's objectives in developing tourism are set out in the 1975–1980 Five Year Plan: to earn foreign exchange, increase employment in rural arts and crafts, and to reduce regional income disparities by appropriate siting of tourist facilities and by encouraging regional and intraregional tourism. The development of internal transportation infrastructure, such as the Kathmandu to Pokhara road, should help to achieve these latter objectives.

Cognizant of the fact that low-budget travelers do not bring much foreign exchange into the economy, the government has encouraged affluent visitors by developing such specialty wildlife viewing sites as Tiger Tops, Elephant Camp, and Gaida Wildlife Camp—all within Royal Chetwan National Park. The Dhukikhel Mountain Resort, just one hour from Kathmandu, is ideal for viewing the Himalayas, and is another attempt to capture the tourist currency.[15]

Nepal's most controversial effort, however, is the single government-controlled casino at the Soaltee Oberoi Hotel on the outskirts of Kathmandu. It has become a major attraction, especially for Indian tourists, who are several countries away east or west from any alternative casino.[16] Nepali citizens are not allowed in the casino, because the reason for its existence is to entertain tourists and earn foreign exchange.[17]

Actually, Nepal has a rather good foreign exchange situation and so it is rather ironic that the biggest claimant on it is the tourist industry. In

1979, 30 percent of the foreign exchange spent went to support tourism.[18] By 1983, tourism's demands for imports consumed 70 percent of
the US$50 million earned by tourism.[19] Because of this, the government
is investigating possibilities for import substitution, but the opportunities
to cut down much on imports are not apparent. As former tourism minister Harka Gurung wryly observed, "One can't talk about percentages
unless there are alternatives."[20]

French consultants have been instrumental in Nepal's tourism planning and the French constitute the second largest group of foreign tourists in Nepal. In 1979, the government commissioned a study by PATA to
develop Pokhara and two other valleys as tourist centers. This has
become an important first step toward diffusing tourism from its present
over-concentration in the Kathmandu Valley.

Since the political system is not an open, competitive one, it is difficult
to generalize about the political problems tourism may have created, but
they no doubt encouraged the government's interest in emphasizing
mountain tourism, which would reduce the tourist pressure on the
Kathmandu Valley. But, as we shall see later, mountain tourism has its
own problems. Clues to political problems lie in other facets of the tourism plan adopted or the aid sought.

UNESCO aid is designed to protect and preserve major cultural sites
from automobile pollution, theft, or destruction of national antiquities
by souvenir-hungry tourists. The Pacific Area Travel Association has also
evinced interest in recent years in national historic preservation. In fact,
in 1980 and 1981 the first and second PATA Heritage Awards were given
to Nepali projects. In 1983, the PATA International Tourism and Heritage Conservation Conference was held in Nepal.

PATA's efforts, begun in 1977, were designed to counter charges that
tourism destroys culture. Its first award went to the Dwarika Village
Hotel, a modest complex, but one that has utilized Nepali treasures and
antiquities in its design and decoration. Although one may wonder if it is
really conservation in the purest sense to utilize "16th century screens"
and "14th century inlaid window frames" in a hotel,[21] in the context of
Nepal's stage of development that is probably as close to museum protection as they could have. Unfortunately, doors, windows, and whole walls
were hacked up for foreigners to cart away in the 1960s. Moreover, the
Dwarika Village Hotel has committed 50 percent of its earnings to preservation work.

In 1981, the PATA Heritage Award went to three cities in Nepal for
their restoration. Bhaktapur, a city that is being restored by a joint
Nepali-German project begun in 1974, has completed its first phase of
preservation. The restoration has not only secured and protected the site,

it has also brought more tourists and new sources of employment in the handicrafts bazaar and cafe.[22]

As one whose travels to Nepal were in the mid-1960s and early 1970s, this writer thinks that on balance tourism has unquestionably meant more preservation of artifacts than their destruction. Even the plunder of some homes and temples by Nepalis for carvings to sell to tourists might have as easily come about for use as firewood in some quarters of Nepal.

It is encouraging that the government's desire to preserve its heritage is being supported both financially and in terms of expertise by some international organizations. It is also just, for the international community and particularly the tourists will benefit at least as much as the Nepali citizens whose immediate development priorities are directed more toward mere survival.

Unfortunately, there are points at which Nepali survival and tourist needs are juxtaposed. A still wider range of Nepal is affected by the tourist pressure on food supplies. Consumption by tourists frequently causes shortages of milk and meat for the local population. This situation may worsen in the near future as the government strives to reduce foreign exchange leakage through imports and seeks to introduce the quality controls that may make more Nepali foodstuffs "fit" for international-standard hotels and restaurants. Even among Nepali groups supportive of tourism, problems can occur. Begging, prostitution, black marketeering, and drug dealing have been common spillover effects of concern to the government, religious authorities, and overall population.[23]

Mountain Tourism

Mountaineering may avoid some of the social problems of tourism concentrated in Kathmandu. Trekkers stay longer, live off the local economy, and may help diffuse some of the tourism receipts to the 95 percent of the population that makes a living from agriculture. Mountain tourism may allow local communities with too many people overworking too little tillable land (83 percent of the land is Himalayan or sub-Himalayan) to switch to tourist-related services as guides, porters, and food-stall entrepreneurs. Sherpa guides currently earn two times the national average despite the seasonality of their work. Bridges, roads, sanitation, health and rescue improvements, and electricity have tended to develop more quickly in areas of interest to tourists.

There are costs in mountain tourism, however. First, much of the work is seasonal. Although such tourism supports 40 trekking agencies and employs 350 people full-time, over 7,000 are employed only during trekking season.[24] Second, scarce food supplies in remote areas may be diverted to trekker tourists, resulting in hardship, inflation, and accelerated malnutrition for some. However, many Sherpas have bought yaks—important sources of protein—with their earnings. But the yaks create fodder shortages. Deforestation, pollution, tourist security, and health become major hurdles of mountain tourism.

The government is ill-equipped to deal with problems such as deforestation in the remote areas. Nepal's forests are common property and thus are seen as no one's responsibility.[25] Moreover, since the forest is common land and farmland is private, there are no incentives to reforest areas that are cut over. From 1964 to 1975 over a third of Nepal's forest disappeared. Perhaps two-thirds are gone by now. This is despite the fact that Nepal has one of the world's lowest rates of energy consumption. Yet most of the energy consumed is in the form of wood. As a political problem, it is most difficult to tackle. Government control in forested areas is uneven and irregular at best. Although up to half of all landslides are caused by deforestation, alternative energy sources are difficult to find. The village level is appropriate for doing something about the problem, but the village that deforests is not always the one that bears the price. Nor does the problem remain Nepal's. Floods in India and Bangladesh are sometimes the result of Nepal's inability to manage the forests.[26]

The tourist immensely compounds the deforestation problem. Although only about 16 percent of all Nepal's tourists come for trekking and mountain-climbing, they still constitute over 25,000 a year! Each trekker needs about 234 pounds of firewood for a 15-day trek and support staff about half that much. Currently only 7 percent carry their own fuel—usually oil.[27]

Two other problems upset the ecology. The first is pollution. Because no one wants to carry anything longer than needed, litter is dropped along trails. The increase in litter even on Mt. Everest has been dramatic, with sanitation problems a close second. "The Trashing of Shangri-La," as it has been called, is at last getting attention.[28] Probably the groups most involved in the situation and most prepared to do something about it are not the government but the trekking associations. One encouraging sign of responsibility came in 1984 when a team of Nepalese Sherpa guides, trekking companions, and international supporters developed an expedition designed to take more off the mountains than they brought. More than 1,000 bags of trash were brought off of just the lower elevations of Mt. Everest. Another expedition also took place in 1984, supported by the Earth Preservation Fund. According to the group's organizer, a Sherpa, "It is not very glamorous to come to the world's highest peak to pick up trash. But unless we begin to, we are worried people may not come at all."[29]

A plan to deal with the problem on a permanent basis has not been determined. Mountain explorers like the late Sir Edmund Hillary favored a tax earmarked for mountain cleanup. Such an approach would create jobs for villagers in the process. The Tourism Ministry fears that such a tax might lead to a decline in mountain climbing. In 1982 the government collected nearly US$400,000 from royalties and trekking fees, a small portion of which went to the Nepal Mountaineer Association and the National Parks. All the more reason, say tax advocates, why one should not jeopardize the beauty and loveliness of an area that a $3 head tax might prevent.

Other suggestions such as dispersal of climbers, which is favored by the International Union of Alpinists, might postpone mountain tourism's decline and alleviate the worst deforestation, but they do not get at the crux of the pollution problem.[30] Further, the government is reluctant to disperse tourists both for security reasons and for the safety of villagers and tourists alike. The government is already desperately overextended in its efforts to monitor tourism and is not eager to compound its problems.

One possibility that the government is considering would reduce the exploring experience but stabilize the environment somewhat. That is to require bottled fuels and to develop permanent campsites complete with latrines on some of the most frequently used routes. That this can be done unobtrusively and thereby keep environment and experience intact has been demonstrated in the U.S. National Parks. Should the government decide on such a course the implementation of such a program is still many years off.

Another social problem associated with mountain tourism is less well recognized. This is a phenomenon known as "trekker medicine." In some areas far from government clinics, villagers have come to depend on free medical advice and medicine given by tourists. The problem as two doctors have described it is that, although the tourist is pleased to be helpful and the villager is grateful for medicine, it may be counterproductive in the long run.

> Trekker medicine is often practiced by tourists who have no specialized medical knowledge, but who have come to Nepal equipped with powerful and sometimes dangerous drugs supplied by doctors in their own countries. Amateur treatment for illness is common and can be harmful. . . . Trekkers rarely see the good or bad results of their treatment as they must move on to a new village every day. . . . A Nepali villager loses both if he recovers or gets worse. If he recovers he will turn away from medical services provided by the Government, as he will learn that he does not need to go to a hospital or a health post; tourists will provide. If his illness gets worse he will turn away from Western medicine in any form and he will begin to lose faith in this form of healing.[31]

Though the public has had little or no opportunity to applaud or deplore government action with respect to tourism since Nepal permits no political parties or free press to function, the Nepal government has tried, it would appear, to keep a concept of the public interest in mind as it has developed tourism. That becomes harder and harder to do as programs expand and their social impact is felt belatedly. Also, tourism has a way of frequently being in either a boom or bust mode in developing countries—neither of which is conducive to thoughtful development.

Nepal has tried to anticipate such problems, for example banning further hotel construction in 1979, lifting it in 1981, and again banning construction in 1984.[32] Tourism is a very hard industry to fine tune, however, for infrastructure takes a long time to develop and bribes in the hotel industry are as commonplace as in all other sectors of the economy. Today overcapacity of luxury hotels is coupled with a shortage of power, planes, and petrol. Yet the government has every incentive to develop tourism successfully as the Royal Family is heavily invested in every phase of its operations from tour operators to the casinos.[33]

One worrisome note: Nepal may be heading toward more resort development.[34] That would probably be a mistake. Whereas wildlife viewing and trekking build on what Nepal already has, resorts require what it has not—roads, planes, imported fixtures, and conveniences—and they divert resources from the basic needs of citizens to the recreational comforts of leisure visitors. That is bad economics and in the long run it is bad politics.

BHUTAN

Tourism in Bhutan today is reminiscent in many ways of the pattern in which Nepal tourism began in the late 1950s. Though Bhutan has not encouraged trekking, both countries were extremely impoverished nations who opened to tourism by being very selective and permitting only a few affluent visitors, curious about the exotic and remote culture of their mountainous kingdoms. There, the Bhutanese insist, the similarities end. Bhutan feels that Nepal has sold its soul for tourism, something the Bhutanese argue will not happen in Bhutan. Harka Gurung contends that Bhutan is simply putting the best face it can on its small tourism program, and that Bhutan's tourism is limited less by Bhutan's goals than by the fact that India will not approve any more permits to Bhutan. It may be too soon to characterize Bhutanese tourism development.[35]

Certainly its apparent reasons for allowing tourism are most unusual: its political independence may depend on it. Bhutan's tourism program is the youngest and most limited in South Asia. In fact, Bhutan might have chosen to remain isolated and dependent upon India had not developments occurred in neighboring Sikkim that led to Indian takeover of Sikkim in 1973. Both Sikkim and Bhutan had treaties with India, written in 1949–1950, which recognized a degree of Indian hegemony. However Bhutan has always been the more independent of the two, and in fact secured United Nations membership under Indian sponsorship in 1956.[36]

Sikkim's loss of independent identity in 1973 was followed shortly thereafter by Bhutan's decision to open its doors, however cautiously, to commercial interests and outside visitors. The decision may also reflect the interests of the young, western-educated ruler, Jigme Singye Wangchuk. In any case, the Organization of the National Tourism Promotion and Bhutan Travel Agency were created in 1974 and placed under the direction of a member of the royal family, the ruler's representative in the Ministry of Finance. Although Bhutan maintains only three embassies abroad—in India, Bangladesh, and at the United Nations in New York—the Bhutan Travel Agency has a division, called the Bhutan Travel Service, in New York.[37]

To the degree that other nations and their traveling citizens see Bhutan as a separate political entity, Bhutan's legitimacy as an independent country is enhanced. Tourism then provides a form of political leverage against potential Indian territorial ambitions. Also, the small number of tourists constitute Bhutan's largest and chief source of foreign exchange. Figures differ but tourism contributes from US$630,000 to $1,000,000 annually to the tiny kingdom.[38]

More than any other South Asian country, Bhutan has chosen to cater to a select clientele of higher-income tourists. Aware and critical of Nepalese tourism development, Bhutanese planners built limited, high-quality facilities and restricted tourists to those on expensive group tours. The government allows only about 200 tourists at a time and only three or four towns are open to foreigners. Even then there are some Bhutanese who are raising objections to their presence. In the 1980s, protests were voiced in the National Assembly,[39] which has led to foreigners being banned from most festivals.

Though luxury tourism is often a mistake for developing nations, Bhutan has cast tourism to its specifications rather than the other way around. It has provided comfortable facilities, but not extravagant ones, and by catering to affluent travelers it has assured that tourism pays its way. The clientele is given a sampling of Bhutanese culture but few concessions are made to the visitor's non-Bhutanese interests. Hence, there are handicrafts available but not girls, casinos, nightclubs, or amusement parks. Relatively little employment is generated from the small scale of Bhutanese tourism but a comparatively high return on investment is achieved. If it were larger it would be harder to control. Corruption is a problem in Bhutan and a larger tourism program would probably encourage it as has happened elsewhere. Kept small, tourism has also remained the monopoly of the king's relatives.[40]

A more sizeable tourism program would also be extremely vulnerable to India's reactions. Bhutan still depends on India for tourist access and India has on occasion proved an obstacle to their entry to Bhutan. India has postponed an air route from Calcutta and continues to control exit passes from India to Bhutan.[41] As it is, Bhutan accomplishes most of its political objectives and some economic ones as well from the small program. Moreover, the affluent clientele is probably a more influential one than larger numbers of low-income travelers would be.

Bhutan has gambled that it can use tourism to protect its tenuous independence from India. In doing so it has also gambled that it can protect its cultural integrity from tourists. If it succeeds it may also win the most important jackpot, the retention of its youth, who today show signs of disaffection from the traditional lifestyle of Bhutan. Tourism can be an instrument for both modernization and cultural preservation. In Bhutan the experiment unfolds.

The political dimensions of Bhutanese and the other tourism policies have certainly not been exhausted by the material in this and the preceeding chapters. Subnational politics has been all but ignored; international and regional collaboration and competition have scarcely been mentioned. The role of labor exportation to the Middle East has had a profoundly negative effect on the quality of low and modestly skilled labor in the tourism industry in Pakistan, India, Bangladesh, and Sri Lanka, even as it has boosted or strained the capacity of airline service to the region. Labor remittances have offered an alternative source of foreign exchange to tourism and other exports. This has not been studied here.

Still, the political dimensions have been explored for Nepal and Bhutan and the other nations in South Asia in greater detail than will be possible for other areas and political systems in this volume—and that has been deliberate. From these seven nations with their varied terrain, cultures, and sizes have emerged seven distinctly different combinations of political objectives, needs, and impacts derived from using or attempting to use tourism as a force for national development.

What all of the preceeding chapters illustrate are not only the complex political dimensions important in understanding tourism policy and why it is or is not supporting national objectives. This scrutiny also demonstrates the salience and importance of tourism policy even in an area and among nations not notably significant in terms of global tourism. If tourism has these kinds of repercussions, interests, and political goals, by what rationale can tourism continue to be ignored by social scientists in areas like Europe, Japan, Africa, or the Caribbean, where its political and economic dimensions loom so much larger? The countries treated here were not selected because they represented the countries where political considerations were most salient. Rather, they were selected because they illustrate that even in countries not known for their tourism development, tourism is playing an often enormous political role.

9

Exploring Alternative Strategies for Tourism Development: Is There a Better Way?

As PREVIOUS chapters have illustrated, developing tourism is not nearly as simple or as certain as most policymakers assume when tourism is adopted as a development strategy. Moreover, as case studies demonstrate, political needs often drive economic plans, sometimes with disastrous effects as in the Philippines, in other cases with mixed or even positive effects as in Bhutan.

Furthermore, although tourism can build on natural resources, their presence or even absence does not determine the success of a tourism policy. The mini-state of Singapore and the British crown colony, Hong Kong, reap far more from international tourists than do any of the countries considered in this book. Yet neither has the tourist attractions, historical and religious treasures, scenic diversity, or cultural riches of the nations considered in these case studies. What they do have is superbly convenient locations and political stability.

Far too often tourism policy and infrastructure development proceeds from an inventory of beaches, historical sites, and political intentions to bid for future mega events like the Olympics, Asian Games, or major conferences. If natural tourist attractions were all that mattered, Uganda, South Africa, and Haiti would be top contenders and Singapore would have no visitors at all.

Tourism policy cannot be compartmentalized, adopted, and implemented in a vacuum. It is too critically dependent on the acceptance by the host population, internal political stability, and the fickle tastes of outsiders. Therefore it is imperative that these actual preconditions be thoroughly understood before tourism development proceeds or expands or becomes a commitment to a single development path.

When this is understood several factors become clear. First, the strident critique of multinational firms in the travel industry is misplaced. These firms are not the villains for promoting a type of tourism that provides the criteria by which tourism policies are currently evaluated—numbers of arrivals and amount of revenue achieved. They can deliver high volume and high gross foreign exchange earnings if there is political stability. Until policymakers demand figures on net foreign exchange earnings and alternative possible returns on capital and labor projected for investment in tourism, they will not be provided. Such figures are, after all, difficult to calculate and multinational firms cannot be obliged to collect data contrary to their own interests. Government planners and particularly tourism departments and agencies must be required to move beyond simplistic gross figures.

Second, even in developed countries tourism development has not been understood as the complex social and political phenomenon it truly is. Economic considerations—short-term ones at that—have dominated policy-making. Recently, nations such as New Zealand, the United States, and Canada are becoming more aware of the dangers of that approach.

The situation, however, is much more complex and potentially tragic in developing nations where economic resources and political stability are often in short supply and where almost the entire infrastructure for tourism will be built with foreign goods, controlled by foreigners, and used by foreigners and where all too often profits will not remain in the country.

Third, hosts and guest populations need to not only be considered in the planning for their successful co-existence, they must come to positively value each other if tourism is to be a stable and long-term component of the economy. That will require careful study. Too often only the tourist is considered and then only in terms of comforts most already enjoy in abundance at home. The local population is seen only narrowly as a source of labor supply.

Even without clear villains, there can be victims of tourism development and usually they are the local population tourism was ostensibly designed to help. I say ostensibly because not even an autocrat builds a tourism program on the announced premise of providing an oasis for strangers to enjoy at bargain rates. Unfortunately, that is often all that is created.

A Franco, a Marcos, or a Duvalier may always exploit tourism for their own personal political needs. There is no easy way to control that except with a clear notion of what tourism's dynamics are; then it may be possible to challenge such building sprees and other excesses and to guide development into more economically and socially constructive channels. Ultimately, even their motives and solid development could be made more compatible. The opposition to ill-conceived development plans cannot be expected to come wholly or even primarily from public sector agencies although those in planning offices must themselves understand what constitutes appropriate tourism development.

Interest groups, other political elites, local communities, and, ideally, the leadership must understand that tourism is absurdly easy to sabotage and that it can be vulnerable if development is not handled well. In addition, and especially in the absence of countervailing forces, international aid and loan consortiums also need to monitor tourism development in the countries with which they interact. Yet here again, because tourism is not a basic needs sector, it is little understood even in development circles until it goes awry. This was belatedly acknowledged by the World Bank when it discontinued direct tourism development loans in 1980.

Unfortunately, most how-to-do-it kits for tourism development have come in the form of advice from the World Tourism Organization or large travel industry firms interested in promoting this or that destination. As shown in the case studies of Sri Lanka, Nepal, and the Philippines, their advice is often at its best only concerned with large-scale, mass, or charter tourism and at its worst self-serving and misleading. In any event these organizations are concerned quite naturally with developing tourism and not with using tourism as a vehicle for development. Some may ask, can a policy do both? Theoretically, yes it can.

But in developing nations only a small percentage of the domestic population has discretionary funds for travel, so tourism is almost never a policy area in such countries primarily to provide facilities for local residents. Only under the short-lived Janata government in India was that a primary objective. It can then be justified in poor countries only as it contributes to the general economy. It is on this criterion that tourism is crudely measured and on this basis that so many national policies are found inadequate.

In this chapter, the focus is on tourism options and on an exploration of ways in which alternative visions of tourism are and could be implemented. Because so many forms of tourism currently exist, any call for totally new directions needs to specify what should go and what should remain.

One thing this chapter will not decry is mass travel. Not only is mass travel here to stay but in and of itself it is not the problem. Indeed, it is ironic that many who write disparagingly of tourists are in other spheres quite concerned about the masses. After all, if the masses are worth our concern when they are impoverished, should one begrudge them a chance to travel in one of the least costly modes, the group tour?

I rather identify with Meg Greenfield's essay "In Praise of the Tourist," which champions the tourist as "vulnerable, normal, traditional and undramatic" in a world too often malevolent and hysterical. She even despairs of making them more sensitive to the mores of their destination, which I am not yet prepared to do.

> For even if we succeed in eliminating downright indecency, we will never be able to overcome the truly terrible aggregate appearance of our tourists. But I no longer want to. I have decided I like it better the way it is. . . .
>
> The snobbish assumption is that the tourist presence is a desecration of the sites they have come to inspect, but I have concluded this is an inversion of the truth. The tourists, in their way, humanize the monuments and redeem the history of the place upon which they have descended.[1]

The problem is less who travels; in fact, in many societies tourism would be a better and less destabilizing force if more had access to the discretionary funds necessary for travel. The world needs more, not fewer, tourists. Therefore, this writer is a bit suspicious of those policy-makers who would have tourism confined to small groups of individual tourists of the "upscale" variety. The assumption is that more affluent tourists are better for a destination, because they bring in more cash relative to the intrusiveness of their presence. Hawaii, Bhutan, and the Philippines under Marcos have argued for directing tourism in such channels. As the case studies have illustrated, however, luxury tourism tends to require more imports, to be more capital-intensive, to be more dependent on outside control of capital, to encourage more of a sense of conspicuous consumption, and to result in a greater sense of relative deprivation than more modest facilities. Moreover, the infrastructure for such tourists rarely is used by other than the elite of a given destination be it in the developed world of Hawaii or the developing nation of the Philippines.

So mass tourism in and of itself cannot be the undifferentiated or exclusive target; rather, it is many of the current practices, development, and control surrounding it. Even if one wanted to develop tourism alternatives that were not mass in character, one would still be forfeiting 95 percent of all tourists to the status quo. So although many alternatives may be small in scale, they cannot set the boundaries for tourism policy.

MAJOR CONCERNS OF ALTERNATIVE TOURISM ADVOCATES

It is probably impossible to categorize all the variants of tourism now hovering under the umbrella of "alternative tourism," but it should be possible to explore at least some of the basic concerns that encouraged these alternatives. The issue should be not just alternatives to current large-scale tourism, but appropriate alternatives. That is a more complicated concept, because appropriate alternatives may be culture-specific.

Many programs calling themselves alternative tourism are concerned with scale. The high-rise luxury hotel with its impersonal nature is alien to those who see it as an irritating rather than relaxing venue, launching tourists into tour buses with assembly-line precision. Home-like surroundings, where companionship can thrive are to some the very definition of alternative tourism. Home stays and bed-and-breakfast programs are designed to humanize rather than commoditize the host-guest relationship. They may be less expensive, but even when they are not they are able to meet individual needs and respond to both host and guest preferences. High-rise facilities may be the most practical and appropriate lodgings, however, where space is at a premium, like Singapore or Hong Kong, and where power and water supplies are adequate. On beaches or in the mountains such places may be aesthetically intrusive, economically unwise, and a drain on scarce power and water resources.

Sometimes the issue is cost. Pensions, family-owned small hotels, hostels, churches, university dorms, and campgrounds are also defined by some as alternative tourism. These accommodations and sometimes no-frill transportation are designed to facilitate mass travel, not supplant it. Based on the assumption that people want to see the destination rather than the interior of their hotel room or the movie on the plane, such tourism has thrived in Europe and the United States.

The irony is that in the very developing countries that are building the most lavish hotels far fewer facilities exist for the budget traveler. Such nations have been quick to copy Intercontinentals and Hiltons, but not campgrounds or economy lodgings. This happens not because the latter are uneconomic. Actually, they are highly successful and certainly more appropriate to the international and the domestic traveler, requiring less expensive infrastructure to build and less energy and imports to maintain. That they are not being constructed reflects elite tastes, political objectives, and, in some cases, private economic considerations. Most of the ruling elite select accommodations fitting their tastes, which are usually upper middle class and Western. A Hyatt or an Intercontinental hotel can be opened with a flourish. To some, it symbolizes a world-class destination. Forty or so modest motels built with the same investment, designed for use throughout the country by both national and international visitors, do not showcase national grandeur as well, though it might be a healthier reflection of the country's priorities.

Because of the political pretensions of many leaders, the infrastructure built for tourists is generally in the luxury category. Once the visitor opts for inside plumbing he or she may have few choices. This is paradoxical for the Western tourist, who, contrary to travel industry or regime rhetoric, does not need this sybaritic luxury; the government does, for reasons that have precious little correlation with development.

As Robert Wood explains, what currently is the status quo need not be the case. Other options are feasible.

> In Southeast Asia much more than in Europe, the hotel sector is sharply bifurcated between cheap, traditional style facilities and expensive, "international standard" hotels. Every government in non-socialist Southeast Asia has opted for capital-intensive, international standard hotels as the basis of its tourist industry. This is a political choice, entailing the subsidy of the hotel sector by the state, which has a number of cultural ramifications. A strong case could be made for developing a type of tourism based on modernizing and expanding the traditional accommodation systems of the region, for example, the losmen in Indonesia.
>
> Given the extremely high import content of the luxury hotels . . . the net foreign exchange gains of luxury tourism are often quite small.[2]

The smaller scale and more basic accommodations are seen as important for alternative tourism whether tourists arrive as individuals, small groups, or large tours. An exception is the large convention, which, as long as it remains subsidized by tax incentives, is likely to require large-scale facilities. Even business travelers are increasingly seeking out small, uncrowded but comfortable accommodations in good apartment hotels or in special wings of more conventional hotels. Whereas the business traveler, forced to travel frequently, recognizes the more soothing psychic and physical comforts of human-scale environments, the chief impetus to those critical of the conventional large hotel is aesthetic and ecological.

Aside from the question of appropriateness of such enormous luxury hotels in the midst of urban ghettos in the developing or developed world, they are particularly ecologically wasteful, not to mention impractical in developing nations. Power outages and water shortages are a fact of life in most such countries. Lobbies with waterfalls and massive pools require obscene amounts of power and water to run. In one poignant Public Broadcasting System video, *Who Pays for Paradise?*, residents of Gabon and the Ivory Coast were shown hauling water on their heads in front of hotels with lavish pools. Moreover, virtually all the equipment has been imported and is subsidized by government tax concessions.[3]

The luxury hotel in the developing nation requires excessive monetary support, disproportionate water, energy, food, land, and construction materials—all items in scarce supply. In some island destinations, reefs are dynamited and fishing destroyed so that beaches can be widened and swimming improved.

Special interest tourism has also been called alternative tourism. A major and growing variant is sport tourism. The Honolulu Marathon, for example, brought over nine million dollars to the community in 1984 between when runners flew in and when they limped out.[4] Golfing, diving, bird watching, fishing, and skiing bring people of kindred interests together even as such activities encourage receiving countries to protect and preserve what the tourists came to enjoy. Trips to the Holy Land, archaeological tours, travel for nostalgic purposes such as the Reunion for Peace trips of veterans in the Philippines, *Roots* tours to Gambia, religious pilgrimages, or other such specially motivated tourism tend to foster travel by individuals deeply interested in at least some aspect of the countries they visit, as opposed to the undifferentiated group tour.

Of course, sex tours represent an unhealthy and deeply resented variant of the special interest tour, and one that creates social and sometimes political problems for both the receiving country and the tourist-generating party. Not all alternative tours are necessarily appropriate.

Alternative tourism may also be concerned with authenticity. Conventional tourism has been justifiably criticized as encouraging fantasy, escapism, pseudo-events, and what Dean MacCannell has called "staged authenticity" and "re-constructed ethnicity."[5] Most would acknowledge that fantasy and escapism have their place in life, and places like Disneyland, Monaco, and Tivoli Gardens do wonders for one's spirit and capacity for play and amusement. But luxurious enclaves in desperately poor countries, financed in whole or in part by government, delude visitors and further impoverish the citizens. They convey an unreal image of the visitor to the host culture and a misleading impression of the conditions in the country to the visitor.

Pseudo-events may be harmless, as Aloha Week is, designed to enhance Hawaii with parade and musical events during the low season. Other genuine celebrations and rituals, however, may be corrupted and trivialized either by changing them, by altering their time frame, repeating them too often, making them more dramatic, or even allowing nonbelievers to see them and merchants to hawk souvenirs of the event. Celebrations that were once spontaneous and a source of joy to the participants have become paid shows for visitors. Examples abound from Indonesia to Spain.

In 1984, Reverend Peter Holden of the Ecumenical Coalition on Third World Tourism, expressed at the Vatican Conference on Tourism the problem of tourism too often corrupting and displacing the authentic with the contrived. Few attending understood it as a problem as long as it was someone else's beliefs that were being caricatured. When Holden explained it in terms of how they would feel if someone tried to turn the Holy Mass or Communion into a tourist attraction—boiled down to 15 minutes, for which tickets were sold, cameras were flashing, and people were being sold plastic relics—the other delegates became apoplectic. "That couldn't be done to the Holy Mass!" "There's no comparison." They still did not understand, but their reaction is not unlike the hurt and dismay others feel at the commoditization of the sacred in their cultures.[6]

"Staged authenticity" is related to the pseudo-event. In most cases tourists like to believe that they are being told the truth about a destination or are getting a taste of what the place is or was all about. Few may be well enough informed to distinguish the accurate from the inaccurate, which leads to the selling of "staged authenticity." Williamsburg and Plimouth Colony are examples of where an authentic past has been reconstructed with more or less attention to accuracy and detail.

Less careful examples of "staged authenticity" include such spectaculars as that sponsored by the Church of Latter Day Saints. "This is Polynesia," a popular and expensive attraction at their Polynesian Cultural Center in Laie, Hawaii, may be harmless, but it is not particularly accurate.[7] Many "authentic" tribal, native, and national dance performances put on for tourists all over the world are in this category. They may be perfectly good as entertainment, but many would be considered patronizing or crude stereotyping by the people that are supposedly being represented.

"Reconstructed ethnicity" has some of the characteristics of "staged authenticity" in some tourist situations. "Reconstructed ethnicity" has been defined by MacCannell as "the maintenance and preservation of ethnic forms for the entertainment of ethnically different others."[8]

In the Philippines, Thailand, and Indonesia, and at Hawaii's Polynesian Cultural Center, this has taken the form of the quasi-cultural amusement park, where major tribal groups are represented, and "typical" dwellings, dances and handicrafts are displayed. Although purporting to be authentic, the real emphasis is on making nonmodern groups look quaint and colorful. Treated as an attraction rather than ethnography, this approach could be rather innocuous, especially when compared with the alternative, which may be guided tours fanning out through one's village, peering in windows and snapping photographs of picturesque scenes.[9] Some groups find the cultural composites like Nayong Filipino or Mini Indonesia crude and trivial because they represent the dominant group's decisions as to what is superficially interesting about the minority groups' cultures.

Where tourists are brought directly to a remote ethnic or tribal group a different problem arises. The brochures that lured travelers may be equally inadequate and may reinforce an ethnic identity that is static at best and more commonly inaccurate. Sometimes the expectations of visitors are comical, but at other times they encourage the freezing of an evolving society into what can become a caricature of its former identity.

> It is difficult to find concrete benefits in this type of ethnic tourism for the people whose life is the attraction. The economic structure is such that most of the money involved does not change hands at the site. . . . Also, the kind of changes that are necessary to develop a group for ethnic tourism rarely improves the lives of its members as sometimes occurs in development for other forms of tourism, i.e. historical shrines.[10]

Even when the group's qualities and values are extolled, there is still a reification of a moment of the culture as permanent and unchanging. MacCannell calls a group "museumized" when this happens.[11] If it takes place at another site, however, as with the Polynesian Cultural Center or the Philippine government's Nayong Filipino, those hired to act out a cultural role can at least treat it as a modeling or acting job. When one's own home is the stage set, there is little escape and one is caught living a role created by others, for others, and for which there is little compensation.

Coping with authenticity without destroying and trivializing the genuine is a major concern of alternative tourism but it is difficult to achieve. One group, including this writer, consciously concerned with the need for alternative tourism, visited a fairly remote village north of Chiang Mai, Thailand. Even though the group traveled by small jeepneys (unobtrusive but scarcely appropriate for the muddy, mountain roads), carried its own food so as not to deplete local supplies, and tried to be courteous and adaptable, it was still an awkward encounter that bridged neither cultural differences, life-styles, nor led to any real understanding. The visitors came, asked many personal questions, looked around, and left. The experience may have been authentic. The larger issue is, did it really do host or guest any good in an experiential sense?

Among those interested in authenticity and alternative tourism, there is another debate over handicrafts, visual arts, and the performing arts. Some decry all changes that appear after the onslaught of tourists and particularly those that are meant to appeal directly to the visitor. For example, are the Indian Christmas ornaments, even if finely done and utilizing traditional materials, a bastardization of craft skills? Some say yes, because Christmas is an alien holiday, and though Indian Christians do exist, these crafts are not from their heritage. Others argue no, that Indians can respond to the market. Not all their work must come from Moghul or Hindu traditions; it is rather the quality of the work that distinguishes good crafts from airport art. A hastily and shoddily carved statuette of the Hindu God Ganesh may be culturally authentic, but more a reflection of the loss of craftsmanship than changes in theme.

Disturbing to others is the growing tendency of crafts once given as gifts, like Pacific tapas, now to be items of trade. Is this type of commoditization of culture to be deplored or encouraged? Disagreement exists. Sometimes, there creeps into the litany of tourist ills a certain "noble savage" perspective where critics bemoan the loss of purity and innocence and subsequent attendant commercialization of "once dignified, proud peoples." At the same time, Westerners may not lose much sleep over decisions to sell their own antiques and quilts, or change architectural style and furnishings with almost whimsical abandon. Who guards the guardians?

It is a worthwhile goal to pursue authenticity and cultural preservation, but when one group—governmental or private—attempts to define precisely what that shall entail, the cultural coalition can quickly break down.

Robert Wood sees it as a methodological problem. "It is striking how much of the writing on the cultural effects of tourism treats culture as a unified reality set against the alien intrusion of tourism. In part this is a unit-of-analysis question: the tendency to study small-scale locales rather than larger social units."[12] Using nation-states does not resolve this problem, however, for some nations are quite small. Nor should one argue that minorities are expendable, even though they are a statistically tiny percentage of the whole nation. Unfortunately, tourism does not come simply to nations, though national governments tally the rewards. It often comes to "small-scale locales" and is no less an invasion simply because the tourists arrive casually dressed and with bucks rather than bullets. Wood is correct about the methodological problem from the standpoint of research, but that is an academic question that in no way diminishes the obligations of policymakers to their constituents.

Wood later identifies the central research question. "Rather than looking for international tourism's impact on some undifferentiated notion of culture, we need to ask how tourism becomes a factor in these oppositions and helps shape the outcomes of conflict."[13]

Surely, too, the preservation of culture must mean more than simply tradition. Franz Fanon expressed it well when he stated: "Culture has never the translucidity of custom; it abhors all simplification. In its essence it is opposed to custom, for custom is always the deterioration of culture."[14]

Perhaps it makes an essential difference if the people affected by tourism have a voice in determining its impact on their lives. This leads to still another aspect on the alternative tourism agenda: who controls the industry?

Control is a tricky concept, for it operates at several levels. Some nations enjoy local control in terms of ownership of the basic infrastructure for the tourism industry. That is small comfort, however, if like Antigua, looking forward to a brisk holiday season, a country discovers that Pan Am has dropped the small nation from its routes. Similarly, local control in the hands of a powerful few may be as intimidating as taking on Hilton International if advocates with resources are not available to represent the public interest in a more generic sense.

In some instances control involves an ownership issue, in others a question of indigenous or expatriate labor, in other instances the prerogatives of management, and equally as critical a public voice in the pace, mode, direction, and monitoring of the industry. From the case studies in Asia and the surveys from public sector tourism development, it is clear that control in a fundamental way is often denied those most affected and most vulnerable.

The documentary *Fire on the Water* makes this point in a particularly poignant way. Vietnamese refugees came to Texas shores to make a living in the already marginal shrimp fishing business. Competition with American fishermen who felt their own livelihood threatened led to violence. Desperately poor Vietnamese fishermen trashed the bay by over-fishing, even in spawning areas. The end result was that the fishing industry dramatically declined and leisure or resort boating is in the process of replacing it. Some, including the director of the film, suggest this was exactly as scripted. Some who sold rusting hulks to the Vietnamese were on hand when the Americans and Vietnamese fought each other to a standstill. With the shrimp gone, the same individuals bought coastal land cheaply for tourist development.[15]

The problem of control is particularly acute in developing nations where so many possess so little, including political clout. Tourism is very seldom a public issue until it runs amuck. As such, political elites are seldom constrained in their tourism initiatives by ordinary citizens. As we have seen in the Philippines, authoritarian societies are not just unhindered by public concerns, but if the elite places a priority on a particular style of tourism, planning ministries and technocrats are a flimsy barrier against the modern Marie Antoinettes or Napoleons.

Currently, Hawaii is struggling with how to balance the interests of those who earn from tourism with those who burn from it—in inflation, increased crime, congestion, and water shortages.[16] Unfortunately, the latter seldom have the political access of the advocates.

Even in democratic India, mega events like Asiad '82 were beyond parliamentary monitoring, while local land grabs in Goa or the evictions of fishermen in Orissa meant that even when tourism initiatives are not large-scale, those most basically affected for their food and shelter can still be powerless to affect the outcome of tourism.[17]

The poignancy of the affected and their powerlessness is captured in Cecil Rajendra's poem.

WHEN THE TOURISTS FLEW IN

The Finance Minister said
    "It will boost the Economy
    The dollars will flow in."

The Minster of Interior said
    "It will provide full
    and varied employment
    for all the indigenes."

The Minister of Culture said
    "It will enrich our life . . .
    contact with other cultures
    must surely
    Improve the texture of living."

The man from the Hilton said
    "We will make you a second Paradise;
    for you it is the dawn
    of a glorious new beginning!"

When the tourists flew in
    our island people
    metamorphosized into
    a grotesque carnival
    —a two-week sideshow

When the tourists flew in
    our men put aside
    their fishing nets
    to become waiters
    our women became whores

When the tourists flew in
    what culture we had went out the window
    we traded our customs
    for sunglasses and pop
    we turned sacred cermonies
    into ten-cent peep shows

When the tourists flew in
    local food became scarce
    prices went up
    but our wages stayed low

> When the tourists flew in
>> we could no longer
>> go down to our beaches
>> the hotel manager said
>> "Natives defile the sea-shore"
>
> When the tourists flew in
>> the hunger and the squalor
>> were preserved
>> as a passing pageant
>> for clicking cameras
>> —a chic eye-sore!
>
> When the tourists flew in
>> we were asked
>> to be "side-walk ambassadors"
>> to stay smiling and polite
>> to always guide
>> the "lost" visitor . . .
>> Hell, if we could only tell them
>> where we really want them to go![18]

Alternative tourism is also concerned with social impact of the tourist on the host society. Unlike the PATA tourism conference that had as its theme "The Consumer, the Only One that Really Matters," to some involved in alternative tourism, the host society must ideally benefit from the encounter or at least not suffer from it. In a developed society, that may mean encouraging tourism that consists of locally owned and managed establishments, assuring that city, county, and park resources be adequately compensated for tourism, and in sponsoring quality tourist experiences that local resident and visitor alike can enjoy. It may mean encouraging the tourist to use local transportation so that it is kept well utilized and up-to-date for all. It may mean developing the kinds of tours that attract the kind of visitors who add to, rather than detract, from the quality of life. Although all such considerations are valid in developing nations, the gap between the standard of living provided the tourist and the resident population may be 500 years apart in quality.

Whether in the desert, the mountains, or the seashore, alternative tourism is also attempting to cope with questions about the carrying capacity of a destination. A case in point is beautiful Hanauma Bay just a few miles from densely populated Honolulu. It is a protected zone where the spectacular fish and the reef are to be left undisturbed—except for the 12,000 visitors that come to the small bay every day. By feeding the fish, there has been no problem to date in keeping them in the populated area, but the quality of experience in snorkeling flipper-to-flipper on a Sunday afternoon is considerably diminished. Already, proposals to curtail traffic and congestion at the site have been attempted. More ideas are needed. More than aesthetics are at stake in the fragile deserts or mountain regions where insensitively developed or too elaborate tourism initiatives can threaten permanent damage to the more delicate terrain.[19]

One of conventional tourism's saddest impacts in the developing world is the schism between leisured tourists and the impoverished host culture. One form of alternative tourism is that which facilitates two-way travel and low-cost domestic tourism. Social tourism has been used to describe those tours as well as ones designed for students, handicapped, workers, veterans, and other groups unable to afford conventional travel.[20] Some such travel is specifically designed to alleviate stress or extreme deprivation. Examples include travel and home stays for children from battle-torn Northern Ireland or trips to the countryside for ghetto youth. Upward Bound is an American program of travel and adventure designed for troubled adolescents.

Some define their efforts at alternative tourism as involving a basic effort to incorporate within the travel experience, whatever its scale, a sensitivity to the culture and values of the destination, a curiosity as to the genuine living conditions of the people, a recognition of the common humanity of visitor and resident, and the encouragement of respect and non-exploitative relationships between host and guest.

Alternative tourism then means a variety of concerns and responses, some focused on the tourist, some on the host culture, some on the natural environment, and some on the political environment. Various groups and governments prioritize these issues quite differently. Even within the travel industry there is a growing recognition that such concerns are not only legitimate, but represent opportunities as well as challenges to the long-term development of the industry.

Tourism has been a force for preservation of both natural beauty and manmade wonders. It has provided new markets for crafts and musical traditions once threatened by extinction. Although this book has been extremely critical of many of the policy decisions taken to support tourism, it would be an over-reaction to argue as some do that tourism is only a spoiler (see Fig. 9.1). The challenge is to convince the international travel industry and governments to think in new and innovative ways to make the industry more socially responsible and thereby more qualitatively satisfying to the visitor, more compatible with local needs and interests. Tourism need not be only a zero-sum game, where someone wins at another's expense. Variable-sum games are in the long-range best interests of the industry, the consumer, and the resident. Ignoring this plays into the hands of desperate terrorists, as the Philippines so clearly illustrates. At this juncture, enough cases have been outlined, enough

Figure 9.1. Tourism balance sheet

Benefits	Costs
Economic	**Economic**
Foreign exchange	Inflation
Build on the existing infrastructure	Foreign exchange leakage
Developed with local products and resources	Seasonality of tourism
Spread development	Unemployment
Complement product of other economic activities	Susceptible to political changes, rumors, spread of disease, economic fluctuation
Employment: full time, part time, seasonal, unskilled	Unbalanced economic development
	Demonstration effects
	Visual pollution
	Destruction of resources
Sociocultural	**Sociocultural**
Broadening of education	Misunderstanding
International peace and understanding	Stereotyping
Breakdown of language barriers, social or class barriers, religious barriers, racial barriers	Xenophobia
	Social pollution
Appreciation of one's own and other sociocultural elements	Commercialization of the culture
	Commercialization of religion
	Commercialization of the arts
	Demonstration effects
	Prostitution
	Conflicts
	Crime

This table represents a sample of the kind of costs and benefits attributed to tourism in the 1960s and 1970s. But it does not balance; or is it supposed to?

SOURCE: Jafar Jafari. "Understanding the Structure of Tourism." In *Tourism and Culture: A Comparative Perspective,* edited by Eddystone C. Nebel III, 67. New Orleans: University of New Orleans, 1983.

concerns highlighted, that it seems appropriate to consider not where we are and how we got there, but where do we go from here.

WHERE DO WE GO FROM HERE?

The Role of Governments

Though a few governments like the United States have left the bulk of tourism promotion and development to the private sector, even there the pattern has changed as cities, counties, states, and regions compete for tourism just as they cooperate in many areas of promotion and research. Some functions, particularly environmental protection, cannot be left to the private sector because of the shorter time frame and market considerations of the latter.[21] Government has a potentially enormous and positive role to play in terms of the scale, cost, pace, control, and quality of tourism.

Unfortunately, governments take whatever elitist, distributive, or redistributive values they hold in other sectors into tourism development. Still, most have developed policies that call for consumer protection, zoning, environmental controls, and fair trade. These are important in tourism development. Government planners should incorporate growth into their infrastructure development, but it is increasingly clear that tourism should be integrated into as diverse an economy as is possible. The fickleness of the industry and its vulnerability to terrorism, political instability, and economic recession means that it should never be permitted to create a monoculture, particularly in island destinations that often assume they can have no other option.

Gradual tourism development is far better for maintaining a balanced and diversified economy. Moreover, it allows local capital a continuing chance to invest. Destinations that embarked on crash tourism development as in Korea, the Philippines, and the Republic of China did so at the expense of local control. "The sheer scale and pace of hotel development in many of these regions has been such as to exclude the possibility of such development being carried out by domestic firms alone."[22] Gradual development prevents stresses and strains on expanding infrastructure, and allows residents and the travel industry to become acquainted without undue pressure. Countries as dissimilar as Switzerland and Bermuda illustrate that where tourism is allowed to proceed gradually, the residents do not get as tired of tourists and are less likely to take advantage of them. Also, tourists do not get satiated with the latest "in" destination and forget it after one visit. Finally, the values of the host society are more likely to be respected and protected if development is phased.

Governments should take care that incentives to foreign investment are not made at the expense of local capital, and that concessions in the form of tax holidays are not at the front end of development. Incentives stacked too early in the investment cycle can be disastrous for the economy and a disincentive to continued good management, yet this is the current general pattern. "Because the major benefits of Transnational participation in the tourist industry are likely to occur during the initial stages of their involvement, the host country may wish to renegotiate the terms of a contract after a relatively short and pre-determined period of time."[23] Helping local business thrive through enterprises such as regional or cooperative airlines and reservation chains can reduce dependence on foreign timetables and profit margins.

Until recently, it has been assumed that the proper nationalist response to foreign investment has been to limit foreign equity either entirely or to a minority share. More recent evidence suggests that foreign management contracts without any equity involvement, although quite common in the developing world, have been a source of dissatisfaction in many countries. For example, in a study of transnational corporate participation in Caribbean tourism, it was discovered that in every case where transnational corporation (TNC) operations were unsatisfactory to the government, the TNC was not financially involved; in every satisfactory case there was financial involvement.[24]

Although not all developing nations can or will choose to avoid transnational management contracts, the United Nations study of transnationals suggests that their use should be temporary.[25] In fact, a government should reconsider its tourism program's emphasis on large-scale TNC involvement if the TNC is unwilling to invest its funds. It may be that a different scale and type of tourism is warranted or that government-sponsored tourism is too risky at that juncture. It may also mean that the plan is appropriate but that the TNC feels free to dictate terms, in which case a government should prudently seek competition among TNCs.

Some governments have also sought negotiating advice from the United Nations and the World Tourism Organization. Although these organizations are not entirely free of bias, they represent more disinterested advice than the TNCs or the travel industry in general. As the United Nations study discovered in conjunction with management contracts:

> There may be a serious imbalance of knowledge and expertise between TNCs and owners of hotels in developing countries, particularly in the case of small countries at an early stage in their development. It would therefore be advisable for these countries to have recourse to impartial and expert advice during contract negotiations. It is also important for a developing country to relate the cost of these contracts to its policy objectives. Management fees may be excessive in relation to the return on capital, especially since most of the risk is usually borne by the host country, either through direct equity participation or through guarantees or loans.[26]

Just knowing what options exist is an essential but overlooked element in governments seeing that they stay in charge of their tourism sector and that tourism supports rather than retards overall national development. For example, in the Caribbean some governments levy an excess profit tax on TNCs to use for local training. Indigenization of the labor force, particularly supervisory and management positions, is very important in encouraging acceptance of tourism as well as providing quality employment for local residents.

Governments are tackling the propensity to import in several ways. Some limit imports almost entirely, while others like India link the relatively few imports allowed to a percentage of foreign exchange earned.[27]

Governments have a fundamental role in promoting domestic tourism. Too often governments in developed countries assume that economic well-being and the private sector make the government's role unnecessary. They may not recognize indirect subsidies to the industry. In the United States and some other nations, for example, business travel is supported through preferential tax deductions. In developing nations domestic tourism is usually seen as a frill that is at best an excuse for rhetoric rather than policy. Where a policy, it often takes the form of currency limitations and taxes that make outbound travel prohibitively expensive. Such protectionist policies may encourage some domestic travel, but curbing the freedom to travel usually results in similar counter measures by other countries.

In case studies from both developing and developed countries, it is apparent that domestic tourism can be an important economic and political force for stabilizing tourism's role in development, encouraging national pride and integration, and providing employment, quality leisure, and health and environmental benefits. The presence of large numbers of domestic tourists also operates to reduce the barriers that can develop when tourists are always leisured and culturally different outsiders.

Hawaii encourages domestic tourism by giving preferentially low rates on hotels and transportation to kama'ainas (residents) and having free or discounted rates for popular tourist attractions. Fiji and Jamaica see that rates for foreigners subsidize considerably lower rates for domestic tourists.

The government ultimately sets the ground rules for domestic tourism. Rest, leisure, holidays, and paid leave are in many national constitutions. "The Constitutions of Spain and Malta stipulate that citizens not only are entitled to rest and paid leave, but cannot relinquish those rights under any circumstances."[28] Generally, those constitutions that have such rights are of fairly recent origin. The United States, for example, has no such provision, but much of its labor legislation and union activity have protected the right to paid leave.

Still, domestic tourism is a minority activity, even in much of the developed world. In the United States, for example, only a bare majority take an annual vacation. International tourism, for all the vast increases, is also still confined to a relative few despite its enormous economic and political influence. Consider the political realities implicit in these two contrasting statements: "Although a global phenomenon, international tourism remains a minority activity. Over 95% of the world's people *did not* cross an international boundary in 1976, only 19% has ever flown in a plane," and "In 1981 world spending for domestic and international travel exceed world spending for military purposes."[29]

Government can also do much to mitigate the environmental impact of tourism. Indeed, it is probably the only body with the authority or will needed to do so. That does not mean it must assume all costs. Through its regulatory and taxing power, government can do a great deal with protective zoning and insistence on appropriate planning. Implementation remains, however, a serious problem, especially in countries with endemic corruption.

Fragile political institutions are as vulnerable to the abuse of tourism legislation as any other type of policy. To the extent that the government planning process has aligned itself with consultants, feasibility studies, or master plans prepared in conjunction with aid consortiums, the World Tourism Organization, or the United Nations Development Project, the publicity surrounding such reports offers the government, the tourism agency, or ministry and interest groups a means of monitoring and investigating subsequent implementation. Totally in-house planning can get rather badly waylaid by political interests that are too strong for administrators to challenge, as was clear in the Philippines under former President Marcos. In authoritarian settings like the Philippines under Marcos and with the chief abusers of policy at the pinnacle of power, it is doubtful whether anybody could have curtailed such aberrations. There is, however, no evidence any major group tried, including the International Monetary Fund.

Governments are also in the best position to protect historical, ecological, and cultural treasures from exploitation. Many are doing so. But pressures to open sites to tourists often are acceded to before the necessary security is in place. Many world-class historical sites are in danger in places like Pakistan, where valuable ruins are left unguarded or with a lone, easily bribed caretaker. One literally walks on pot shards, bangles, and dishes of a 5,000-year-old civilization as one tours the ancient site of Harappa, near Lahore.

At a minimum, tribes, minority peoples, and other strata of the population also need control to regulate their exposure to tourists, or the government needs to respond to the wishes of these groups as to the role they want in tourism, if any. Some groups have more clout than others. Some Native American tribes in the United States, for example, the Navajos, have tribally owned resorts on their reservations. Others, such as the members of Taos Pueblo in New Mexico, charge admission to the hordes of tourists moving through their settlements, peering in homes, and taking endless pictures of their picturesque poverty. Still others, like the Hopis of Arizona, allow access but prohibit all photography and sketching. Aborigine groups in Australia, the Maoris of New Zealand, hill tribes of India, Thailand, and the Philippines, and the Masai of Kenya are only a few of the tribal groups struggling to come to terms with tourism and their government's policy toward it and them.

It is an interesting sidelight to the impact of tourism that even among governments notably uninterested or unsuited to protecting ethnic diversity, tourism operates to enlarge the government's interest and involvement in culture. This, in turn, gives the ethnic group a leverage it otherwise would not enjoy. For example, the historical treatment of Hawaiians in Hawaii since the missionary days of the 1820s has been one that most would admit bordered on genocide at worst, exploitation and deculturation at best. But, the development of tourism encouraged the government to sell the ethnicity of Hawaiians as a part of its marketing of Hawaii as a destination. In the process, Hawaiians *as Hawaiians* began to be more successful in their claims to economic and cultural protection by the state. A similar process occurred in Bali, where touristic considerations dissuaded the Indonesian government from attempting to push Islamicization and the Indonesian language on the Hindu island.[30]

Preventing the exploitation of women, or increasingly children and young men, is far easier than dealing with the problem of sex tours and prostitution after the private sector gets a vested interest in their continuance. Every government has statutes that allow it to intervene on behalf of public health and safety. Whether prostitution is prohibited or licensed and taxed, it can and should be regulated. Moreover government promotion and the licensing of hotels and tour agencies should insist they market in such a way that sex is not promised or sold in the process. A comparision of two American states, Hawaii and Virginia, illustrates the point.

The Hawaii Visitors Bureau has an advertising campaign that builds an ambiguous, sexually inviting image into a lovely photograph of Hawaii's charms. On each poster or advertisment is a pretty, supposedly Hawaiian woman provocatively posed with a single flower lei in a clinging *pareau* (which is in marked contrast to the baggy muumuus worn in Hawaii). A remote waterfall or wall of vegetation forms the backdrop. The caption: "The Beauty Remains to be Seen." Does the slogan mean that beauty in the picture? Or does it mean that Hawaii is more than a pretty girl and a waterfall? The ad promises beauty and romance, not fun, sports, cultural diversity, great shopping, or even the famous beaches. It is designed to attract single men, not couples, not the elderly, not even single women.

The "Virginia is for Lovers" campaign is in stark contrast. There we see young toddlers holding hands on a beach, couples swimming, teens horseback riding, and couples over 50 having a candlelit dinner. The implication is clear: Virginia is for all ages, for those who love life, beauty, and a good time. A romantic ambience is there, but you bring your love, you do not rent a partner at your destination!

Hawaii adds to its narrow marketing image by its "Hawaiian Girls" calendars, its scratch-'n-sniff postcards—scratch the nude girl on the card and she exudes one of Hawaii's popular flower scents (makes "cents," but is in bad taste)!

Governments with no compunctions about censorship could include marketing in their oversight. This is especially important where the government is negotiating charters with international tour operators who specialize in "sunlust" tourism. Thailand, the Philippines, and Korea have paid dearly for their sleazy reputations in diminished length of visitor stays, reduced diversity of arrivals, dependence on sex tourism, and in social controversy, disease, crime, and abused and illegitimate children. Tallying only the easily quantifiable statistics can be a serious mistake. Failing to monitor resident reactions and only considering visitor motivation and satisfaction can easily lead to government acquiescence in a pace and style of tourism development that will create in the future a politically and economically expensive backlash.[31]

Riots in Jamaica have seldom hinged on tourism issues, but given the government's insensitivity to the dignity of their own people, surely it is only a matter of time.

> You can rent a lovely life in Jamaica by the week. It starts with a country house or a beach cottage hilltop hideaway that comes equipped with gentle people named Ivy or Maude or Malcolm who will cook, tend, mend, diaper and launder for you. Who will "Mr. Peter," please you all day long, pamper you with homemade coconut pie, admire you when you look "soft" (handsome), giggle at your jokes and weep when you leave.[32]

Step'n Fetchit is evidently alive and well in the Caribbean!

The government should also consider publishing brochures and encouraging orientation films for visitors, especially where the tourist-generating culture is quite different from the host culture as it is in many developing nations. This is done in only a handful of countries, but could save a great deal of potential misunderstandings between tourist and resident. Most tourists have no desire to offend, but few know where topless bathing is appropriate (Mediterranean, yes; Sri Lanka, no), where one covers up to go in a temple (Thailand and many other places) and where men must strip to the waist to enter one (South India), where it is a gross act of rudeness to touch someone on the head or point your toe at them (Thailand), and the list goes on. How to give to charity without encouraging begging, where and how much to tip, basic information on the country's history and political system—all this information fulfills a need that the government can provide more logically than the private sector.

An account like this of government's role-and-duty to intervene in tourism is hamstrung by its inability to convey the turbulence of the tourism political environment. Neither policy nor government is static. Both get shaped by a myriad of competing claims and influences, some controllable, some not. Governments change, some on a regular basis, most of them according to rhythms of their own. International economic and political events force changes, reactions, and initiatives that were not foreseen. In some political systems, prominent issues on the tourism political agenda of one government level will be ignored at another level. Characteristically, in developing nations, the national government will regard tourism as more salient, at least at the early stages of development, than other levels. In the United States just the opposite is true. There a progressive, bipartisan myopia concerning tourism's role in the system develops as one moves from the cities and states most aware of tourism to the national level.

Policy implementation will be more effective in some directions and some points in time than others. It, too, needs regular monitoring. For example, 30 years ago the great herds of African animals were being slaughtered in obscene numbers by tourists on safari, as well as by professional hunters who would sell animal skins, teeth, or tusks for fashions or souvenirs. Policies gradually responded to the cries of environmentalists, and hunting safaris were replaced by photo safaris. Today, the animals have become a hazard in some areas—to the ecology in general and to livestock and agriculture in particular. Also, despite the vast acreage set aside for the animals, most, reasonably enough, congregate near water holes. Tourists congregate where the animals are and the effect is that most animals and tourists in game parks crowd into less than eight percent of the park land. The ambiance is scarcely more adventurous than Sunday afternoon at the local zoo! It is a policy problem that can only get worse as tourist and animal populations grow.

Although most governments have tourism policies that can best be summarized as "bring us more," the responsible policies of the future are going to concern the allocation of leisure and tourism space. Already the U.S. national parks have been forced to declare limitations on the number permitted in the popular parks at any one time. Rationing of tourist experiences may well become common in the next century.

What Can Groups Do?

Although the government can and should do a great deal to develop tourism, interest groups have an important role in prodding and independently developing information, resources, tours, surveys, and other research that can encourage diversification of the industry and monitor both industry and government performance. How much groups can do is a function of (1) the salience of tourism, (2) the economic and political resources of various groups, and (3) the scope for pluralist interest group activity. Some international groups are more free to investigate tourism problems than domestic groups in authoritarian or socialist countries.

Rather than attempt to detail the activities of the myriad of governmental and nongovernmental organizations that are dealing in some way with tourism, this section will chart the growth of just one network that is attempting to encourage responsible tourism.

Church groups in Asia discovered in the 1970s that whether their functional focus was education, development, labor, women, or public health, they kept coming across tourism's impact on their research area. School children were dropping out of school to beg from the tourists or to act as guides. Development specialists watched as scarce community funds were diverted to hotel construction, beach improvements, or resort infrastructure. Labor organizations increasingly got complaints about labor safety at construction sites hastily thrown together for crash tourism development. Accidents at the round-the-clock construction of Manila's luxury hotels and convention center were covered up. Labor conditions at Asiad '82 were ignored by all but the leftist press.[33]

Reports of over 100,000 prostitutes in Manila and over 1,000,000 in Thailand triggered interest in the sex tours. Prostitution has long been associated with military bases in the area but tourism's impact has many times eclipsed the impact of the bases as a source of prostitution. Subic Bay Naval Base in the Philippines may account for most of the 12,000 prostitutes in the area, but this is less than one-eighth the number catering to tourists in Manila alone. Diseases like syphilis, supergonorrhea, and AIDS and problems of illegitimate and sexually abused children have concerned church workers involved in projects affecting public health. Although these various core areas of church activities were becoming aware of tourism's negative impacts on their particular projects, few were aware of how it impinged on other facets of the church's work.

Penang Conference

One of those few, Reverend Ron O'Grady, called together a small group in 1975 to the first conference on tourism held in Asia. The Penang Conference met as part of a half-year study of tourism sponsored by the Christian Conference of Asia. The conference generated more questions than conclusions, but it was one of the first groups to probe the facile statements of the tourist industry and the sanguine rhetoric of the national tourism offices to explore what tourism meant to the lives of ordinary Asians.

This first conference entitled its report "Tourism: the Asian Dilemma." The group recognized that tourism had both positive and negative impacts. Yet it was not then prepared to condemn or applaud tourism's developmental impact.

The Penang Conference had at least three important consequences. Clearly the most important was that it succeeded in putting tourism on the political and social agenda of the churches of Asia.[34] This was no mean feat. The conference was little noted, but its conference report sold out quickly. A nerve had been touched. Tourism had become a credible, legitimate topic of concern.

The second outcome of the Penang Conference was aimed less at institutions than individuals. A Code of Ethics for Tourists (Fig. 9.2) was produced. "This Code of Ethics was based on the premise that so long as there are foreign tourists in Asia, those tourists ought to seek to behave in such a manner that is not offensive to their Asian hosts and in the process both hosts and tourists may be culturally enriched."[35] This simple code has enjoyed amazing success. It has been translated into over a dozen languages and has been reprinted in church, travel trade, and airline magazines as well as tour brochures and government promotional material. Most people appreciate the information, so there is little risk that tasteful and nonthreatening suggestions for tourist behavior will be resented.

The third major result of the Penang Conference was to encourage the organization of a truly international workshop on tourism in developing countries. The response to the Penang report and the Code of Ethics were but two indicators that the timing for such a conference was right and appropriate.

The Manila Conference

In September 1980 the second major conference, the International Workshop on Tourism, was held in Manila, the Philippines. The 30 participants from Asia, the Pacific, the Caribbean, Africa, and a few tourist-generating countries graphically illustrated the change in political climate toward tourism that had taken place in the intervening five years. No longer were they equivocal about tourism's impact on national development. "The one most glaring thing that surfaced from the deliberations of the workshop was that tourism wreaked more havoc than brought

Figure 9.2. A Code of Ethics for Tourists

1. Travel in a spirit of humility and with a genuine desire to learn more about the people of your host country.

2. Be sensitively aware of the feelings of other people, thus, preventing what might be offensive behavior on your part. This applies very much to photography.

3. Cultivate the habit of listening and observing, rather than merely hearing and seeing.

4. Realize that often the people in the country you visit have time concepts and thought patterns different from your own; this does not make them inferior, only different.

5. Instead of looking for that "beach paradise," discover the enrichment of seeing a different way of life through other eyes.

6. Acquaint yourself with local customs—people will be happy to help you.

7. Instead of the Western practice of knowing all the answers, cultivate the habit of listening.

8. Remember that you are only one of the thousands of tourists visiting this country and so do not expect special privileges.

9. If you really want your experience to be "a home away from home," it is foolish to waste money on traveling.

10. When you are shopping, remember that the "bargain" you obtained was only possible because of the low wages paid to the maker.

11. Do not make promises to people in your host country unless you are certain you can carry them through.

12. Spend time reflecting on your daily experiences in an attempt to deepen your understanding. It has been said that what enriches you may rob and violate others.

Source: Ron O'Grady, *Third World Tourism,* Singapore, Christian Conference of Asia, 1980.

benefits to recipient Third World countries."[36] The report continued in this vein, exploding what it viewed as the myths of tourism, namely that the industry was a good source of foreign exchange, employment, of cultural understanding.

The contrast with the World Tourism Conference meeting in Manila at the same time could not have been more complete. The WTO was engaged in extolling the values of international tourism and its own role as an organization, research, and consulting core to the industry.

Both conferences were in the city whose very skyline and profile had been altered in the previous five years by the domination of the administration's political uses of tourism over the development needs of its poverty-stricken citizens. But the delegates to these conferences saw selectively. The WTO conference delegates saw a city of unmatched glamour, of lavish hotels, conference, and exhibition centers presided over by a president and first lady attentive to the every whim of their influential convention guests.

The delegates to the International Workshop on Tourism saw the contrast between the rosy rhetoric of tourism's contribution to development extolled in the controlled press and the lives of those evicted for tourism beautification schemes, the teenage whores who gave the fancy hotels an alternative source of income through kickbacks, and the unspoken chasm between gross tourism revenues and net tourism income after all the foreign exchange leakages had been subtracted.

This conference also published a report, *Third World Tourism,* destined to be the most popular publication ever produced by the Christian Conference of Asia. In this report, a different set of questions were posed to those asked at Penang: "Can tourism be salvaged?" "Is there something that can be scavenged from the scrap heap of tourism which can be turned towards the development of people?"[37]

Over 100 recommendations were endorsed by the conference, ranging from economic to social to cultural. The overall thrust of these recommendations was to reduce the dependence on transnational corporations and imports; increase net economic benefits from tourism through import substitution, create less exploitative and erratic wages, insure better distribution of economic gains and employment opportunities; encourage more participation and control of tourism by those affected by it. It also recommended educating the media and the government to adopt non-sexist, non-racist, and non-paternalistic stereotypes in the development of tourism. The report also pledged to support an active program of research and network formation to sustain such interest and work to implement their goals.[38]

The Manila Workshop Report reached conclusions that largely coincide with the critique some social scientists had begun making ten years earlier, but the report reached countless thousands whose instincts were activist rather than academic. The participants organized themselves into a network developing public awareness campaigns against sex tours, doing case studies on the impact of tourism, lobbying politicians and other influentials, and producing information for use by other activist groups.

More than the flurry of activity that often follows a stimulating conference, the Manila Conference recognized that the task before it was long-range in nature and required a permanent institutional base. The conference appealed to churches, development groups, trade unions, women's organizations, and youth groups to combine forces in a tourism monitoring network that is international in scope, activist in orientation, and ecumenical in spirit.

The appeal succeeded. The Ecumenical Coalition on Third World

Tourism (ECTWT) was formed in 1981. The coalition was organized by the Christian Conference of Asia, the Federation of Asian Bishops' Conference, the Pacific Conference of Churches, and the Caribbean Conference of Churches. It was later joined by the Consejo Latinoamericano de Iglesias, the All American Conference of Churches, and the Middle East Council of Churches.[39]

The ECTWT established a small secretariat in Bangkok charged with building a global network for action, developing a resource and information center, and exploring alternative directions for tourism development and control. The secretariat quickly established *Contours,* a small quarterly magazine that serves as an information conduit for what is happening to tourism or because of it. In less than two years, a mailing list of over 1,500 individuals and organizations had been established, links had been created with numerous church and non-church related organizations dealing with tourism, a library and research center was developed, an audiovisual clearinghouse organized, and still another international conference executed.[40]

Chiang Mai Conference

The Chiang Mai Conference of 40 participants drawn from 20 countries met in northern Thailand April and May 1984. It differed from the two earlier conferences in two main ways. First, its focus was not on inquiry or diagnosis but options:

> While Penang revealed the dilemma and Manila made the damning judgment, Chiang Mai has begun the process of searching for answers. We know the questions now. The participants of the Chiang Mai Workshop did not spend their time asking questions about tourism; they tried to search for answers and made commitments to action. . . . There emerged in Chiang Mai a *Hope* that some steps can be taken to build a new kind of tourism . . . which respects human rights, which values human culture and which returns just rewards to the people who offer services.[41]

This conference focused not only on alternatives to tourism organization as it presently exists but had a geographical emphasis on Asia. As such it was to be part of a series of conferences that had both a theme and a specific geographical orientation. For if anything has been learned about tourism it is that even common problems may require culture-specific responses. Even in a country like Canada, research has shown that there are different levels of carrying capacity for similar destinations based on local values and differing levels of tolerance for outsiders.[42]

Although Asia was much too broad a designation to be much of a delineator of concerns, the focus meant that most of the participants were Asian and most of the experiments with alternative tourism were or would be taking place in an Asian context. The other non-Asian participants had expertise either with their own programs of sending tourists to Asia or with developing strategies including films and brochures, government policies, or orientation programs that would make the host-guest encounter more genuinely enriching for both.

The Report of the Workshop on Alternative Tourism with a Focus on Asia was released within months of the Chiang Mai Conference and the *Resource Handbook on Alternative Tourism* was published in 1985, by the Christian Conference of Asia. New regional tourism conferences were held in Fiji; Bad Boll, Germany; San Anselmo, California; and Wellington, New Zealand, organized by former participants. Audiovisuals are being sold and speeches delivered. The web is growing.

In Europe the Tourism Ecumenical Network (TEN) has a similar agenda and there is much collaboration among ECTWT and other such groups. A future emphasis of ECTWT will move beyond exclusive reliance on church funding and toward financial and policy participation from a variety of sources. In Asia particularly, exclusive dependence on the churches—no matter how much discretion and freedom ECTWT is given—tends to reduce the organization's political base. What the organization has lacked in diverse funding has been largely offset by its ability to channel its energies into substantive program development rather than devote vast chunks of time to liaison or administrative tasks. Keeping that task-orientation while expanding the coalition's base of support will be the next institutional challenge.

Currently, there is so much to do and so few organizations involved that concerned groups dealing with tourism have spent little if any time in turf or jurisdictional battles. But as one finds in international organizations internecine strife is always a threat, particularly if the inspired talent that launches an organization is not continued with able and complementary leadership.

The United Nations, environmental groups, and some women's and labor organizations have begun to make tourism an agenda item. Space does not permit a full exploration of their tourism initiatives. What the Ecumenical Coalition on Third World Tourism's experience illustrates is that isolated groups, committees, and individuals are becoming aware of the political and social problems associated with tourism and that once they can be put in touch with each other, the union is catalytic. The dynamics of networking assure a geometric progression of activities and influence that go well beyond the sum of individual group endeavors.

The Role of the Individual in Appropriate Tourism

It used to be that travel, particularly the Grand Tour of Europe, was the capstone to the liberal education of an elite few. Travel was a way to see world-class art first hand, to visit historical sites, to meet authors, to practice one's French and Italian, and to explore leisurely and at some depth totally different cultures.

That is no longer true for most tourists. Even if that were their motivation, the tourist culture prepared by the host country isolates and prevents most such experiences. Today, the vast bulk of tourists have very little liberal arts education, possess scant if any foreign language skills, and tend to travel with a sense of acquisitiveness that measures number of destinations, souvenirs, photos, and suntans rather than friends made, personal growth, or understanding achieved. Like the tourist destinations, the individual tourist tallies the superficial and the quantifiable and discounts or ignores the net value of travel. Both need to relearn what is worth tallying if tourism is to be the experience it could be.

The anti-capitalist critique argues that it is the alienation of the tourist from the workplace that leads to the frenzied touring and escapist lifestyle. "The key to this riddle is to realize that the tourists are actually fleeing from their home countries as opposed to being fatally lured to foreign shores. The real absurdities lie in the places they live rather than in the ones they are going to."[43] That may be, but it is not unique to capitalism. No less acquisitive are those from socialist countries, where it could be argued that living conditions make rest and relaxation no less a goal.

This analysis does not attempt to suggest a cure for travel in the reshaping of the societies from whence the travelers come. To assert that tourism is less than it could be is a long way from concluding that all travel is escapist and escapism is unrelievably bad for those who escape and those who must host the escapees.

Yet, even the travel industry is urging that marketing focus less on fulfilling fantasies and more on the notion that travel is a durable good that prepares one for a fit and active life. It makes sensible travel a type of status like a healthy trim body. The argument is obviously self-serving for the industry. To the extent travel is a necessity and not a frill, it will not be eliminated at the first sign of recession. The reasoning may, however, dovetail with those concerned with tourism's negative impact. To the extent that travel is important it can be planned, prepared for, savored, and evaluated. The stigma of the gauche tourist can be used as a prod for insisting on quality information. The rapidly increasing number of guidebooks on the market suggest that this is already happening.

Even if countries do not insist on tours having pre-tour briefings, tours can conduct such orientations or prepare careful guidelines for responsible travel that include destination-specific suggestions for behavior. Airlines can allow short films, as Lufthansa does, that encourage the tourist to see the host culture as a sensitive and complex society worthy of respect and dignity.[44] The extra cost involved may be minimal if it prevents embarrassing incidents, increases visitor satisfaction, and facilitates acceptance of such groups overseas. Some tour groups have also found the post-tour debriefing an important aspect of responsible tourism. It allows the traveler an opportunity to reflect, assimilate, and integrate the travel impressions while at the same time enjoying and sharing an important developmental experience with others.

In some cases this may lead to a sustained group involvement with the host culture. One Australian tour group, Just Travel, uses part of the post-tour debriefing to decide how to spend what was left of the contingency fund set up for the trip. It could be divided among participants, but usually it is donated to some needy group or worthy project seen in the course of the tour.

Commercial groups may discover that the post-tour debriefing has the practical benefit of providing useful feedback while encouraging more repeat travel by satisfied clients who enjoy the more personalized service. Where this is not feasible a simple mail questionnaire may suffice.

Information is critical. Thus far, the discussion has been on ways the individual tourist can be better informed. Sometimes individuals in the host culture or at specific visitor attractions must initiate the information and insist that the tourist respect local customs. Often this can be done through community interpretation programs that inform both visitor and resident about a site in ways that convey respect for the site and the rules and customs surrounding it. Hawaii has been particularly active in developing a network of organizations that interact with tourists and the community in such a way that everyone benefits.[45]

Tourism education is also essential for residents. In the past this has generally taken the form of articles, talks, and programs emphasizing the economic importance of tourism and encouraging friendliness toward the tourist. It is equally important that such education emphasize the importance of demonstrating the dignity and culture of the host society, reinforcing the notion that tourists should be shown the quality and richness of the host civilization. To that end, religious customs and dress should not be changed for the tourists; artifacts and historic and archaeological sites should be carefully protected and preserved, and residents should behave with dignity and hospitality. It should be emphasized to residents that tourists are apt to behave inappropriately out of ignorance rather than deliberate rudeness; that they may be insecure and uncertain. Their leisure and affluence is probably unusual for them so they may behave strangely. Most of their lives, these people have to work hard too.

Activist individuals like Ron O'Grady and Peter Holden have been the sparks that have stimulated numerous organizations dealing with tourism such as the ECTWT and TEN or tourist-related activities within organizations based on labor, ecology, or the concerns of women. Academic journals focused on tourism have also been largely the creation of a single individual or a concerned few. Their emphasis on quality research has not obscured a bias for relevance or a concern with the impact of tourism on the quality of life. *Annals of Tourism Research,* the brainchild of anthropologist Jafar Jafari, and *Tourism Recreation Research,* the product of environmentalists Tej Vir Singh and Jagdish Kaur, are now venerable institutions in tourism research. In their early years, however, it was the tenacity and imagination of a few individuals that mattered. Today, both journals have subscribers in more than 60 countries.

Many key individuals within the travel industry, such as Arthur Frommer, have also encouraged responsible tourism with an attention to the impact tourism has on both host and guest.[46] Most must contend with both governments and businesses that are poorly attuned to these issues. Sometimes the official neglect is benign, more often it is not, as when hastily thought out energy policies in the 1970s jeopardized the economic health of scores of U.S. communities dependent on tourism.

Even when regions have introduced tourism gradually with care and sensitivity as Bermuda has, continual monitoring is essential lest orderly growth be assumed automatic and quality controls a foregone conclusion. In 1984 Bermuda signed a contract for a Club Med resort. Like the People's Republic of China, Bermuda is betting that it can introduce more variety into its tourist infrastructure without social cost. It is a hotly contested viewpoint in Bermuda, as befits a democratic society concerned about its number one industry.[47] In the PRC, debate is shrouded in secrecy.

Studying tourism policies is more than a way of comparing strategies of tourism development. It is also a way of exploring local, national, and international politics, and of examining strengths and weaknesses in the policy process of various societies. It is a way of studying political culture and social values and assessing theories of development and ideological assumptions. It is also a way of dissecting the actual as opposed to the rhetorical freedom of maneuver of individuals and groups within the political process.

Notes

CHAPTER 1

1. Somerset R. Waters, *Travel Industry World Yearbook: The Big Picture 1986,* Vol. 30, p. 7.

2. David L. Edgell, Sr., *International Tourism Prospects, 1987–2000,* p. iii.

3. Ibid.

4. Ibid., preface.

5. Linda K. Richter, "Tourism Politics and Political Science: A Case of Not So Benign Neglect."

6. Linda K. Richter, "State-Sponsored Tourism Development: A Growth Area for Public Administration."

7. Waters, *Travel Industry World Yearbook . . . 1986,* Vol. 30, p. 4.

8. Arend Lijphart, "Tourist Traffic and Integration Potential."

9. Tord Hoivik and Turid Heiberg, "Centre-Periphery Tourism and Self-Reliance."

10. Robert Stock, "Political and Social Contributions of International Tourism to the Development of Israel"; George Young, *Tourism, Blessing or Blight?;* Linda K. Richter, *Land Reform and Tourism Development: Policy-Making in the Philippines.*

11. Ronald Francisco, "The Political Impact of Economic Dependence on Tourism in Latin America."

12. Stock, "Political and Social Contributions," p. 33.

13. Young, *Tourism, Blessing or Blight?,* p. 173.

14. Mary Lord, "Chun's Option: To Crush or Concede"; "High-Stakes Games: Are the Olympics at Risk?"

15. David L. Edgell, Sr., "International Tourism and Travel," p. 174.

16. Stock, "Political and Social Contributions," p. 33.

17. Cord D. Hansen-Sturm, "Trade in Services in a U.S.-Israel Limited Free Trade Area." Testimony, p. 2.

18. Barbara Sturken, "The World Bank Well Runs Dry."

19. Hansen-Sturm, "Trade in Services." Testimony, p. 16.

20. Ibid., p. 4.

21. Ibid., p. 14.

22. *New York Times,* October 27, 1981.

23. Hansen-Sturm, "Trade in Services." Testimony, p. 2.

24. Linda K. Richter, "The Political Uses of Tourism: A Philippine Case Study."

25. Edda Henson, "World Tourism Organization in Asia and the Pacific"; Jafar Jafari, "Creation of the Intergovernmental World Tourism Organization."

26. Public Broadcasting System, *World: Who Pays for Paradise?,* June 1978.

27. John Dunning and Matthew McQueen, "Multinational Corporations in the International Hotel Industry"; Centre on Transnational Corporations, *Transnational Corporations in International Tourism.*

28. Harry G. Matthews, *International Tourism: A Political and Social Analysis.*

29. Dean MacCannell, *The Tourist: A New Theory of the Leisure Class.*

30. Linda K. Richter and William L. Waugh, Jr., "Terrorism and Tourism as Logical Companions."

31. Richter, *Land Reform and Tourism Development.*

32. Ibid.

33. Ibid.

34. Salah Wahao, "The Legal Protection of the Tourist."

35. Thomas A. Dickerson, "Travel Law: Securing Travelers' Rights and Remedies."

36. Patrick Schul and John L. Crompton, "Search Behavior of International Vacationers: Travel-Specific Lifestyle and Sociodemographic Variables."

37. John R. Kelly, "Leisure and Quality: Beyond the Quantitative Barrier in Research," pp. 300–301.

38. Christopher Holloway, *The Business of Tourism,* p. 66.

39. Interview with staff of Department of Tourism in Islamabad, Pakistan, August 1977.

40. Douglas Ashford, "The Structural Analysis of Policy or Institutions Really Do Matter," p. 82.

41. Albert Hirschman, "Policy-Making and Policy Analysis in Latin America: A Return Journey."

42. World Bank, *Tourism, Sector Working Paper,* p. 13.

43. Charles W. Lamb and John R. Crompton, "Qualitative Measures of Program Success."

44. "Tourism Travels to the Third World," *Dollars and Sense,* p. 15.

45. Dennison Nash, "Tourism as an Anthropological Subject," p. 465; Nash, "Tourism as a Form of Imperialism." See also Emanuel E. De Kadt, *Tourism: Passport to Development?*

46. *Contours,* Vol. 1, No. 3, 1983, p. 15.

47. Cor Westland, "The Development of National Free Time Policies," pp. 357–358.

48. Ibid., p. 359.

49. Elwood L. Shafer, "Policy Issues in Outdoor Recreation Research," p. 368.

50. Ibid., p. 360.

51. Ibid., p. 371.

52. The classic study of American pluralism is Robert Dahl's study of New Haven, Connecticut, *Who Governs?*

53. Abraham Pizam, "Tourism's Impact: The Social Costs to the Destination Community as Perceived by Its Residents," pp. 8–12. The need for such studies as Pizam's was also acknowledged as an exception in Suzanne D. Cook, "Research in State and Provincial Tourist Offices," p. 157.

54. Richter, "Not So Benign Neglect."

55. Linda K. Richter, "The Political Dimensions of Tourism."

56. Cynthia Enloe in her outstanding study, *The Politics of Pollution in a Comparative Perspective,* broke down the political process into a few components and compared these across several societies. That approach provides the opportunity for systematic cross-cultural comparison. Hers was also one of the first studies by a political scientist to mention tourism as a political topic.

Formal tourism policies can be compared and discussed with a panel of political experts in a modified Delphi study. This would be worth doing and possibly have some predictive value if experts on a nation's politics showed any interest in its tourism policy. They do not. Polls or questionnaires submitted to national regional and local tourism programs in several countries could also generate a lot of data about the scope and administration of government-directed tourism, but access, cooperation, cost, and elusive political factors make this approach impractical for several nations. Still another possibility is an edited work in which a variety of scholars could each specialize in the tourism development politics for a particular country and write according to a prearranged organization and analytical agenda. This has worked well for many comparative administration studies, but finding political scientists abroad who are working on tourism is no easier than finding them in the United States. Thus, the groundbreaking disciplinary work of Valene Smith in her book, *Hosts and Guests: The Anthropology of Tourism,* is also not feasible for political science at this stage. Smith did not organize the book into a common analytical agenda other than to include analyses that were germane to anthropology nor did she attempt to delimit the inquiry to a particular level of analysis or geographical area.

The only place there appears to be tentative signs of interest among American political scientists is in the field of public administration. Both practitioners and public administration scholars are following the lead of elected officials in cities and states concerned that tourism development provide the economic vehicle to lure visitors, film crews, and mega-conventions, and influence industry relocations by confirming a certain locale or region as a desirable destination. There were two tourism-related panels and a mobile workshop at the 1988 American Society for Public Administration Conference, a sure indication of public sector recognition of the topic of tourism.

57. Edgell, *International Tourism Prospects,* p. 11.

58. The Haj trip of Muslims to Mecca turned into a bloody nightmare when Iranian Shiites reportedly rioted in opposition to Saudi politics and provoked a counterattack that led to the death of hundreds in the summer of 1987.

59. Governor's Conference on Tourism, Honolulu, Hawaii, December 11, 1984.

CHAPTER 2

1. Peter Van Ness, "Black, White and Grey in China Research."

2. Mentioned in Ian Middleton, ed., *China, A Seatrade Study.* More recent articles I have found, however, commended the Chinese for improvements in data collection and the release of information, but even they remain wary and acknowledge the many contradictions that exist in the statistics. Murray Bailey and Jill Hunt, "China, National Report No. 117," pp. 5–6.

3. Linda K. Richter, "The Political Implications of Chinese Tourism Policy."

4. Di-chen Gao and Guang-rui Zhang, "China's Tourism: Policy and Practice."

5. Ibid.

6. John Fraser, *The Chinese People,* p. 68.

7. The dates of the Cultural Revolution differ in various accounts. The Chinese see it ending with the arrest of the Gang of Four in 1977.

8. Arne J. de Keijzer and Frederic M. Kaplan, *China Guidebook, 1980–1981,* p. 21.

9. Gao and Zhang, "China's Tourism."

10. De Keijzer and Kaplan, *China Guidebook,* p. 21.

11. Ibid.

12. *Christian Science Monitor,* May 26, 1987. See also "China Inbound," for a description of the efforts to cope with entry, exit, and transport problems.

13. Middleton, *China, A Seatrade Study,* p. 85.

14. Interview with Dexter J. L. Choy, School of Travel Industry Management, Honolulu, September 4, 1984.

15. Robert C. Fisher and Leslie Brown, *Fodor's People's Republic of China;* Murray Bailey and Jill Hunt, "China, National Report No. 117," p. 16.

16. *Manhattan Mercury,* January 14, 1982.

17. Middleton, *China, A Seatrade Study,* p. 85.

18. Ibid.

19. Peter R. Moody, Jr., "Political Liberalization in China: A Struggle Between Two Lines," p. 34.

20. Yet by 1984, Maxim's French restaurant was open in Beijing and a Club Med was under construction in southern China.

21. *China Daily,* October 20, 1984.

22. Somerset R. Waters, *Travel Industry World Yearbook: The Big Picture, 1986,* Vol. 30, p. 106.

23. Somerset R. Waters, *Travel Industry World Yearbook, The Big Picture, 1984,* Vol. 28, p. 5.

24. Barbara Letson, *China Solo.*

25. "Overpricing: China Learns to Exploit."

26. *Christian Science Monitor,* March 19, 1987.

27. Interviews with travel industry officials in the People's Republic of China, December 1981.

28. Interview with Kent Weideman, Diplomat-in-Residence, East-West Center, November 1984.

29. John Bryden, *Tourism and Development: A Case Study of the Commonwealth Caribbean.*

30. Simon Leys, *Chinese Shadows,* p. 3.

31. Jill Hunt, "Tourism: Competition Comes to the Industry," p. 99. See also Nai-tao Wu, "Tibet Opens to the Outside World."

32. *Christian Science Monitor,* March 19, 1987.

33. Roy C. Buck, "The Ubiquitous Tourist Brochure."

34. Fox Butterfield, *China, Alive in the Bitter Sea,* pp. 12–13.

35. Ibid., p. 24.

36. Ibid.

37. Leys, *Chinese Shadows,* p. 1.

38. Gao and Zhang, "China's Tourism."

39. Donald H. Graham, "Doing Business in the People's Republic of China," a speech presented at the Harvard Business School 16th Continuing Education Seminar, Nevada, 1980.

40. Dexter J. L. Choy and Chuck Y. Gee, "Tourism in the PRC—Five Years After China Opens its Gates."

41. "Tourism: A Review." By 1986 both such figures were available, although the net earnings were not available and raw foreign exchange earnings still rough. See Bailey and Hunt, "China National Report No. 117," p. 11.

42. Interviews conducted with Chinese tourism officials in Tianjin, December 1981.

43. Choy and Gee, "Tourism in the PRC—Five Years After China Opens its Gates."

44. Leys, *Chinese Shadows,* p. 4.

45. "China Still Seeks Improvements."

46. Gao and Zhang, "China's Tourism."

47. Ze-yu Zhang, "China's Growing Tourist Industry."

48. De Keijzer and Kaplan, *China Guidebook,* p. 154.

49. *China International Tourism Conference Souvenir Book.*

50. "China," *Travel Age West,* September 7, 1981.

51. Dean MacCannell, *The Tourist: A New Theory of the Leisure Class,* p. 85.

52. Dexter J. L. Choy, "Rejoinder to Linda K. Richter's Political Implications of Chinese Tourism Policy."

53. *Asiaweek,* August 21, 1981, pp. 32–33.

54. Julian Baum, "Chinese Policy: Open Door Inward," p. 17; Tie-Sheng Wang and Li-Cheng Ge, "Domestic Tourism Development in China: A Regression Analysis"; Adam Pilarski, "Notes on Domestic Tourism Development in China." See also Bailey and Hunt, "China, National Report No. 117," p. 15; "CITS Progress and Problems," p. 48.

55. Baum, "Open Door Inward." See also Guo-jian Han, "More Chinese Touring at Home."

56. De Keijzer and Kaplan, *China Guidebook,* p. 154.

57. Gao and Zhang, "China's Tourism."

58. *Asia Travel Trade,* January 1984, pp. 13–15.

59. Waters, *Travel Industry World Yearbook, 1986,* p. 10.

60. Ibid., p. 106.

61. Interview with Kent Weideman, Diplomat-in-Residence, East-West Center, November 1984.

62. Zhang, "China's Growing Tourist Industry."

63. Interview with China Holidays tour escort, December 1981.

64. *The Travel Agent.*

65. Far Eastern Economic Review, "China," *Asia Yearbook, 1979,* p. 174.

66. "China: The Second Time Around."

67. Ibid. See also Middleton, *China, A Seatrade Study,* p. 84.

68. Wayne Nafziger in a memo to me, August 4, 1987; Peter Van Ness, "Black, White and Grey," p. 30.

69. Butterfield, *Bitter Sea,* p. 281.

70. Ibid.

71. *China Daily,* October 22, 1984.

72. Chuck Y. Gee and Dexter J. L. Choy, "The First China International Travel Conference."

73. Wan Fu, "The Present Situation and Prospects of China's Tourism," a speech presented at the Kunming International Travel and Tourism Conference, November 25–28, 1981.

74. *Christian Science Monitor,* April 8 and November 14, 1983; *China Tourism,* July 1983; "CITS Progress and Problems," p. 48.

75. Ke-hua Han, "Chinese-Style Tourism." By late 1984 Chinese-style tourism included a floating casino, a Club Med, and a campaign against chopsticks as being unhygenic. *Honolulu Advertiser,* December 24, 1984.

76. Gao and Zhang, "Report of the Third National Seminar on Tourist Economics," p. 153.

77. Ibid.

78. *China Daily,* October 22, 1984.

79. Gao and Zhang, "Report of the Third National Seminar on Tourist Economics," p. 153.

80. Ibid.

81. Ibid., p. 155.

82. *Keesings' Contemporary Archives.*

83. David Bonavia, "China '80," pp. 48, 55.

84. Gao and Zhang, "Report of the Third National Seminar on Tourist Economics," p. 154; Wayne Nafziger, memo to me, August 4, 1987.

85. Waters, *Travel Industry World Yearbook, 1986,* p. 105.

86. "Turning to Training," *Asia Travel Trade,* April 1984.

87. Waters, *Travel Industry World Yearbook, 1986,* p. 106.

88. "Turning to Training," p. 19.

89. Ibid.

90. Linda K. Richter, *Land Reform and Tourism Development: Policy-Making in the Philippines;* Harry Matthews, *International Tourism, A Political and Social Analysis.*

91. Interview with Kent Weideman, Diplomat-in-Residence, East-West Center, November 1984. Prices have continued to rise sharply in the mid-1980s.

92. Philip Frick McKean, "Towards a New Theoretical Analysis of Tourism: Economic Dualism and Cultural Innovation in Bali"; Margaret Byrne Swain, "Cuna Women and Ethnic Tourism: A Way to Persist and an Avenue to Change."

93. Richard Wolters, "China Laying the Groundwork for a New Style of

Tourism." In fact even "class" as a term is retained in distinctions among levels of comfort on boats and planes.

94. A point made throughout Fox Butterfield's book, *China, Alive in the Bitter Sea.*

95. Leys, *Chinese Shadows,* pp. 19–20. Though Leys was writing of tourism in the PRC in the early seventies, his comments remain generally valid today.

96. Butterfield, *Bitter Sea,* p. 31.

97. Dennison Nash, "Tourism as a Form of Imperialism."

98. Bonavia, "China '80," p. 50.

99. Twenty Authors From Abroad, *Living in China.*

100. Leys, *Chinese Shadows,* p. 91.

101. Molly Schuchat, "State Tourism in China and the U.S.A."

102. Noel Kent, "Tourism, A New Kind of Sugar"; Linda K. Richter, "Tourism and Political Science: A Case of Not So Benign Neglect."

103. Leys, *Chinese Shadows,* p. 8.

104. Far Eastern Economic Review, "China," *Asia Yearbook, 1980,* p. 163.

105. The Japanese are also the most numerous group. Somerset R. Waters, *Travel Industry World Yearbook: The Big Picture, 1984.*

106. Derek Davies, "Traveler's Tale."

107. Ibid.

108. Lowell Dittmer, "China in 1981: Reform, Readjustment, Rectification"; Takashi Oka, "Peking Attempts to Allay Taiwan's Fears of Being Gobbled Up."

109. Bailey and Hunt, "China, National Report No. 117," pp. 11–12.

CHAPTER 3

1. This chapter is a revised, updated, but very abridged composite of several studies I have done on Philippine tourism. For more detailed political analysis of tourism organizations and their administrature milieu, see my book, *Land Reform and Tourism Development: Policy-Making in the Philippines.* My article, "The Political Uses of Tourism: A Philippine Case Study," examines at greater length the political needs of the Marcos regime served by tourism. This chapter is based on 138 interviews and other research done in the Philippines in 1976 and 1977, while I was on a Fulbright Research grant. During that time I was a Visiting Research Associate of the University of the Philippines, College of Public Administration. In 1987 more interviews were conducted at the Department of Tourism and among interest groups affected by tourism policy.

2. Reagan, as governor of California, had been a friend of the Marcos' since the opening of the Philippine Cultural Center in Manila in the early 1970s. The First Couple had invited many celebrities but Governor Reagan was the only prominent American politician to accept, perhaps as a way of bolstering his presidential ambitions with foreign contacts. It would be over a decade before he realized that such notorious friends were a political liability.

3. See Carl Lande, ed., *Rebuilding a Nation: Philippine Challenges and American Policy.*

4. Leticia Magsanoc, "The View from the Tourist Belt."

5. Carl Lande, *Leadership, Factions and Parties: The Structure of Philippine Politics.*

6. Jose Aspiras, "Tourism in 1973 . . . A Success All the Way."

7. Oriol Pi-Sunyer, "The Politics of Tourism in Catalonia," p. 61.

8. The Department of Tourism became the Ministry of Tourism in 1978 after the president had developed his own martial law variant of a parliamentary system. Its internal dynamics and leadership were not changed by the terminology any more than martial law was affected by parliamentary labels. The labels reverted to department and secretary following the ratification of the 1986 Constitution. In discussing the tourism body the term "department" will be used, and "secretary" will be used to designate its head throughout the chapter.

9. Interview with Undersecretary of Tourism, Gregorio Araneta, June 8, 1977.

10. Bernard Wideman, "Overbuilt, Underbooked."

11. Macrina Leuterio Ilustre, "Metro Manila Opens Its Arms to the World's Top Financiers."

12. Wideman, "Overbuilt, Underbooked."

13. Department of Tourism, *Accomplishment Report, 1976,* p. 38.

14. *Asia Travel Trade,* October 1976, p. 65.

15. *Bulletin Today,* September 6, 1983, p. 19.

16. *Bulletin Today,* September 9, 1983, p. 19.

17. Interviews with hoteliers, November 1976–July 1977. See also Presidential Decree No. 867 and *Asia Travel Trade,* March 1983, p. 34.

18. *Asia Travel Trade,* October 1976, pp. 50–51.

19. Department of Tourism, *Accomplishment Report, 1976,* p. 14.

20. Confidential interviews in Manila, January 1977.

21. Primitivo Mijares, *The Conjugal Dictatorship of Ferdinand and Imelda Marcos,* pp. 120–121.

22. Linda K. Richter, "Philippine Policies Toward Filipino Americans."

23. Department of Tourism, "Invitation to a Traditional Philippine Christmas."

24. Interview with Vic Portugal, Research and Statistics Division, June 1977.

25. Commentary by Teodoro Valencia, *Filipino Reporter,* March 13–19, 1981, p. 12. The *Filipino Reporter* was a pro-Marcos paper published in New York.

26. Interview with Vic Portugal, June 1977.

27. Department of Tourism, *Accomplishment Report, 1976,* pp. 42–43.

28. *Manila Journal,* July 23–29, 1978.

29. Official, Philippine Consulate in Hawaii, October 29, 1984.

30. Presidential Letter of Instruction, No. 331, October 29, 1975.

31. *Times Journal* (Manila), January 10, 1977; "The Number 1 Market," *Far Eastern Economic Review,* January 2, 1977, pp. 42–44; *Datafil,* 16–30 November 1976, p. 1931, reports tourist arrivals from ASEAN region were up 98 percent over 1975.

32. *Bulletin Today,* March 14, 1977.

33. Interview with mayor of Manila, Ramon Bagatsing, May 26, 1977.

34. Confidential interviews March–June 1977.

35. Ibid.

36. Interview, June 1977. I was most fortunate to have been included in planning sessions during the two months before the PACOM conference and I was an observer throughout the meeting.

37. Rodney Tasker, "Campus Confrontation."

38. Judy Bredemeier, "Convening Where Asia Wears A Smile," p. 27.

39. Robert E. Wood, "Ethnic Tourism, the State, and Cultural Change in Southeast Asia," p. 371.

40. *International Tourism Quarterly,* No. 4, 1982, p. 11.

41. *Asia Travel Trade,* May 1984, p. 39.

42. *Bulletin Today,* May 26, 1982.

43. *Honolulu Star-Bulletin,* November 12, 1984, section A-9.

44. Linda K. Richter, "The Philippines," in *Colliers Encyclopedia Yearbook 1984.* The communists are also finding the rampant prostitution associated with tourism to be a major irritant to exploit. See also Francisco Nemenzo, "Rectification Process in the Philippine Communist Movement."

45. *Fookien Times Yearbook, 1976,* p. 6.

46. Interview with personnel of *Bulletin Today,* February 1977.

47. Rodney Tasker, "Journalist Vindicated."

48. Department of Tourism, *Accomplishment Report, 1973–1975,* p. 4.

49. Interviews. See also the recommendations in William L. Thomas, "Progressive Rather than Centralized Tourism: A Recommendation for Improving International Tourism in the Philippines."

50. Department of Tourism Planning Service, *The Tourism Investments Priorities Plan, 1977–1981, Final Revision.*

51. *Bulletin Today,* December 2, 1976.

52. Interview with Gregorio Araneta, June 8, 1977.

53. Interviews in La Union and Agoo in May 1977.

54. Araneta contends that his non-Ilocano background worked against him and for Aspiras in the selection of a Secretary of Tourism. Interview, June 1977; see also "The Wedding of the Year."

55. Interviews with Araneta and the personnel managers of the Department of Tourism and the Philippine Tourism Authority, 1977.

56. I read all their resources in two days, but often just read other things in there just to see if there was some function assigned to them I had missed. There was not.

57. Interview with Marawi City Tourism Coordinator Mitz Ramusen, May 1977.

58. See Linda K. Richter, *Land Reform and Tourism Development.*

59. Ibid.

60. Interview with Colonel Cacdac, General Manager of the Philippine Tourism Authority, June 7, 1977.

61. Department of Tourism, *Accomplishment Report, 1976,* pp. 6–7.

62. *Business Day* (Manila), September 20, 1977, p. 2.

63. Department of Tourism, *Accomplishment Report, 1976,* p. 21.

64. For background on the government's corporativism policy see Robert Stauffer, "Philippine Corporativism: A Note on the New Society."

65. Interview with Dr. Eryl Buan, Associate Dean of the Asian Institute of Tourism, January 18, 1977.

66. Interview with an official working with tourism policy in the National Economic Development Authority (NEDA).

67. Interview with hotel manager, 1977.

68. There was some controversy about whether highway personnel and machinery were used to build the lengthy driveway for the Mayan Imperial. Wideman, "Overbuilt, Underbooked"; and various interviews in Manila, June 1977. By 1987 other scandals had emerged concerning the hotel.

69. *Business Day,* May 26, 1977, p. 1.

70. *Stars and Stripes,* November 26, 1977.

71. Orlando Sacay, *Samahang Nayon,* p. 63.

72. Matt Miller, "Will PAL Remain National Airlines?"

73. *Pacific Travel News,* February 1974. See also *Bulletin Today,* December 30, 1973, p. 6.

74. *Asia Travel Trade,* January 1977.

75. *Bulletin Today,* August 6, 1977, p. 17. See also *Manila Journal,* September 4–10, 1977.

76. *Business Day,* July 13, 1977, p. 1.

77. *Bulletin Today,* July 15, 1977.

78. Miller, "Will PAL Remain National Airlines?," p. 10.

79. *Manila Journal,* January 22–29, 1979.

80. *Asia Travel Trade,* May 1984, p. 11.

81. Mijares, *Conjugal Dictatorship,* pp. 200–202.

82. Orlando Mercado in a speech at the East-West Center, Honolulu, October 26, 1984.

83. *Newsweek,* July 13, 1981.

84. *Asia Travel Trade,* March 1983, p. 34.

85. Linda K. Richter, "Tourism by Decree."

86. *Contours,* Vol. 1, No. 4, 1983.

87. Ralph Waldo Emerson, "Essay on Self-Reliance," p. 70; Linda K. Richter, "The Hobgoblin Factor in International Tourism."

88. Harry G. Matthews, *International Tourism, A Political and Social Analysis.*

89. Richter, "Tourism By Decree."

90. James Barber, *The Presidential Character.*

91. Interview with Undersecretary of Tourism Narzalina Lim, February 2, 1987.

92. Ibid.

93. Ibid.

94. Ibid.

95. Margot J. Baterina, "Promoting Tourism on a Small Budget."

96. Interview with Undersecretary of Tourism Narzalina Lim, February 2, 1987.

97. Baterina, "Promoting Tourism."

98. Interview with Undersecretary of Tourism Narzalina Lim, February 2, 1987.

99. Interview with Director of Malacañang Palace, February 5, 1987.

100. Personal observation, January 1987; see Belinda A. Aquino, *The Politics of Plunder,* for an excellent analysis of the dynamics and techniques by which President Marcos amassed his illegal Philippine fortune.

101. Tourism brochures.

102. Interview with Undersecretary of Tourism Narzalina Lim, February 2, 1987.

103. *Philippine News,* May 1987.

104. *Philippine Panorama,* May 24, 1987.

105. Baterina, "Promoting Tourism," p. 16.

106. Interview with Undersecretary of Tourism Narzalina Lim, February 2, 1987.

107. Baterina, "Promoting Tourism," p. 16.

108. Claude A. Buss, *Cory Aquino and the People of the Philippines.*

CHAPTER 4

1. James Elliott, "Politics, Power, and Tourism in Thailand," p. 381.

2. See especially William J. Siffin's classic study, *The Thai Bureaucracy: Institutional Change and Development;* and Fred W. Riggs' impressive work, *Thailand: The Modernization of a Bureaucratic Policy.*

3. John Girling, "Thailand in Gramscian Perspective," pp. 394–395.

4. Somerset R. Waters, *Travel Industry World Yearbook: The Big Picture, 1986,* Vol. 30, p. 103; "Thailand: Boomtime in Bangkok."

5. Tourism Authority of Thailand, *Annual Statistical Report on Tourism in Thailand, 1983,* pp. 17, 23; Somerset R. Waters, "Thailand," in *Travel Industry World Yearbook: The Big Picture, 1983,* Vol. 27, p. 99.

6. "Thailand: Boomtime in Bangkok," p. 18.

7. Elliott, "Politics, Power, and Tourism in Thailand," p. 381.

8. Tourism Authority of Thailand, *Annual Report, 1983,* p. 23.

9. Elliott, "Politics, Power, and Tourism in Thailand," p. 381.

10. "Thailand, Sex as a Travel Motivator," p. 49.

11. Ibid.

12. Tourism Authority of Thailand, *Annual Statistical Report on Tourism in Thailand, 1983.*

13. *Asia Travel Trade,* June 1983, p. 49.

14. Duangkamol Chansuriyawong, *Alternative World* (Bangkok).

15. Tourism Authority of Thailand, *Annual Statistical Report on Tourism in Thailand, 1983,* p. 59.

16. Chansuriyawong, *Alternative World* (Bangkok).

17. "Relying on Everyone Else."

18. "Thailand: Market Probe," 1983, p. 51.

19. Elliott, "Politics, Power, and Tourism in Thailand," p. 385.

20. Ibid., pp. 385–386. See also Fred Riggs, *Thailand.*

21. "Relying on Everyone Else," p. MP27. See also William J. Siffin, "The Essential Character of the Contemporary Bureaucracy."

22. Tourism Authority of Thailand, *Annual Report, 1983,* p. 11.

23. Ibid.

24. Ibid.

25. Ibid.

26. Suchitra Punyaratabandu-Bhakdi, "Thailand in 1983."

27. "Thailand: Market Probe," 1980; "Thailand: Boomtime in Bangkok," p. 18.

28. Tourism Authority of Thailand, *Annual Report, 1983,* p. 23.

29. Waters, "Thailand," in *Travel Industry World Yearbook 1980–81: The Big Picture,* p. 109.

30. Tourism Authority of Thailand, *Annual Report, 1983.*

31. Ibid., pp. 31–32.

32. Elliott, "Politics, Power, and Tourism in Thailand," p. 386.

33. "Sex Tourism to Thailand."

34. Tourism Authority of Thailand, *Annual Report, 1983.*

35. "Thailand: Tripling the Tourist Police," p. 49.

36. Tourism Authority of Thailand, *Annual Report, 1983.*

37. *International Tourism Quarterly,* No. 2, 1984, p. 23.

38. Ralph Wahnschafft, "Formal and Informal Tourism Sectors: A Case Study in Pattaya, Thailand," p. 431.

39. *International Tourism Quarterly,* No. 2, 1984, p. 14.

40. Tourism Authority of Thailand, *Annual Report, 1983,* p. 10.

41. "Thailand: Market Probe," 1980.

42. *International Tourism Quarterly,* No. 2, 1984, p. 23.

43. Ibid.; *International Tourism Quarterly,* No. 2, 1980.

44. Robert E. Wood, "The Economics of Tourism," p. 8.

45. Brewster Grace, *A Note on Thailand,* p. 5.

46. Centre on Transnational Corporations, *Transnational Corporations in International Tourism,* p. 84.

47. Tourism Authority of Thailand, *Annual Report, 1983.*

48. Erik Cohen, "Marginal Paradises: Bungalow Tourism on the Islands of Southern Thailand."

49. Erik Cohen, "Jungle Guides in Northern Thailand." My own experience among the tribal villages of Northern Thailand supports Cohen's analysis.

50. Truong Thanh-Dam, "The Dynamics of Sex Tourism: The Case of Southeast Asia."

51. "Where They Don't Lock up Their Daughters."

52. Marjorie A. Muecke, "Make Money not Babies: Changing Status Markers of Northern Thai Women."

53. Ibid.

54. Ibid.

55. Erik Cohen, "Thai Girls and Farang Men: The Edge of Ambiguity."

56. "Sex Tourism to Thailand."

57. Underground film made in Thailand called *Business in Bodies.*

58. "Thailand: Market Probe," 1983, p. 1.

59. *Asia Travel Trade,* May 1982, p. 46.

60. "Sex Tourism to Thailand."

61. "Thailand: Market Probe," October 1981, p. MP3.

62. "Thailand: Market Probe," August 28, 1981, p. 20.

63. Ibid.

64. Cohen, "Thai Girls and Farang Men."

65. "Thailand: Boomtime in Bangkok," pp. 17–18.

CHAPTER 5

1. The Aitareya Brahmana as quoted in Tej Vir Singh, *Tourism and the Tourist Industry.*

2. R. P. Naik, "Role of Government in Tourism," p. 29.

3. "Does India Have to be Sold?"

4. Interview with Jerry Panzo, Public Relations Director of Hawaii Visitors Bureau, September 1984.

5. George Young, *Tourism: Blessing or Blight?*, p. 173.

6. Speech by Toufique Siddiqi, East-West Center, Honolulu, September 18, 1984.

7. Linda K. Richter and William L. Richter, "Policy Choices in South Asian Tourism Development."

8. Linda K. Richter, *Land Reform and Tourism Development: Policy-Making in the Philippines.*

9. Somerset R. Waters, *Travel Industry World Yearbook: The Big Picture, 1984,* pp. 98–99.

10. M. M. Anand, *Tourism and the Hotel Industry in India: A Study in Management.* It should be noted that since 1981 travel between India and Pakistan has increased as both countries have sought to encourage a normalization of their relations with each other.

11. Sudhir H. Kale and Katherine M. Weir, "Marketing Third World Countries to the Western Traveler," p. 4.

12. Waters, *Travel Industry World Yearbook, 1986,* p. 101.

13. Tord Hoivik and Turid Heiberg, "Centre-Periphery Tourism and Self-Reliance."

14. See Harold Isaacs, *Scratches on Our Minds: American Images of China and India.*

15. Anand, *Tourism and the Hotel Industry in India,* p. 52.

16. Kale and Weir, "Marketing Third World Countries to the Western Traveler," pp. 2–4.

17. Anand, *Tourism and the Hotel Industry in India,* pp. 51–52.

18. Ibid., pp. 52–53.

19. W. D. Patterson, quoted in Anand, *Tourism and the Hotel Industry in India,* p. 25.

20. Robert Hardgrave, "India."

21. *U.S. News and World Report,* December 3, 1984, p. 45.

22. Government of India Planning Commission, "Draft Five Year Plan 1978–1983," pp. 215–216.

23. R. K. Raju, "The Year of a Million Tourists," pp. 4–5.

24. Waters, *Travel Industry World Yearbook, 1986,* pp. 98–99.

25. Kale and Weir, "Marketing Third World Countries to the Western Traveler," p. 5.

26. Madhoo Pavaskar, "Employment Effects of Tourism and the Indian Experience," is the most conservative estimate, while figures in Sheila Kumar, "Tourism: Boon or Bane?," are the most optimistic; B. R. S. Gupte, "Tourism, a Multi-dimensional Industry," p. 23.

27. Pavaskar, "Employment Effects of Tourism," p. 36.

28. U.S. General Accounting Office, "Funding Constraints Require A New Approach to Support Tourism Information for Foreign Visitors," p. 5; Ilkka A. Ron Kainen and Richard J. Fararo, "United States Travel and Tourism Policy."

29. Linda K. Richter, "State-Sponsored Tourism Development: A Growth Area for Public Administration."

30. A. K. Bhatia, *Tourism in India*, pp. 47–48.

31. Ibid., pp. 84–90. The Ministry of Tourism and Civil Aviation also appoints a tourism astrologer, presumably as backup for the Planning Office. *India's Who's Who 1984.*

32. Bhatia, *Tourism in India*, pp. 53, 70.

33. Ibid., p. 53.

34. "Tourism Haryana."

35. Tej Vir Singh, "On Planning Towns, Tourism, and Environment."

36. *Eastern Economist*, May 12, 1978, p. 930.

37. Ibid.

38. Richter and Richter, "Policy Choices."

39. Waters, *Travel Industry World Yearbook, 1986*, p. 101.

40. Raju, "The Year of A Million Tourists," p. 5.

41. Ibid.

42. Ibid.

43. "Strong Growth But Problems Remain," p. 38.

44. Centre on Transnational Corporations, *Transnational Corporations in International Tourism*, p. 63.

45. Ibid.; Bhatia, *Tourism in India*, pp. 133–134.

46. *Eastern Economist*, May 12, 1978, p. 930.

47. *Eastern Economist*, October 19, 1979, p. 801.

48. Naik, "Role of Government in Tourism."

49. *The Travel Agent*, January 8, 1981, p. 2.

50. Waters, *Travel Industry World Yearbook: The Big Picture, 1984*, pp. 98–99.

51. Anand, *Tourism and the Hotel Industry in India*, p. 36.

52. Selig Harrison, *India: The Most Dangerous Decades*.

53. Bhatia, *Tourism in India*, p. 81.

54. Pavaskar, "Employment Effects of Tourism."

55. "Product Update South Asia," p. S1.

56. *Asia Travel Trade*, July 1980.

57. *Indian Tourist*, April 1971, pp. 6–7.

58. Ibid.

59. Centre on Transnational Corporations, *Transnational Corporations in International Tourism*.

60. Ibid.

61. Richter and Richter, "Policy Choices."

62. Anand, *Tourism and the Hotel Industry in India,* p. 182.

63. Ibid., p. 189.

64. Ibid.

65. Ibid., p. 190.

66. *Asia Travel Trade,* May 1979, p. MP-2. In 1986 several of these offices were closed. *Asia Travel Trade,* October 1986, p. 40.

67. "India: Market Probe," p. MP16.

68. *International Tourism Quarterly,* No. 4, 1981, p. 10; *International Tourism Quarterly,* No. 2, 1980.

69. *Indian Express,* 1979.

70. *Indian Express,* April 25, 1981.

71. *Indian Express,* October 30, 1982.

72. Tragic exceptions have also included land grabs for tourism development in Goa and Orissa. See "The TATA Land Grab at Candolim"; and "Update on Goa."

73. *Travel Age West,* 1981, p. 14; *Times of India,* July 18, 1981.

74. Clayton Jones, "India's Plan to Expand Tourism Looks Beyond Pilgrimage Tradition," p. 6.

75. Govind Hari Singhania, "Workshop on Tourism."

76. *Travel Age West,* 1981, p. 14.

77. Sharat G. Lin and Nageshwar Patnaik, "Migrant Labor at Asiad '82 Construction Sites in New Delhi."

78. Ajit Bhattacharjea, "A Poignant Month."

79. Hugh Gantzer and Colleen Gantzer, "The Asiad Hotel Bubble." Hotel occupancies had fallen as low as 10 percent at some new luxury hotels even before the assassination of Indira Gandhi and the Bhopal tragedy cut arrivals still lower. Kumar, "Tourism: Boon or Bane," p. 72.

80. "World Business."

81. Linda K. Richter, "The Hobgoblin Factor in International Tourism"; Government of India, Department of Tourism, "Foreign Tourist Survey, 1976–1977," p. iii.

82. *Indian Express,* October 21, 1982, p. 6.

83. *Indian Express,* October 30, 1982.

84. Interview with N. C. Krishan, President of the Indo-American Chamber of Commerce, November 5, 1984.

85. R. Srinivasan, "Computers in India." Speech delivered at the East-West Center, October 25, 1984.

86. Jean Dickinson Gibbons and Mary Fish, "Changing Economic Roles of India's International Visitors."

87. Hugh Gantzer and Colleen Gantzer, "Managing Tourists and Politicians in India."

88. Ibid., p. 118.

89. Centre on Transnational Corporations, *Transnational Corporations in International Tourism,* p. 63.

90. Tej Vir Singh and Jagdish Kaur, "Tourism in the Himalayas."

91. Gantzer and Gantzer, "Managing Tourists."

92. Ibid., p. 125.

93. Ibid., p. 119.

94. Ibid., p. 120.

95. *Asian Recorder,* Vol. 28, No. 14, April 2–8, 1982, p. 16536.

96. Gantzer and Gantzer, "Managing Tourists," p. 122.

Chapter 6

1. *Pakistan Observer,* August 11, 1965.

2. K. A. Hussain, *Seminar on Parks and Playgrounds for National Development,* p. 1.

3. *Pakistan Affairs* 34, No. 9, May 1, 1981, p. 2.

4. Pakistan Department of Tourism, *Annual Report, 1969,* p. 6.

5. United Nations Development Project, *Tourism in Pakistan,* p. 163.

6. Waheed-uz-Zaman, ed., *The Quest for Identity.*

7. "They Still Don't Know Pakistan?"

8. William L. Richter, "The Political Dynamics of Islamic Resurgence in Pakistan."

9. Rafique Akhtar, *Pakistan Yearbook, 1976,* p. 108; interview with Jameel Khan, Deputy Secretary of Tourism, Islamabad, August 15, 1977.

10. *Pakistan Times,* August 31, 1977.

11. *White Paper on the Performance of the Bhutto Regime,* p. 175.

12. Interviews with both American and Pakistani tourism officials, Islamabad, Pakistan, August 1977.

13. Interview with Fuad Butt, July 29, 1977.

14. Interviews with Pakistani travel agents, tourism officials, and hotel operators, 1977.

15. *Pakistan Times,* September 23, 1973.

16. United Nations Development Project, *Tourism in Pakistan,* vol. 1.

17. Ibid., p. 14.

18. Linda K. Richter, "The Impact of Regime Change on Women in Pakistan and Afghanistan." Paper given at the Midwest Political Science Association Meeting in Cincinnati, April 1981.

19. *Pakistan Times,* August 31, 1977.

20. Interviews with Lahore hotel managers, 1977.

21. *Asia,* October 1982.

22. United Nations Development Project, *Tourism in Pakistan,* vol. 1, p. 259.

23. Interview with Mrs. Walji, owner of Pakistan's largest private tour operation, 1977.

24. William L. Richter, "Persistent Praetorianism: Pakistan's Third Military Regime."

25. *Dawn,* November 27, 1980.

26. Interviews with members of Pakistan's Hotel and Restaurant Association, October 1977.

27. V. P. Menon, *The Transfer of Power in India.*

28. United Nations Development Project, *Guidelines for Development,* vol. 2, p. 189.

29. *Pakistan Times,* July 1, 1972.

30. *Tourist World,* Vol. 3, No. 3, March 1963, pp. 39–40; *Pakistan Times,* December 1973.

31. *Pakistan Times,* February 19, 1962.

32. *Dawn,* January 31, 1964.

33. United Nations Development Project, *Program of Action for Development, Tourism in Pakistan,* Vol. 3, p. 15.

34. *Pakistan Times,* September 26, 1974.

35. Impressions from interviewing nearly a dozen middle-range officials in the central and regional tourism offices, 1977.

36. *Pakistan Times,* October 20, 1975.

37. *Pacific Travel,* April 1977.

38. *Viewpoint,* July 29, 1977, p. 13.

39. Interview with Mrs. Walji, 1977.

40. Interview with M. D. Saeed Qureshi, Managing Director of the PTDC, Karachi, 1977.

41. *Viewpoint,* July 29, 1977, p. 13.

42. *Pakistan Times,* April 14, 1970.

43. *Dawn,* October 11, 1977.

44. Somerset R. Waters, *Travel Industry World Yearbook: The Big Picture, 1983,* p. 99; "Pakistan: Handling a Visitor Decline."

45. "New Policy to Promote Domestic Tourism"; *Dawn,* October 11, 1984.

46. *Pacific Travel News,* March 1984.

47. *Holiday,* November 20–November 26, 1982.

48. *Dawn,* November 15, 1982; Masud Nabi Nur, "Tourism Prospects in Pakistan."

49. *Pacific Travel News,* March 1984.

50. Linda K. Richter, "The Potential and Pitfalls of Tourism Planning in Third World Nations: Case of Pakistan."

51. Niaz Mir, "The Second Singapore-to-Be."

52. Somerset R. Waters, *Travel Industry World Yearbook: The Big Picture, 1986,* pp. 101–102.

53. Dean MacCannell, *The Tourist: A New Theory of the Leisure Class.*

54. Begum Viqar-un-Nisa Noon, "Tourism: The First Task."

55. Raguib Siddiqui, "Undiscovered Bangladesh."

56. *Pacific Travel News,* March 1984, p. 74.

57. *Dacca Times,* May 27, 1965.

58. "Bangladesh: Market Probe," p. MP17.

59. Raguib Siddiqui, "Flying without Fuel."

60. Raguib Siddiqui, "Burdened with Overgrowth."

61. *Aviatour,* July 30, 1983.

62. Ross Coggins, "The Development Set," n.p., n.d.

63. "Bangladesh: Market Probe," p. MP17. Pattaya, Thailand is notorious for unbridled growth and prostitution.

64. Ibid., p. 18.

65. *Bangladesh,* Vol. 2, No. 13, January 15, 1979, p. 2.

66. *Aviatour,* July 30, 1983, p. 5.

67. *Dacca Times,* July 12, 1981; *Pacific Travel News,* March 1984, p. 74.

68. Aaron Wildavsky and Naomi Caiden, *Planning and Budgeting in Poor Countries.*

69. *Aviatour,* April 30, 1983.

70. Ibid.

71. Linda K. Richter, "State-Sponsored Tourism Development: A Growth Area for Public Administration."

CHAPTER 7

1. Nimalasiri Silva, "Policies and Programmes for Tourism," p. 9.

2. Ibid., p. 12.

3. *Pacific News,* January 27, 1984.

4. Susantha Goonatilake, *Tourism in Sri Lanka: The Mapping of International Inequalities and Their Internal Structure Effects.*

5. *International Tourism Quarterly,* No. 4, 1981, p. 12.

6. *The Travel Agent,* September 17, 1979.

7. *Pacific News,* January 27, 1984.

8. *Asia Travel Trade,* August 1977: Supplement, p. 2.

9. *Pacific Travel News,* March 1984: 42–48, 12–25.

10. *Pacific News,* January 27, 1984.

11. Silva, "Policies and Programmes," p. 15.

12. Ibid.

13. H. N. S. Karunatilake, "Foreign Exchange Earnings from Tourism," p. 27.

14. Goonatilake, *Tourism in Sri Lanka,* p. 13.

15. Ibid., p. 15.

16. Ibid., p. 24.

17. Ibid., p. 13.

18. Ibid., p. 21.

19. Interview with Maureen Seneviratne, Sri Lankan writer and tour developer, at Conference on Alternative Tourism, Chiang Mai, Thailand, April 29, 1984.

20. Karunatilake, "Foreign Exchange Earnings from Tourism," pp. 27–28.

21. A pioneering effort to alert tourists to the impact of their behavior and encourage them not to give to beggars has been a film produced in Germany for use on charter flights to Sri Lanka. It is one of a series of films designed to educate tourists on their effect in developing nations.

22. Selvy Thiruchandran, "Tourism at What Cost."

23. Shireen Samarasooruya, "Access to Income From Tourism for Women."

24. *Pacific Travel News,* March 1978, p. 42.

25. D. Radke, *Contribution of International Tourism to the Economic Development of Sri Lanka.*

26. "Product Update: Sri Lanka."

27. Noel Kent, "Tourism: A New Kind of Sugar"; Linda K. Richter, *Land Reform and Tourism Development: Policy-Making in the Philippines.*

28. *International Tourism Quarterly,* No. 4, 1983, pp. 14–15.

29. S. W. R. de A. Samarasinghe, "Sri Lanka in 1983: Ethnic Conflict and the Search for Solutions."

30. "Sri Lanka After the Riots."

31. Far Eastern Economic Review, November 27, 1981, p. 70.

32. "Sri Lanka After the Riots," p. 17; Far Eastern Economic Review, "Sri Lanka," *Asia Yearbook, 1987,* p. 247.

33. Goonatilake, *Tourism in Sri Lanka.*

34. Ceylon Tourist Board, "Come Share Our Way of Life." The government is, however, showing increased intolerance of criticism of the industry. *Business Traveler,* for example, was banned for mentioning Sri Lankan brothels. *Asia Travel Trade,* May 1984, p. 58.

35. Far Eastern Economic Review, "Maldives," *Asia Yearbook, 1980,* p. 244.

36. *International Tourism Quarterly,* No. 2, 1987, pp. 60, 70.

37. "Special Report on the Maldives, No. 45."

38. Far Eastern Economic Review, "Maldives," *Asia Yearbook, 1982.*

39. *International Tourism Quarterly,* No. 1, 1983, pp. 59–70.

40. Ibid., No. 2, 1987, p. 69.

41. Ibid., No. 1, 1983, p. 62.

42. Ibid.

43. Far Eastern Economic Review, "The Maldives," *Asia Yearbook, 1987,* p. 195.

44. *International Tourism Quarterly,* No. 2, 1987, pp. 57–71.

CHAPTER 8

1. Byrn Barnard, "Nepal Tourism." Dr. Rishikesh Shaha noted that the first blow to Nepali-Tibetan trade was the result of the British opening of a trade route in 1903–1904, which allowed Tibet to bypass Nepal and trade directly with India through Kalimpong.

2. "National Report No. 51, Nepal."

3. It was my pleasure to take this astounding road at that time. Tourists had a choice of rickety buses or gaily decorated but overcrowded trucks. The scenery was ample compensation for the truck ride, which took over 12 hours to cover the 125 miles of winding mountain roads.

4. F. F. Baumgartner et al., "Trekking-Tourism in Nepal."

5. "Nepal: Market Probe," 1980.

6. "Nepal."

7. *Asia Travel Trade,* October 1980.

8. Aaron Wildavsky, "Why Planning Fails in Nepal"; Aaron Wildavsky and Naomi Caiden, *Planning and Budgeting in Poor Countries.*

9. *Asia Travel Trade,* October 1980.

10. *International Tourism Quarterly,* No. 1, 1979, p. 39.

11. *Asia Travel Trade,* October 1980, p. 2.

12. Interview with Harka Gurung, former Nepal Minister of Tourism, Honolulu, December 19, 1984. See also Barbara Sturken, "The World Bank Well Runs Dry."

13. Dili Raj Uprety, "Mountain Tourism in Nepal," p. 40.

14. "Nepal."

15. *Pacific Travel News,* March 1984.

16. "Nepal: Market Probe," 1981.

17. *Pacific Travel News,* July 1980.

18. *International Tourism Quarterly,* No. 1, 1979, p. 37.

19. Shyan Bahadur, "Sharing the Tourist Dollar."

20. Interview with Harka Gurung, former Nepal Minister of Tourism, Honolulu, December 19, 1984.

21. *Pacific Travel News,* July 1980.

22. Shirley Fockler, "Nepal: Preserving the Past."

23. Interview with Deputy Mayor of Kathmandu, Mrs. Kanchen Mala Chalisey, October 17, 1984.

24. *Pacific Travel News,* March 1984.

25. Michael B. Wallace, "Managing Resources That Are Common Property: From Kathmandu to Capital Hill," p. 220.

26. Ibid., p. 222.

27. Imtiaz Muqbil, "The Trashing of the Road to Shangri-La," p. 8.

28. Ibid.

29. *Pacific Travel News,* July 1984, p. 56.

30. Muqbil, "Trashing the Road to Shangri-La," p. 8.

31. Penny Dawson and James Uhrig, "Trekker Medicine in Nepal," p. 6.

32. *Pacific Travel News,* July 1984, p. 56; "Nepal: Market Probe," 1981.

33. Interview with Mrs. Kanchen Mala Chalisey, Deputy Mayor of Kathmandu, October 17, 1984.

34. "Market Probe: Nepal," 1980, p. 19.

35. Far Eastern Economic Review, "Bhutan," *Asia Yearbook, 1982,* p. 119; interview with Harka Gurung, former Nepal Minister of Tourism, Honolulu, December 19, 1984.

36. V. H. Coelho, *Sikkim and Bhutan.*

37. Michael Kaufman, "Basketball is Big in Bhutan."

38. *Asia Travel Trade,* January 1984, p. 27; Far Eastern Economic Review, "Bhutan," *Asia Yearbook, 1982,* p. 119.

39. Far Eastern Economic Review, "Bhutan," *Asia Yearbook, 1982,* p. 119.

40. Far Eastern Economic Review, "Bhutan," *Asia Yearbook, 1980,* pp. 142–143; interview with Harka Gurung, former Nepal Minister of Tourism, Honolulu, December 19, 1984.

41. Far Eastern Economic Review, "Bhutan," *Asia Yearbook, 1982,* p. 119.

CHAPTER 9

1. Meg Greenfield, *Newsweek,* July 15, 1985, last page.

2. Robert E. Wood, "International Tourism and Cultural Change in Southeast Asia," pp. 576–577.

3. PBS documentary, *World: Who Pays for Paradise?*

4. *Honolulu Star-Bulletin,* December 10, 1984.

5. Dean MacCannell, "Reconstructed Ethnicity: Tourism and Cultural Identity in Third World Communities."

6. Interview with Peter Holden, Executive Director of the Ecumenical Coalition on Third World Tourism, Honolulu, November 13, 1984.

7. Theodore B. Brameld, *Tourism as Cultural Learning.*

8. MacCannell, "Reconstructed Ethnicity," p. 385.

9. Interview with Manu Paul, Maori activist, Honolulu, November 12, 1984.

10. MacCannell, "Reconstructed Ethnicity," pp. 386–387.

11. Ibid., p. 388.

12. Wood, "International Tourism and Cultural Change," p. 565.

13. Ibid., p. 566.

14. Franz Fanon, *The Wretched of the Earth,* p. 180.

15. Talk given by Director Robert Hillmann about his film documentary, *Fire on the Water,* East-West Center, Honolulu, December 6, 1984.

16. This was illustrated at the Governor's Conference on Tourism, December 10 and 11, 1984. Most of those affected adversely by tourism were not among the 500 representatives voting, nor were they among the 3,000 invited. The agenda was also under the control of industry advocates and reflected the narrow discussion parameters they could tolerate. On many issues, like a proposed hotel tax or a contemplated convention center, only the industry view was advanced despite the appearance of balance in the titles of the speeches given.

17. *Contours,* Vol. 1, No. 3, 1983, pp. 6–7.

18. Cecil Rajendra, "When the Tourists Flew In."

19. Tej Vir Singh and Jagdish Kaur, *Studies in Tourism, Wildlife Parks and Conservation.* See also Max Preglau, "Tourism Kills Tourism: Environmental, Cultural, and Economic Consequences of Tourism."

20. Arthur Haulot, "Social Tourism: Current Dimensions and Future Developments."

21. Jafar Jafari, "Understanding the Structure of Tourism." See also Organization for Economic Cooperation and Development, *The Impact of Tourism on the Environment.*

22. Centre on Transnational Corporations, *Transnational Corporations in International Tourism,* p. 83.

23. Ibid.

24. Paul Chen-Young and Associates, *Transnationals and Tourism in the Caribbean,* p. 63.

25. Centre on Transnational Corporations, *Transnational Corporations in International Tourism,* p. 83.

26. Ibid., p. 61.

27. Ibid., p. 86.

28. World Tourism Organization, as quoted in *Contours,* Vol. 9, No. 3, p. 15.

29. Charles L. Geshekter, "International Tourism and African Development: Some Reflections on Kenya"; Patrick Schul and John L. Crompton, "Search Behavior of International Vacationers: Travel-Specific Lifestyle and Sociodemographic Variables."

30. Robert E. Wood, "Ethnic Tourism, the State and Cultural Change in Southeast Asia."

31. *International Tourism Quarterly,* No. 3, 1979, p. 9; Bryan H. Farrell, "Tourism's Human Conflicts: Cases From the Pacific."

32. H. Michael Erisman, "Tourism and Cultural Dependency in the West Indies."

33. Sharat G. Lin and Nageshwar Patnaik, "Migrant Labor at Asiad '82 Construction Sites in New Delhi."

34. Peter Holden, ed., *Report of the Workshop on Alternative Tourism with a Focus on Asia.*

35. Ibid., p. 6.

36. Ron O'Grady, ed., *Third World Tourism,* p. 3.

37. Ibid., pp. 3–4.

38. Ibid., pp. 31–35.

39. Holden, *Report of the Workshop on Alternative Tourism with a Focus on Asia.*

40. Ibid.

41. Ibid., p. 8.

42. Karen Cooke, "Guidelines for Socially Appropriate Tourism Development in British Columbia."

43. "Visions of Poverty, Visions of Wealth."

44. Ibid.

45. Community Interpretation and Tourism Seminar, September 12 and 14, 1984, Honolulu, Hawaii.

46. Arthur Frommer, *The New World of Travel, 1988,* pp. 6–13.

47. Mr. Colin Selley, Former Tourism Minister of Bermuda at Hawaii Governor's Conference on Tourism, December 11, 1984.

Bibliography

Books, Monographs, and Yearbooks

Akhtar, Rafique. *Pakistan Yearbook 1976*. Karachi: East and West Publishing Co., 1976.

Anand, M. M. *Tourism and the Hotel Industry in India, A Study in Management*. New Delhi: Prentice-Hall of India, 1976.

Aquino, Belinda A. *The Politics of Plunder: The Philippines Under Marcos*. Manila: Great Books Trading Co., 1987.

Ashford, Douglas. "The Structural Analysis of Policy or Institutions Really Do Matter." In *Comparing Public Policies: New Concepts and Methods,* edited by Douglas Ashford, 82. Beverly Hills: Sage, 1978.

Bangladesh. Vol. 2 (no. 13): 2 (January 15, 1979).

Barber, James. *The Presidential Character*. Englewood Cliffs, N.J.: Prentice-Hall, 1972.

Bhatia, A. K. *Tourism in India*. New Delhi: Sterling, 1978.

Bhoosan, B. S. *The Development Experience of Nepal*. Delhi: Concept Publishing Co., 1979.

Brameld, Theodore B. *Tourism as Cultural Learning*. Washington, D.C.: University Press of America, 1977.

Bryden, John. *Tourism and Development: A Case Study of the Commonwealth Caribbean*. Cambridge: Cambridge University Press, 1973.

Buss, Claude A. *Cory Aquino and the People of the Philippines*. Stanford, Ca.: Stanford Alumni Assoc., 1987.

Butterfield, Fox. *China, Alive in the Bitter Sea*. New York: Bantam Books, 1982.

Centre on Transnational Corporations. *Transnational Corporations in International Tourism*. New York: United Nations, 1982.

Chen-Young, Paul, and Associates. *Transnationals and Tourism in the Caribbean*. Jamaica, 1977.

China International Tourism Conference Souvenir Book. 1983.

Coelho, V. H. *Sikkim and Bhutan*. Delhi: Indian Council for Cultural Relations, 1967.

Cohen, Erik. "Hill Tribe Tourism." In *Highlanders of Thailand,* edited by John

McKinnon and Wanat Bhruksasri, 307–325. Kuala Lumpur: Oxford University Press, 1983.

Cook, Suzanne D. "Research in State and Provincial Tourist Offices." In *Travel, Tourism and Hospitality Research: A Handbook for Managers and Researchers,* edited by J. R. Brent Richie and Charles Goeldner, 157. New York: John Wiley & Sons, 1987.

Dahl, Robert Alan. *Who Governs? Democracy and Power in an American City.* New Haven: Yale University Press, 1986.

De Kadt, Emanuel, ed. *Tourism: Passport to Development?* New York: Oxford University Press, 1979.

De Keijzer, Arne J., and Frederic M. Kaplan. *China Guidebook 1980–1981.* New York: Eurasia Press, 1980.

De Silva, G. M. P. "Investment in Tourist Industry in Sri Lanka." In *The Role of Tourism in the Social and Economic Development of Sri Lanka,* edited by G. M. P. De Silva. Colombo: Social Science Research Centre, 12 August 1978.

Edgell, David L., Sr. "International Tourism and Travel." In *International Business Prospects, 1977–1999,* edited by Howard F. Van Zandt, 163–189. Indianapolis: Bobbs-Merrill, 1978.

———. *International Tourism Prospects, 1987–2000.* Washington, D.C.: U.S. Department of Commerce, U.S. Travel and Tourism Administration.

———. *International Trade in Tourism, A Manual for Managers and Executives.* Washington, D.C.: U.S. Department of Commerce, October 1985.

Edwards, Anthony. *International Tourism Development Forecasts to 1985.* London: The Economist Intelligence Unit Ltd., 1976.

Ellahie, S. Maqbool, ed. *Seminar on Parks and Playgrounds for National Development.* Islamabad, 1973.

Emerson, Ralph Waldo. "Essay on Self-Reliance (1841)." In *Harvard Classics.* Vol. 5, 70. New York: P. F. Collier & Son, 1909.

Enloe, Cynthia H. *The Politics of Pollution in a Comparative Perspective.* New York: David McKay Co., 1975.

Fanon, Franz. *The Wretched of the Earth.* New York: Grove Press, 1966.

Far Eastern Economic Review. "Bhutan." *Asia Yearbook, 1980.* Hong Kong: Far Eastern Economic Review, 1980.

———. "Bhutan." *Asia Yearbook, 1982.* Hong Kong: Far Eastern Economic Review, 1982.

———. "China." *Asia Yearbook, 1978.* Hong Kong: Far Eastern Economic Review, 1978.

———. "China." *Asia Yearbook, 1979.* Hong Kong: Far Eastern Economic Review, 1979.

———. "China." *Asia Yearbook, 1980.* Hong Kong: Far Eastern Economic Review, 1980.

———. "China." *Asia Yearbook, 1981.* Hong Kong: Far Eastern Economic Review, 1981.

———. "China." *Asia Yearbook, 1987.* Hong Kong: Far Eastern Economic Review, 1987.

———. "Maldives." *Asia Yearbook, 1980.* Hong Kong: Far Eastern Economic Review, 1980.

———. "Maldives." *Asia Yearbook, 1982.* Hong Kong: Far Eastern Economic Review, 1982.

———. "The Maldives." *Asia Yearbook, 1987.* Hong Kong: Far Eastern Economic Review, 1987.

———. "Nepal." *Asia Yearbook, 1980,* p. 251. Hong Kong: Far Eastern Economic Review, 1980.

———. "Nepal." *Asia Yearbook, 1982,* p. 209. Hong Kong: Far Eastern Economic Review, 1982.

———. "Sri Lanka." *Asia Yearbook, 1987.* Hong Kong: Far Eastern Economic Review, 1987.

———. "The Philippines." *Asia Yearbook, 1976.* Hong Kong: Far Eastern Economic Review, 1976.

Finney, Ben, and Karen Ann Watson. *A New Kind of Sugar: Tourism in the South Pacific.* Honolulu: East-West Center, 1976.

Fisher, Robert C., and Leslie Brown. *Fodor's People's Republic of China.* New York: David McKay Co., 1979.

Fodor. *India, Nepal, and Sri Lanka.* New York: Fodor Travel Guides, 1984.

Fookien Times Yearbook, 1976. Manila: Fookien Times Yearbook Publishing Co., 1976.

Fookien Times Yearbook, 1986. Manila: Fookien Times Yearbook Publishing Co., 1986.

Franda, Marcus. *Quiet Turbulence in the Seychelles. Part I: Tourism and Development.* American University Field Staff Reports No. 10, 1979.

———. *The Seychelles, Unquiet Islands.* Boulder: Westview, 1982.

Fraser, John. *The Chinese People.* New York: Summit Books, 1980.

Frommer, Arthur. *The New World of Travel, 1988.* New York: Prentice-Hall, 1988.

Geshekter, Charles L. "International Tourism and African Development: Some Reflections on Kenya." In *Tourism and Economic Change: Studies in Third World Societies,* edited by Mario Zamora, Vinson H. Sutlive, and Nathan Altschuler. Williamsburg, Va.: Department of Anthropology, College of William and Mary, 1978.

Godbey, Geoffrey. "Planning for Leisure in a Pluralistic Society." In *Recreation and Leisure: Issues in an Era of Change,* edited by T. L. Goodale, 165–177. State College, Pa.: Venture Publications, 1982.

Goonatilake, Susantha. *Tourism in Sri Lanka: The Mapping of International Inequalities and Their Internal Structure Effects.* No. 19. Colombo: People's Bank of Sri Lanka, January 1978.

Grace, Brewster. *A Note on Thailand.* American University Field Staff Reports, Southeast Asia Series, Vol. 22, No. 4, 1974.

Gray, Spalding. *Swimming to Cambodia.* New York: Theatre Communications Group, 1985.

Gurung, Harka. *Nepal: Dimensions of Development.* Kathmandu: Sahayogi Press, 1984.

Hanna, Willard A. *Tourism in Southeast Asia.* American University Field Staff Reports, Southeast Asia Series, Vol. 15, No. 13, December 1967.

Harrell-Bond, Barbara. *A Window on an Outside World: Tourism as Development in the Gambia.* American University Field Staff Reports, No. 19, 1978.

Harrison, Selig S. *In Afghanistan's Shadow: Baluch Nationalism and Soviet Temptations.* Washington, D.C.: Carnegie Endowment for International Peace, 1981.

———. *India: The Most Dangerous Decades.* Princeton, N.J.: Princeton University Press, 1960.

Henson, Edda. "World Tourism Organization in Asia and the Pacific." In *Fookien Times Yearbook, 1980,* 194–196. Manila: Fookien Times Yearbook Publishing Co., 1980.

Holden, Peter, ed. *Report of the Workshop on Alternative Tourism with a Focus on Asia.* Bangkok: Ecumenical Coalition on Third World Tourism, 1984.

Holloway, Christopher. *The Business of Tourism.* 2nd ed. London: Pitman, 1986.

Hussain, K. A. *Seminar on Parks and Playgrounds for National Development.* Islamabad, 1973.

India's Who's Who 1984. 1446–1456.

Issacs, Harold. *Scratches on Our Minds: American Images of China and India.* New York: J. Day Co., 1958.

Jafari, Jafar. "Understanding the Structure of Tourism." In *Tourism and Culture: A Comparative Perspective,* edited by Eddystone C. Nebel III, 67. New Orleans: University of New Orleans, 1983.

Judd, Dennis R. *The Politics of American Cities,* 3rd ed. Boston: Little, Brown, 1988.

Karunatilake, H. N. S. "Foreign Exchange Earnings from Tourism." In *The Role of Tourism in the Social and Economic Development of Sri Lanka.* Colombo: Social Science Research Centre, 12 August 1978.

Keesings' Contemporary Archives. March 13, 1981: 30771.

Kelly, John R. "Leisure and Quality: Beyond the Quantitative Barrier in Research." In *Recreation and Leisure: Issues in an Era of Change,* edited by T. L. Goodale. State College, Pa.: Venture Publications, 1982.

Kendall, K. W. and Turgut Var. *The Perceived Impacts of Tourism: The State of the Art.* Paper No. 6. Honolulu: Tourism Research Publications, 1984.

Kent, Noel. "Tourism, A New Kind of Sugar." In *A New Kind of Sugar: Tourism in the Pacific,* edited by Ben Finney and Karen Ann Watson, 169–198. Honolulu: East-West Center, 1976.

———. *Hawaii: Islands Under the Influence.* Monthly Review. 1984.

Kochanek, Stanley. *Business and Politics in Pakistan.* N.p., n.d.

Lamb, Charles W., and John R. Crompton. "Qualitative Measures of Program Success." In *Recreation and Leisure: Issues in an Era of Change,* edited by T. L. Goodale, 326–338. State College, Pa.: Venture Publications, 1982.

Lande, Carl H. *Leadership, Factions and Parties: The Structure of Philippine Politics.* Yale University, Southeast Asia Series, Monograph No. 6. New Haven, Conn.: Yale University, 1965.

Lande, Carl H., ed. *Rebuilding a Nation: Philippine Challenges and American Policy.* Washington, D.C.: Washington Institute, 1987.

Letson, Barbara. *China Solo.* Arlington, Va.: Jadetree Press, 1984.

Leys, Simon. *Chinese Shadows.* New York: Penguin, 1982.

Lieber, Stanley R., and Daniel R. Fesenmaier, eds. *Recreation Planning and Management.* State College, Pa.: Venture Publications, 1983.

MacCannell, Dean. *The Tourist: A New Theory of the Leisure Class.* New York: Schocken Books, 1976.

McKean, Philip Frick. "Towards a New Theoretical Analysis of Tourism: Economic Dualism and Cultural Innovation in Bali." In *Hosts and Guests: The Anthropology of Tourism,* edited by Valene L. Smith, 93–108. Oxford: Basil Blackwell, 1978.

Malloy, Ruth Lor. *Travel Guide to the People's Republic of China.* New York: William Morrow & Co., 1980.

Matthews, Harry G. *International Tourism, A Political and Social Analysis.* Cambridge, Mass.: Schenkman Publishing Co., 1978.

Menon, V. P. *The Transfer of Power in India.* Princeton, N.J.: Princeton University Press, 1957.

Middleton, Ian, ed. *China; A Seatrade Study.* Colchester, England: Seatrade Publishing, Ltd., 1979.

Mijares, Primitivo. *The Conjugal Dictatorship of Ferdinand and Imelda Marcos.* San Francisco: Union Square Publications, 1976.

Nash, Dennison. "Tourism as a Form of Imperialism." In *Hosts and Guests: The Anthropology of Tourism,* edited by Valene L. Smith, 33–48. Oxford: Basil Blackwood, 1978.

Nebel, Eddystone C., III, ed. *Tourism and Culture: A Comparative Perspective.* New Orleans: University of New Orleans, 1983.

Neher, Clark, ed. *Modern Thai Politics.* Cambridge, Mass.: Schenkman Publishing Co., 1976.

Nemenzo, Francisco. "Rectification Process in the Philippine Communist Movement." In *Armed Communist Movements in Southeast Asia,* edited by Lim Joo-Jock and S. Vani., 71–101. New York: St. Martin's Press, 1984.

1983 Philippines Statistical Yearbook. Manila: NEDA, 1983.

Nuñez, Theorn. "Touristic Studies in Anthropological Perspective." In *Hosts and Guests: The Anthropology of Tourism,* edited by Valene L. Smith, 207–216. Oxford: Basil Blackwood, 1978.

O'Grady, Ron, ed, *Third World Tourism.* Singapore: Christian Conference of Asia, 1980.

Olson, Mancur, *The Logic of Collective Action.* Cambridge: Harvard University Press, 1971.

Perera, Lakshimi. "Case Study: Hikkaduwa." In *The Role of Tourism in Social and Economic Development of Sri Lanka,* 47–56. Colombo: Social Science Research Centre, 12 August 1978.

Philippine Yearbook, 1983. Manila: NEDA, 1982.

Phongpaichit, Pasuk. *From Peasant Girls to Bangkok Masseuses.* Geneva: International Labor Organization, 1982.

Preglau, Max. "Tourism Kills Tourism: Environmental, Cultural, and Economic

Consequences of Tourism." In *Tourism and Culture: A Comparative Perspective,* edited by Eddystone C. Nebel III, 35–64. New Orleans: University of New Orleans, 1983.

Qadir, Abdul. *Development Directory of Pakistan.* Vol. 1. Karachi: Abdul Qadir, 1964.

Radke, D. *Contribution of International Tourism to the Economic Development of Sri Lanka.* Occasional Paper. Berlin: German Development Institute, 1975.

Reiter, Rayna Rapp. "The Politics of Tourism in a French Alpine Community." In *Hosts and Guests: The Anthropology of Tourism,* edited by Valene L. Smith, 139–147. Oxford: Basil Blackwood, 1978.

Richter, Linda K. *Land Reform and Tourism Development: Policy-Making in the Philippines.* Cambridge, Mass.: Schenkman Publishing Co., 1982.

———. "Philippines." In *Colliers Encyclopedia Yearbook 1984.* New York: MacMillan Educational Publishing Co., 1985.

———. "The Political Dimensions of Tourism." In *Travel, Tourism and Hospitality Research: A Handbook for Managers and Researchers,* edited by J. R. Brent Ritchie and Charles R. Goeldner, 215–229. New York: John Wiley & Sons, 1987.

Riggs, Fred W. *Thailand: The Modernization of a Bureaucratic Policy.* Honolulu: East-West Center Press, 1966.

The Role of Tourism in Social and Economic Development of Sri Lanka. Colombo: Social Science Research Centre, 12 August 1978.

Sacay, Orlando. *Samahang Nayon.* Manila: National Publishing, 1974.

Sarna, S. R., and S. P. Ahuja, eds. *Tourism in India: A Perspective to 1990.* New Delhi: The Institute of Economic and Market Research, 1978.

Seth, Pran Nath. *Successful Tourism Planning and Management.* New Delhi: Cross Section Publisher, 1978.

Shafer, Elwood L. "Policy Issues in Outdoor Recreation Research." In *Recreation and Leisure: Issues in an Era of Change,* edited by T. L. Goodale, 365–372. State College, Pa.: Venture Publications, 1982.

Siffin, William J. "The Essential Character of the Contemporary Bureaucracy." In *Modern Thai Politics,* edited by Clark Neher, 399–400. Cambridge, Mass.: Schenkman Publishing Co., 1976.

———. *The Thai Bureaucracy: Institutional Change and Development.* Honolulu: East-West Center Press, 1966.

Silva, Nimalasiri. "Policies and Programmes for Tourism." In *The Role of Tourism in Social and Economic Development of Sri Lanka.* Colombo: Social Science Research Centre, 12 August 1978.

Singh, Tej Vir. *Tourism and the Tourist Industry.* Delhi: New Heights Rainbow Book Co., 1975.

Singh, Tej Vir, and Jagdish Kaur. *Himalayas, Mountains, and Men.* Lucknow, India: Print House, 1984.

———. "Tourism in the Himalayas." In *Studies in Tourism, Wildlife Parks and Conservation,* edited by Tej Vir Singh and Jagdish Kaur, 434–442. New Delhi: Metropolitan, 1982.

Singh, Tej Vir, and Jagdish Kaur, eds. *Studies in Tourism, Wildlife Parks and Conservation.* New Delhi: Metropolitan, 1982.

Smith, Valene L., ed. *Hosts and Guests: The Anthropology of Tourism.* Oxford: Basil Blackwell, 1978.

Swain, Margaret Byrne. "Cuna Women and Ethnic Tourism: A Way to Persist and an Avenue to Change." In *Hosts and Guests: The Anthropology of Tourism,* edited by Valene L. Smith, 71–82. Oxford: Basil Blackwell, 1978.

Thangamani, K. *Studies in Tourism Development Planning.* Mysore: University of Mysore, Institute of Development Studies, 1981.

"Tourism." *Pakistan Yearbook, 1969.* 477–485. Karachi: Karachi National Publishing House Ltd., 1969.

"Tourism." *Philippine Yearbook, 1981.* 595–599. Manila: NEDA, 1981.

Tupounina, Sione, Ron Crocombe, and Claire Slatter, eds. *The Pacific Way: Social Issues in National Development.* Suva: South Pacific Social Science Association, 1975.

Turner, Louis and John Ash. *The Golden Hordes.* London: Constable and Co., 1975.

Twenty Authors From Abroad. *Living in China.* Beijing: New World Press, 1979.

United Nations Development Project. "Guidelines for Development." In *Tourism in Pakistan.* SEMA Book Two. New York: United Nations, 1974.

———. "Program of Action for Development." In *Tourism in Pakistan.* SEMA Book Three. New York: United Nations, 1974.

———. *Tourism in Pakistan.* SEMA Book One. New York: United Nations, 1974.

Waheed-uz-Zaman, ed. *The Quest for Identity.* Islamabad: University of Islamabad Press, 1974.

Waters, Somerset R. *Travel Industry World Yearbook: The Big Picture, 1980–81.* New York: Child and Waters, 1981.

———. *Travel Industry World Yearbook: The Big Picture, 1983.* Vol. 27. New York: Child and Waters, 1983.

———. *Travel Industry World Yearbook: The Big Picture, 1984.* Vol. 28. New York: Child and Waters, 1984.

———. *Travel Industry World Yearbook: The Big Picture, 1986.* Vol. 30. New York: Child and Waters, 1986.

Westland, Cor. "The Development of National Free Time Policies." In *Recreation and Leisure: Issues in an Era of Change,* edited by T. L. Goodale, 351–364. State College, Pa.: Venture Publications, 1982.

Wildavsky, Aaron, and Naomi Caiden. *Planning and Budgeting in Poor Countries.* New York: John Wiley & Sons, 1974.

Wills, Garry. *Inventing America.* New York: Doubleday, 1978.

Wilson, David. "The Early Effects of Tourism in the Seychelles." In *Tourism: Passport to Development?,* edited by Emanuel De Kadt, 205–236. New York: Oxford University Press, 1979.

Winkler, James E. *Losing Control: Towards an Understanding of Transnational Corporations in the Pacific Islands.* Pacific Conference of Churches, 1982.

World Almanac. New York: Newspaper Enterprise Association, 1982.

Young, George. *Tourism: Blessing or Blight?* London: Pelican, 1973.

Zamora, Mario D., Vinson H. Sutlive, and Nathan Altshuler, eds. *Tourism and Economic Change: Studies in Third World Societies.* Williamsburg, Va.: Department of Anthropology, College of William and Mary, 1978.

Ziring, Lawrence. "Political Science and Pakistan: 1947–1972." In *Pakistan and Bangladesh: Bibliographic Essays in Social Science,* edited by W. Eric Gustafson. Islamabad: University of Islamabad Press, March 1976.

ARTICLES

Ahmed, Nazimuddun, "Tourism and the Historical and Cultural Heritage of Bangladesh." *World Travel,* no. 150: 36–40 (September–October 1979).

Airey, David. "European Government Approaches to Tourism." *Tourism Management* 4: 234–244 (December 1983).

Akogulu, Tunay. "Tourism and the Problem of the Environment." *Tourist Review* (1971): 18–20.

"Alternative Tourism." *Contours* 1, no. 4 (1983).

Anderson, Paul. "U.S.-China Venture Lets Tourists Explore Rural Area On Their Own." *Wichita Eagle* (1982).

Archer, Brian. "Domestic Tourism as a Development Factor." *Annals of Tourism Research* 5: 126–141 (January–March 1978).

"Asiad's Other Side." *India Today* (June 30, 1982): 74.

"Asia Travel." *The Asia Record* (December 1982): 26.

Aspiras, Jose. "Tourism in 1973 . . . A Success All the Way." *Bulletin Today* (Manila) (December 31, 1973).

Bahadur, Shyan. "Sharing the Tourist Dollar." *Contours* 1, no. 8: 8–9 (1984).

Bailey, Murray, and Jill Hunt. "China National Report No. 117." *International Tourism Reports,* no. 3: 5–30 (1986).

Bailie, J. Gerald. "The Evolution of Canadian International Travel Documentation." *Annals of Tourism Research* 12 (no.4) 563–580: (1985).

"Bangladesh: Market Probe." *Asia Travel Trade* (May 1979): M.P. 17.

Barnard, Byrn. "Nepal Tourism." *Newsletter of Institute of Current World Affairs* (March 1984).

Bastin, Ron. "Integrating Alternative Tourism." *Contours* 1, no. 5 (1983).

"Batasan to Probe Bias Against Filipinos at Top Manila Hotels." *Filipino Reporter* (New York) (December 23–29, 1983).

Baterina, Margot J. "Promoting Tourism on a Small Budget." *Panorama* (Manila): 12, 14, 16 (May 24, 1987).

Baum, Julian. "Chinese Policy: Open Door Inward." *Christian Science Monitor* (May 8, 1987): 17.

Baumgartner, F. F. et al. "Trekking: Tourism in Nepal." *Tourist Review* 34 (no. 3): 26–29 (1979).

Belknap, Jodi. "Wake Up to Bed and Breakfast." *Aloha Magazine* (September/October n.d.): 51–53.

Bhattacharjea, Ajit. "A Poignant Month." *Indian Express* (October 30, 1982): 6.

Bigornia, Jesus. "Empty Hotels: Symbols of Debacle." *Bulletin Today* (Manila) (April 2, 1983): 6.

Block, Elizabeth. "Bangkok Hotels Face Room Glut, Tourist Drought." *Nation's Restaurant News* (August 13, 1984): 175.

Bonavia, David. "China '80." *Far Eastern Economic Review* (September 26, 1980): 48–55, 69.

Bredemeier, Judy. "Convening Where Asia Wears a Smile." *Travel Scene* (October 15, 1980): 27–28.

Britton, Robert A. "The Image of the Third World in Tourism Marketing." *Annals of Tourism Research* (July–September 1979): 318–329.

———. "Making Tourism More Supportive of Small State Development: The Case of St. Vincent." *Annals of Tourism Research* 4 (no. 5): 268–278 (1977).

Buck, Roy C. "The Ubiquitous Tourist Brochure." *Annals of Tourism Research* (March–April 1977): 198.

Burkhart, A. J. "Tourism: Key Issues for the 1980's." *Long Range Planning* 15 (no. 4): 91–97 (1982).

Burn, Henry Pelham. "Packaging Paradise." *Sierra Club Bulletin* 60 (no. 5) (1975).

Butterfield, Fox. "Tibet Opens Up to Tourists, But Only a Few at a Time." *New York Times,* 4 (no. 4) (July 23, 1979).

Carter, Jimmy. "Veto Message." *Congressional Quarterly Weekly Report* (January 10, 1981): 113.

Chansuriyawong, Duangkamol. *Alternative World* (Bangkok) 4: 20 (1987).

Chib, Som N. "Comment on Ichaporia's Tourism at Khajuraho: An Indian Enigma." *Annals of Tourism Research* 11 (no. 3) 507–510 (1984).

———. "Tourism and the Third World." *Third World Quarterly* 2 (no. 2): 283–294 (1980).

"China." *Travel Age West* (September 7, 1981).

"China Hotels: Problems and Prospects." *Asia Travel Trade* (February 1984): 16–24.

"China Inbound." *Asia Travel Trade* (January 1986): 15–19.

"China Investigates Extortion Demands." *Wichita-Eagle Beacon* (December 17, 1983): 11a.

"China is Warming to East Europeans as Well as to Soviets." *Christian Science Monitor,* (November 14, 1983): 12–13.

"China Still Seeks Improvements." *Asia Travel Trade* (May 1983): 24.

"China: The Second Time Around." *ASTA NEWS* (November 15, 1983): 28–36.

China Tourism, No. 37 (July 1983).

Choy, Dexter J. L. "Rejoinder to Linda K. Richter's Political Implications of Chinese Tourism Policy." *Annals of Tourism Research* 10 (no. 4) (1984).

Choy, Dexter J. L., and Chuck Y. Gee. "Tourism in the PRC—Five Years After China Opens Its Gates." *International Journal of Tourism Management* 4 (no. 2): 116–119 (1983).

Chu, Godwin C., and Leonard L. Chu. "Letters to the Editor They Write in China." *East-West Perspectives* 1 (Summer 1979): 2–7.

"CITS Progress and Problems." *Asia Travel Trade* (April 1986): 48–51.

Clarke, Arthur C. "A Land Without Enemies." *Tourmaline: The Magazine of Sri Lanka* 1 (no. 2).

Coggins, Ross. "The Development Set." No publisher indicated.

Cohen, Erik. "Jungle Guides in Northern Thailand." *Sociological Review* 30 (no. 2): 234–266 (May 1982).

———. "Marginal Paradises: Bungalow Tourism on the Islands of Southern Thailand." *Annals of Tourism Research* 9 (no. 2): 403–428 (1982).

———. "Thai Girls and Farang Men: The Edge of Ambiguity." *Annals of Tourism Research* 9 (no. 3): 403–428 (1982).

Cole, Richard G. "Sixteenth-Century Travel Books As a Source of European Attitudes Toward Non-White and Non-Western Culture." *Proceedings of the American Philosophical Society* 116: 59–67 (1972).

Cooke, Karen. "Guidelines for Socially Appropriate Tourism Development in British Columbia." *Journal of Travel Research* 21 (Summer 1982): 22–28.

Creal, James. "A National Tourism Policy: Good Business for America." *National Journal* (October 4, 1980): 1681.

Crocombe, Ron. "Education, Enjoyment, and Integrity in Tourism." *Contours* 1, no. 8 (1984).

Da, He. "Song of the Loess Plateau." *China Tourism, Third Anniversary Issue* No. 37: 26 (July 1983).

Dannhorn, Robin. "Asia's Tourism Catalyst." *Far Eastern Economic Review* (January 21, 1977): 36–37.

Davies, Derek. "Traveler's Tale." *Far Eastern Economic Review* (May 14, 1982): 37.

Dawn. 13 July 1977: 1.

———. 24 May 1982: 3.

Dawn Tourism Convention 1982 Supplement, (November 15, 1982).

Dawson, Penny, and James Uhrig. "Trekker Medicine in Nepal." *Contours* 1, no. 4: 6–7 (3rd Quarter, 1983).

"Definition of Alternative Tourism." *Contours* 1, no. 7: 5 (1984).

"Delhi to Host World Tourism Conference." *India News* (July 9, 1984).

Dent, Keith. "Travel as Education: The English Landed Classes in the Eighteenth Century." *Educational Studies* 1: 171–180 (October 1975).

Dernoi, L. A. "Travelling Light." *Contours* 1, no. 8 (Last Quarter 1984).

———. "Alternative Tourism." *International Journal of Tourism Management* 2 (no. 4): 253–264 (December 1981).

Dickerson, Thomas A. "Travel Law: Securing Travelers' Rights and Remedies." *Trial* 18 (no. 8): 44–47, 73 (August 1982).

Dittmer, Lowell. "China in 1981: Reform, Readjustment, Rectification." *Asian Survey* (January 1, 1982): 33–46.

"Does India Have to be Sold?" *Vidura* 15 (January–February 1978): 28–29.

"Domestic Tourism." *Dawn* (11 October 1981).

"Domestic Tourism in Pakistan." *World Travel,* no. 149: 53–54 (1979).

"Downsiders vs. Optimists." *Newsweek* (October 22, 1984): 51.

Dunning, John, and Matthew McQueen. "Multinational Corporations in the International Hotel Industry." *Annals of Tourism Research* 9 (no. 1): 69–90 (1982).

"East-bloc Tours to China Pick Up." *Christian Science Monitor* (April 1983).

Elliott, James. "Politics, Power, and Tourism in Thailand." *Annals of Tourism Research* 10: 377–393 (1983).

Erisman, H. Michael. "Tourism and Cultural Dependency in the West Indies." *Annals of Tourism Research* 10 (no. 4): 337–361 (1983).

Farrell, Bryan H. "Tourism's Human Conflicts: Cases From the Pacific." *Annals of Tourism Research* 6 (no.2): 122–136 (April–June 1979).

"First International Tourist Conference." *Beijing Review* 25: 6 (July 26, 1982).

Fockler, Shirley. "Nepal: Preserving the Past." *Pacific Travel News* (January 1984): 34–35.

Francisco, Ronald. "The Political Impact of Economic Dependence on Tourism in Latin America." *Annals of Tourism Research* 10 (no. 3): 363–376 (1983).

Gantzer, Hugh, and Colleen Gantzer. "The Asiad Hotel Bubble." *Indian Express* (India) (July 11, 1981): 6.

———. "Lopsided Growth and Over-Centralization." *Indian Express* (August 24, 1981): 6.

———. "Managing Tourists and Politicians in India." *International Journal of Tourism Management* 4 (no. 3): 118–125 (June 1983).

Gao, Di-chen, and Guang-rui Zhang. "China's Tourism: Policy and Practice." *International Journal of Tourism Management* 4 (no. 2): 75–84 (June 1983).

———. "Report of the Third National Seminar on Tourism Economics." *International Journal of Tourism Management* 5: 153–155 (June 1984).

Gee, Chuck Y., and Dexter J. L. Choy. "The First China International Travel Conference." *Annals of Tourism Research* 9: 267–269 (1982).

Gibbons, Jean Dickinson, and Mary Fish. "Changing Economic Roles of India's International Visitors." *Tourism Recreation Research* 9 (no. 1): 5–8 (1984).

Girling, John. "Thailand in Gramscian Perspective." *Pacific Affairs* 57 (no. 3): 385–403 (Fall 1984).

"Goa's Agonda 5 Star Hotel Project." *Contours* 2 (no. 3): 13–15 (1985).

Goldstein, Carl. "Hands Across the Strait." *Far Eastern Economic Review* (August 6, 1987): 18.

Graham, Anton. A Review of *China* by Sarah Allen and Cherry Barnett. *Far Eastern Economic Review* (October 10, 1980).

Gray-Forton, Gregory. "The Conference Business and the Travel Trade." *International Tourism Quarterly*, no. 4: 49–63 (1977).

"The Great Escape." *Time* (June 15, 1981): 40–46.

Gupte, B. R. S. "Tourism, a Multi-dimensional Industry." *Yojana* (May 16–31, 1987): 22–25.

Gurung, Harka. "Tourism Trends in Nepal." *Nepal Industrial Digest* 8 (no. 1): 1–8 (1978).

Han, Guo-jian. "More Chinese Touring at Home." *Beijing Review* 38: 24–25 (September 21, 1987).

Han, Ke-hua. "Chinese-Style Tourism." *Beijing Review* 25 (no. 29): 20–22 (July 19, 1982).

Hanrahan, John. "Fat City." *Common Cause* (May–June 1983): 44–45.

Hansen-Sturm, Cord D. "Our Battle Against Travel Barriers Begins at Home." *The Travel Agent* (July 21, 1983): 1, 7, 27.

Hardgrave, Robert. "India." *Asian Survey* 24 (no. 2): 209–218 (February 1984).

Haulot, Arthur. "Social Tourism: Current Dimensions and Future Developments." *Tourism Management* 2 (no. 3): 207–213 (September 1981).

Hayes, Bernetta J. "The Congressional Travel and Tourism Caucus and U.S. National Tourism Policy." *Tourism Management* 2 (no. 2): 121–137 (June 1981).

"High-Stakes Games: Are the Olympics at Risk?" *Newsweek* (June 29, 1987): 32–33.

Hirschman, Albert. "Policy-Making and Policy Analysis in Latin America: A Return Journey." *Policy Sciences* 6: 385–402.

Hoivik, Tord, and Turid Heiberg. "Centre-Periphery Tourism and Self-Reliance." *International Social Science Journal* 32 (no. 1): 69–98 (1980).

Holiday Special Supplement Tourism Convention 1982. Vol. 5, no. 46: 13–19 (November 1982).

"Home Visits." *Pacific Travel News* (April 1984): 12–19.

Hunt, Jill. "Tourism: Competition Comes to the Industry." *Far Eastern Economic Review* (March 19, 1987): 97–99.

Ilustre, Macrina Leuterio. "Metro Manila Opens Its Arms to the World's Top Financiers." *Examiner* (Manila) (October 1976): 12–17.

"India: Market Probe." *Asia Travel Trade* (1978).

"India: Market Probe." *Asia Travel Trade* (July 1980).

"India: A Tourist Paradise: The Promise of Tomorrow." *India News* (India) (August 6, 1984): 5, 6.

"Interview: Boris Lissanevitch." *Where: Mirror of Nepal* (n.d.).

Jafari, Jafar. "Creation of the Intergovernmental World Tourism Organization." *Annals of Tourism Research* 2: 237–246 (May–June 1975).

Jain, C. B. "Domestic Tourism in India." *World Travel* 152: 38 (1980).

"Japan: Lipstick on the Collar." *Asiaweek* (January 23, 1981): 25–26.

Jones, Clayton. "India's Plan to Expand Tourism Looks Beyond Pilgrimage Tradition." *Christian Science Monitor* (October 12, 1982): 6.

———. "Moonlighting Air Force Builds Sri Lanka's Tourism." *Christian Science Monitor* (January 27, 1982): 2.

"Jose Antonio Gonzalez, Minister of Tourism Philippines," *Asia Travel Trade* (April 1986): 52–53.

Kainen, Ilkka A. Ron, and Richard J. Fararo. "United States Travel and Tourism Policy." *Journal of Travel Research* 25 (no. 4): 2–8 (Spring 1987).

Kale, Sudhir H., and Katherine M. Weir. "Marketing Third World Countries to the Western Traveler: The Case of India." *Journal of Travel Research* 25 (no. 2): 2–7 (Fall 1986).

Katgora, N. J. "Growth Prospects Tremendous." *Tourism and Wildlife* (August–October 1980).

Kaufman, Michael T. "Basketball is Big in Bhutan but Traditions Too Are Prized." *New York Times* (April 29, 1980): 2.

Kaushik, Purushottam. "New Delhi for Home Tourist." *Tourist Trade of India* 12 (no. 3): 17–18 (1977).

Krippendorf, Joel. "Towards New Tourism Policies: The Importance of Environmental and Socio-cultural Factors." *Tourism Management* 3 (no. 3): 135–148 (September 1982).

Kumar, Sheila. "Tourism: Boon or Bane." *Businessworld* (September 24–October 7, 1984): 66–75.

Lee, Mary. "Flow through at Lowu." *Far Eastern Economic Review* (August 7, 1981): 52–53.

Legal, Prithvi Raj. "Economic Impact of Tourism in Nepal: An Input-Output Approach." *Journal of Development and Administrative Studies* (June and December 1982): 149–178.

Lehmann, Nicolas. "Iron Triangle Keeps Tiny Agency from Being Sent to Scrapheap." *Washington Post* (January 16, 1981): A14.

Lenze, Ilse. "Tourism Prostitution in Asia." *ISIS International Bulletin* 13 (November 1979).

"Letter from Bangkok." *Far Eastern Economic Review* (August 4, 1983).

Leung, David. "Pakistan: Five Year Tourism Plan." *Asia Travel Trade* (January 1975): 17.

Lew, Alan. "The History, Policies and Social Impact of International Tourism in the People's Republic of China." *Asian Profile* 15(2): 117–128 (April 1987).

Lewis, John. "They Fall Among Thieves." *Far Eastern Economic Review* (May 1, 1981): 26–27.

———. "A Boom Japan Does Not Want." *Far Eastern Economic Review* (November 7, 1980): 92–101.

Lin, Sharat G., and Nageshwar Patnaik. "Migrant Labor at Asiad '82 Construction Sites in New Delhi." *Bulletin of Concerned Asian Scholars* 14 (no. 3): 23–31 (July/September 1982).

Lijphart, Arend. "Tourist Traffic and Integration Potential." *Journal of Common Market Studies* 2: 251–262 (February 1964).

"The Living Escape: Tourism Explodes in Asia and the Pacific." *Time* (June 15, 1981): 40–46.

Lord, Mary. "Chun's Option: To Crush or Concede." *U.S. News and World Report* (June 29, 1987): 26–28.

McCalip, Bernevia. "The Tourism Industry: Background, Status and Federal Government Initiatives." *Congressional Research Service Report*. No. 80-72E (1980).

MacCannell, Dean. "Reconstructed Ethnicity: Tourism and Cultural Identity in Third World Communities." *Annals of Tourism Research* 11 (no. 3): pp. 375–391 (1984).

Magsanoc, Leticia. "The View from the Tourist Belt." *Focus Philippines* (Manila) (18 November 1972): 46.

"Maldives." *International Tourism Quarterly*, no. 2: 57–71 (1987).

"The Maldives: A Case Study." *International Tourism Quarterly*, no. 1: 59–70 (1983).

Manik, G. S. "A Tax Stifling Tourism." *Indian Express* (April 25, 1981).

"Manila Hotels Suffering." *Asia Travel Trade* (May 1984): 39–41.

"Martinique, The Despoiling of an Island's Heritage." *Contours* 2, no. 3: 4–5 (3rd Quarter, 1985).

"The Merry Month of May." *Asiaweek* (February 13, 1981): 15–16.

Middleton, Victor T. C. "Tourism in Rural Areas." *Tourism Management* 3: 52–58 (March 1982).

Miller, Matt. "Will PAL Remain National Airlines?" Special from *Far Eastern Economic Review* in *Philippine Times* (Chicago) (January 6–12, 1979): 8, 10.

Mir, Niaz. "The Second Singapore-to-Be." *Dawn* (November 24, 1978): 9.

Moody, Peter R., Jr. "Political Liberalization in China: A Struggle Between Two Lines." *Pacific Affairs* 51 (no. 1): 26–44 (Spring 1984).

Muecke, Marjorie A. "Make Money Not Babies: Changing Status Markers of Northern Thai Women." *Asian Survey* 24 (no. 4): 459–470 (April 1984).

Muqbil, Imtiaz. "The Trashing of the Road to Shangri-La." *Contours* 1, no. 7: 7–8 (April–June 1984).

Naik, R. P. "Role of Government in Tourism." *Tourism and Wildlife* (February–April 1978): 4–5, 29.

Nash, Dennison. "Tourism as an Anthropological Subject." *Current Anthropology* 22: 461–481 (October 1981).

"National Report No. 51, Nepal." *International Tourism Quarterly,* no. 1: 31–46 (1979).

"Nepal." *International Tourism Quarterly,* no. 2: 10–11 (1984).

"Nepal Inbound: Access Skill Limits Growth." *Asia Travel Trade:* 20.

"Nepal: Market Probe." *Asia Travel Trade* (October 1980).

"Nepal: Market Probe." *Asia Travel Trade* (September 1981).

"Nepal, National Report No. 120." *International Tourism Reports,* no. 3: 61–74 (1986).

Netterkoven, Lothar. "Mass Tourism from the Industrial Society to the Developing Countries." *Economics* 10: 121–137 (1974).

Neumann, A. Lin. "Hospitality Girls in the Philippines." *Southeast Asia Chronicle,* SRC No. 66, PSC 9 (no. 5): 18–23.

"The New Colonialism: Tourism with No Return." *The Sun* (June 24, 1977).

"New Policy to Promote Domestic Tourism." *Dawn Overseas* (October 7, 1982): 3.

Noon, (Begum) Viqar-un-Nisa. "Tourism: The First Task." *Viewpoint* 4 (August 27, 1978).

"The Number 1 Market." *Far Eastern Economic Review* (January 2, 1977): 42–44.

Nur, Masud Nabi. "Tourism Prospects in Pakistan." *Dawn* (Supplement: Pakistan Tourism Convention) (November 1, 1983).

Oka, Takashi. "Peking Attempts to Allay Taiwan's Fears of Being Gobbled Up." *Christian Science Monitor* (October 1, 1981): 3.

O'Reilly, A. M. "An Overview of the Costs and Benefits of Tourism." *Tourist Review* 38 (no. 1): 25–27 (January–March 1983).

"Overpricing: China Learns to Exploit." *Asia Travel Trade* (October 1979).

"Pakistan, Handling a Visitor Decline." *Asia Travel Trade* (July 1983): 56–57.

"Pakistan: Slow Progress." *Asia Travel Trade* (May 1985): 22–28.

"Pakistan Still Hoping for a Breakthrough." *Asia Travel Trade* (February 1984): 48–49.

"Patches Showing Up in National Parks." *U.S. News and World Report* (June 17, 1985): 69–70.

Pavaskar, Madhoo. "Employment Effects of Tourism and the Indian Experience." *Journal of Travel Research* (Fall 1982): 32–38.

"Philippine Airlines: Now Gonzalez Gets the Airline." *Asia Travel Trade* (June 1986): 38.

"Philippine Resorts Still Building." *Asia Travel Trade* (March 1983): 34–35.

Pilarski, Adam. "Notes on Domestic Tourism Development in China." *Journal of Travel Research* 25 (no. 2): 29–30 (Fall 1986).

Pi-Sunyer, Oriol. "The Politics of Tourism in Catalonia." *Mediterranean Studies* 1 (no. 2): 46–69 (1979).

Pizam, Abraham. "Tourism's Impact: The Social Costs to the Destination Community as Perceived by Its Residents." *Journal of Travel Research* 16: 8–12 (Spring 1978).

"Product Update: South Asia." *Asia Travel Trade* (May 1986): S1–S8.

"Product Update: Sri Lanka." *Asia Travel Trade* (August 1983).

"Protesting the Sexual Imperialists." *Far Eastern Economic Review* (March 14, 1975): 5–6.

Punyaratabandu-Bhakdi, Suchitra. "Thailand in 1983." *Asian Survey* 24 (no. 2): 187–194 (February 1984).

Rajendra, Cecil. "When the Tourists Flew In." *Contours* 1, no. 4 (1983).

Raju, R. K. "The Year of a Million Tourists." *Indian and Foreign Review* 24 (no. 9): 4–5, 27 (February 28, 1987).

Ramirez, Jun. "Tax Plan to Save 15 Big Hotels OK'd." *Bulletin Today* (Manila) (April 22, 1983).

"Relying on Everyone Else." *Asia Travel Trade* (August 1982).

Riaz, Hassan. "International Tourism and Inter-Cultural Communication." *Southeast Asian Journal of Social Science* 3 (no. 2): 25–38 (1975).

Richter, Linda K. "The Fragmented Politics of U.S. Tourism." *Tourism Management* 6 (no. 3): 162–173 (September 1985).

———. "The Hobgoblin Factor in International Tourism." *Contours* 1, no. 5: 8–9 (1984).

———. "Philippine Policies Toward Filipino Americans." *Asian Thought and Society* (November 1982).

———. "The Political Implications of Chinese Tourism Policy." *Annals of Tourism Research* 10 (no. 4): 395–413 (1983).

———. "The Political Uses of Tourism: A Philippine Case Study." *Journal of Developing Areas* 14: 237–257 (January 1980).

———. "The Potential and Pitfalls of Tourism Planning in Third World Nations: Case of Pakistan." *Tourism Recreation Research* 9 (no. 1): 9–13 (1984).

———. "State-Sponsored Tourism Development: A Growth Area for Public Administration." *Public Administration Review* 45 (no. 6): 832–839 (November–December 1985).

———. "Tourism By Decree." *Southeast Asia Chronicle* 78: 27–32 (April 1981).

———. "Tourism Politics and Political Science: A Case of Not So Benign Neglect." *Annals of Tourism Research* 10 (no. 3): 313–335 (1983).

Richter, Linda K., and William L. Richter. "Policy Choices in South Asian Tourism Development." *Annals of Tourism Research* 12 (no. 2): 201–217 (1985).

Richter, Linda K., and William L. Waugh, Jr. "Terrorism and Tourism as Logical Companions." *Tourism Management* (December 1986): 230–238.

Richter, William L. "Persistent Praetorianism: Pakistan's Third Military Regime." *Pacific Affairs* 51: 406–426 (Fall 1978).

———. "The Political Dynamics of Islamic Resurgence in Pakistan." *Asian Survey* 19 (no. 6): 547–557 (June 1979).

Rogers, Penny. "Jamaican Hello." *American Way* (November 1984): 15.

Rosenau, James N. "Le Touriste et Le Terrorist ou Les Deux Extremes du Continuum Transnational." *Etudes Internationales* 10: 231–252 (June 1979).

Rubin, Karen. "India Tourism Development Corporation Launching Overseas Venture." *The Travel Agent* (January 8, 1981).

Samarasooruya, Shireen. "Access to Income from Tourism for Women." *Voice of Women* 2 (no. 1): 7–11, 15.

Samaringhe, S. W. R. de A. "Sri Lanka in 1983: Ethnic Conflict and the Search for Solutions." *Asian Survey* 24 (no. 2): 225 (February 1984).

Sarasohn, Judy. "Bill Establishes New Agency to Promote Foreign Tourism." *Congressional Quarterly Weekly Report* 13: 3548 (December 1980).

———. "Congress, Administration Disagree on Promoting U.S. Travel By Foreigners." *Congressional Quarterly Weekly Report* 14: 1667 (June 1980).

Schuchat, Molly. "State Tourism in China and the U.S.A." *Annals of Tourism Research* 6 (no. 4): 425–434 (1979).

Schul, Patrick and John L. Crompton. "Search Behavior of International Vacationers: Travel-Specific Lifestyle and Sociodemographic Variables." *Journal of Travel Research* 22 (no. 2): 25–30 (1983).

"Selling Sri Lanka." *Asia Travel Trade* (November 1978): MP-20.

Seth, P. N. "Dimensions of Indian Tourism." *Indian and Foreign Review* 13: 13, 16–17 (December 1, 1975).

Sethi, Sunil. "The Way We Were." *India Today* (May 31, 1983): 74–76.

"Set in a Holding Pattern." *Asia Travel Trade* (April 1984).

"Sex Tourism to Thailand." *ISIS International Bulletin,* no. 13 (November 1979).

Sharif, I. H. "Parjatan Run Sloppily." *Dacca Times* (Bangladesh) (July 12, 1981).

Shrestha, Mangal K. "Issues of Development: Policy Reforms in the Nepalese Civil Service." *Journal of Development and Administrative Studies* (June and December 1982): 164–171.

Siddiqui, Raguib. "Burdened with Overgrowth." *Aviatour* (May 28, 1983): 1.

———. "Flying without Fuel." *Aviatour* (April 30, 1983).

———. "Undiscovered Bangladesh." *Aviatour* (September 24, 1983): 1.

Singh, K. M. "Not Yet Cleared for Take-Off." *Far Eastern Economic Review* (September 18, 1981): 130.

Singh, Tej Vir. "On Planning Towns, Tourism, and Environment." *Tourism Recreation Research* 4 (no. 2): 9–14 (1984).

Singhania, Govind Hari. "Workshop on Tourism." *Indian Express* (September 30, 1981).

"Special Report on the Maldives, No. 45." *International Tourism Quarterly,* no. 1: 59–70 (1983).

"Sri Lanka After the Riots." *Asia Travel Trade* 16: 17–22 (January 1984).

"Sri Lanka Still in Decline." *Asia Travel Trade* (June 1986): 28–29.

Stauffer, Robert. "Philippine Corporatism: A Note on the New Society." *Asian Survey* 17: 393–407 (April 1977).

Stock, Robert. "Political and Social Contributions of International Tourism to the Development of Israel." *Annals of Tourism Research* 4: 30–42 (October/December 1977).

"Strong Growth But Problems Remain." *Asia Travel Trade* (October 1986): 37–40.

Sturken, Barbara. "The World Bank Well Runs Dry." *Travel Scene* (November 15, 1980): 14–15.

Tasker, Rodney. "Campus Confrontation." *Far Eastern Economic Review* (September 9, 1977): 8–9.

———. "Journalist Vindicated." *Far Eastern Economic Review* (July 1, 1977): 14.

"The TATA Land Grab at Candolim." *Contours* 1, no. 3: 6–7 (1983).

"Thailand." *International Tourism Quarterly,* no. 2: 12–30 (1984).

"Thailand: Boomtime in Bangkok." *Asia Travel Trade* (January 1988): 17–18.

"Thailand: Market Probe." *Asia Travel Trade* (December 1980).

"Thailand: Market Probe." *Asia Travel Trade* (August 1981).

"Thailand: Market Probe." *Asia Travel Trade* (October 1981).

"Thailand: Market Probe." *Asia Travel Trade* (July 1983).

"Thailand: New Era in Tourism." *Asia-Pacific Travel* (January–February 1980): 42.

"Thailand, Sex as a Travel Motivator." *Asia Travel Trade* (June 1983): 49, 51, 52.

"Thailand: Tripling the Tourist Police." *Asia Travel Trade* (March 1984): 49–50.

"Thailand: What the GIs Left Behind." *Far Eastern Economic Review* (September 1, 1976): 26–28.

Thanh-Dam, Truong. "The Dynamics of Sex Tourism: The Case of Southeast Asia." *Development and Change* 14: 533–553 (1983).

"They Still Don't Know Pakistan?" *Pakistan Tourism Review* 1: 1 (March 1977).

"Third World Project Financing." *Tourism Management* 3 (no. 1): 61–63 (March 1982).

Thiruchandran, Selvy. "Tourism at What Cost." *Voice of Women* 2 (no. 2): 16.

Thomas, William L. "Progressive Rather than Centralized Tourism: A Recommendation for Improving International Tourism in the Philippines." *The Philippine Geographic Journal* (June 1978).

"Tourism." *Far Eastern Economic Review* (September 26, 1980): 69, 76–79.

"Tourism: A Review." *Asia Travel Trade* (January 1984): 13–15.

"Tourism Haryana." *Vidura* 15 (no. 11): 16–17 (January–February 1978).

"Tourism Travels to the Third World." *Dollars and Sense* 36: 14–15 (1978).

"Tourist Club Cornerstone Laid." *Bulletin Today* (Manila) (April 30, 1979): 1.

"Tourists and the Slums." *Contours* 1, no. 3: 10 (1983).

"The Tourist Trap, Who Gets Caught?" *Cultural Survival Quarterly* 6 (no. 3) (Summer 1982).

Turner, Louis. "Tourism and the Social Sciences: From Blackpool to Benidorm and Bali." *Annals of Tourism Research* (April 1974): 180–205.

"Turning to Training." *Asia Travel Trade* (April 1984): 19–21.

UNESCO. "The Effects of Tourism on Socio-Cultural Values." *Annals of Tourism Research* 4: 74–105 (November/December 1976).

Unmat, R. C. "Fostering Tourism: Why Dither." *Eastern Economist* (October 19, 1979): 797.

"Update on Goa." *Contours* 1, no. 7: 14–15 (1984).

Uprety, Dilli Raj. "Mountain Tourism in Nepal." *World Travel,* no. 140: 39–40 (January–February 1978).

Valencia, Teodoro. *Filipino Reporter* (New York) (March 13–19, 1981): 12.

Van Ness, Peter. "Black, White and Grey in China Research." *Far Eastern Economic Review* (February 9, 1984): 30–31.

"Visions of Poverty, Visions of Wealth." Special Issue of the *New Internationalist,* no. 142 (December 1984).

Vokey, Richard. "Dilemma of the Holiday Hosts." *Far Eastern Economic Review* (November 7, 1980): 92–101.

Wahao, Salah. "The Legal Protection of the Tourist." *Tourism Review* (1971): 159–160.

Wahnschafft, Ralph. "Formal and Informal Tourism Sectors: A Case Study in Pattaya, Thailand." *Annals of Tourism Research* 9 (no. 3): 429–451 (1982).

Wallace, Michael B. "Managing Resources that are Common Property: From Kathmandu to Capital Hill." *Journal of Policy Analysis and Management* 2: 220–237 (Winter 1983).

Wang, Tie-sheng and Li-cheng Ge. "Domestic Tourism Development in China: A Regression Analysis." *Journal of Travel Research* 24 (no. 2): 13–17 (1985).

Weaver, Mary Anne. "Mr. Oberoi of India: A Five-Star Hotelier of the Third World." *Christian Science Monitor* (November 14, 1983): 47–48.

"Wedding of the Year." *Asiaweek* (June 24, 1983): 28–29.

Wenham, Julie. "Just Travel: An Experiment in Alternative Tourism." *Contours* 1, no. 5: 6 (1983).

"Where They Don't Lock Up Their Daughters." *Far Eastern Economic Review* (August 4, 1983).

Wideman, Bernard. "Overbuilt, Underbooked." *Far Eastern Economic Review* (January 21, 1977): 72.

Wildavsky, Aaron. "Why Planning Fails in Nepal." *Administrative Science Quarterly* 17: 408–428 (December 1972).

Wolters, Richard. "China Laying the Groundwork for a New Style of Tourism." *Christian Science Monitor* (November 3, 1981): 15–16.

Wood, Robert E. "The Economics of Tourism." *Southeast Asia Chronicle,* no. 78 (April 1981): 2–13.

———. "Ethnic Tourism, the State, and the Cultural Change in Southeast Asia." *Annals of Tourism Research* 11 (no. 3): 353–374 (1984).

———. "International Tourism and Cultural Change in Southeast Asia." *Economic Development and Cultural Change* 28: 561–582 (April 1980).

———. "Tourism and Underdevelopment in Southeast Asia." *Journal of Contemporary Asia* 9 (no. 3): 274–287 (1979).

"World Business." *U.S. News and World Report* (October 3, 1983): 40.

Wu, Nai-tao. "Tibet Opens to the Outside World." *Beijing Review* 42: 16–20 (October 19, 1987).

Zhang, Ze-yu. "China's Growing Tourist Industry." *Beijing Review* 23 (no. 27): 14–17 (July 7, 1980).

Zito, Larna. "Settling Down: Bedouin in the Sinai." *Cultural Survival Quarterly* 6 (no. 3) (Summer 1982).

OFFICIAL PUBLICATIONS

Ceylon Tourism Plan. Colombo: Government of Ceylon, 1967.

Ceylon Tourism Plan Summary. Colombo: Ceylon Tourist Board, 1968.

Commission of the European Communities. "A Community Policy on Tourism." *Bulletin of the European Communities.* Supplement. April 1982.

Concessions, Promotions of Tourism. Colombo: Inland Revenue Department, 1968.

Corazzini, Arthur. "Study of Estimates of Job Generation in the Travel and Tourism Industry." GAO/PAD–83-54. September 30, 1983.

Council of Field Coordinators. Memorandum to Secretary Jose D. Aspiras. June 20, 1974.

Department of Tourism. *Accomplishment Report, 1973–1975.* Manila: National Media Production Center, 1976.

———. *Accomplishment Report, 1976.* Manila: Government Printing Office, 1976.

———. "Invitation to a Traditional Philippine Christmas." Manila: DOT, 1973.

Department of Tourism Planning Service. *The Tourism Investment Priorities Plan, 1977–1981 Final Revision.* January 1977.

Development Budget for Philippine Ministry of Tourism for 1977–1978.

Economic Research and Statistics Section. *Foreign Tourism in Pakistan.* Islamabad: Government Tourism Division, October 1976.

Economic Research and Statistics Section of Tourism Division. *Tourism Growth in Pakistan, 1981.* Islamabad: Government of Pakistan, 1981.

Government of India, Department of Tourism. "Foreign Tourist Survey 1976–1977." Delhi: GOI, 1977.

Government of India Planning Commission. "Draft Five Year Plan 1978–1983." Delhi: GOI, 1978.

Hearing Before the Subcommittee on Business, Trade and Tourism of the U.S. Senate Committee on Commerce, Science and Transportation. Washington, D.C.: U.S. Government Printing Office. April 6, 1984.

Kaspar, C. "Tourism Planning for the Eighties." Berne: AIEST, 1978.

National Tourism Policy Act. Senate Hearings. Washington, D.C.: Government Printing Office, 1979.

Nyrop, Richard F., et al. *Area Handbook for India.* 3rd ed. Washington, D.C.: Government Printing Office, 1975.

Organization for Economic Cooperation and Development. *The Impact of Tourism on the Environment.* Paris: OECD, 1980.

Pakistan Department of Tourism. *Annual Report, 1969.* Islamabad: Government of Pakistan, 1969.

Philippine Tourism Authority. *A Complete Guide for Tourism Investors in the Philippines.* Manila: Government Printing Office, 1973.

"The Philippine Tourism Authority and You." Pamphlet of the Philippine Tourism Authority, n.d.

Philippine Tourism Newsletter. Manila: Department of Tourism.

Presidential Decree, No. 819. Manila. October 1975.

Presidential Decree, No. 867. Manila. January 2, 1976.

Presidential Letter of Instruction, No. 331. Manila. October 29, 1975.

"Regional Report No. 10." The Association of Southeast Asian Nations.

Report 1975–1976 Government of India Ministry of Tourism and Civil Aviation. New Delhi: Government of India, 1976.

Report of the Prospects for Tourism Development in Ceylon. International Bank for Reconstruction and Development, 1968.

"Sri Lanka, Come Share Our Way of Life." Ceylon Tourist Board, n.d.

Sri Lanka Embassy Newsletter. January 1977.

Toole, Julian. "Welcome to Sri Lanka." *Serendib* (monthly). Colombo: Ceylon Tourism Board.

Tourism Authority of Thailand. *Annual Report, 1983.*

———. *Annual Report, 1987.*

———. *Annual Statistical Report on Tourism in Thailand, 1983.*

Tourist Organization of Thailand. "Statistics on Tourism in Thailand 1957–1968."

United States General Accounting Office. "Funding Constraints Require a New Approach to Support Tourism Information for Foreign Visitors." Washington, D.C.: Government Printing Office, September 17, 1982.

White Paper on the Performance of the Bhutto Regime, Vol. II. Government of Pakistan, 1978

World Bank. *Tourism, Sector Working Paper.* June 1972.

Videorecordings

Business in Bodies. An underground film available from the Ecumenical Coalition on Third World Tourism. No director or producer listed.

Fire on the Water. Directed by Robert Hillman.

World: Who Pays for Paradise? Public Broadcasting System. June 1, 1978.

Speeches and Professional Papers

Bertocci, Peter J. "Resource Development and Ethnic Conflict: The Case of the Chittagong Hill Tracts of Bangladesh." Paper presented at the Association for Asian Studies Meeting, March 25–27, 1983.

Buan, Eryl Gil A. "The Asian Institute of Tourism." Speech delivered to PATA chapter, November 12, 1976.

Gonsalves, Paul S. "From Leisure to Learning: A Strategy for India." Paper presented at the Workshop on Alternative Tourism, Chiang Mai, Thailand, April 26–May 9, 1984.

———. "Tourism in India: An Overview." Paper presented at the Workshop on Alternative Tourism, Chiang Mai, Thailand, April 26–May 9, 1984.

Graham, Donald H. "Doing Business in the People's Republic of China." Speech presented at the Harvard Business School, 16th Continuing Education Seminar, Nevada, 1980.

Hansen-Sturm, Cord D. "Trade in Services in a U.S.-Israel Limited Free Trade Area." Testimony before the Subcommittee on Trade of the Ways and Means Committee of the House of Representatives, June 14, 1984.

———. "Travel as an Information Medium." Speech delivered at the annual meeting of the Travel and Tourism Research Association, June 1984.

Kumar, Prem. "Notes on Alternative Tourism in Sri Lanka." A talk presented at the Chiang Mai Conference on Alternative Tourism, Chiang Mai, Thailand, April 26–May 9, 1984.

Melchior, Alejandro. Untitled speech delivered to the Capital Christian Leadership Association, Quezon City, December 1976.

Richter, Linda K. "The Politics of Tourism: A Comparative Perspective." Paper presented at the Midwest Political Science Meeting, Chicago, April 1980.

———. "The Impact of Regime Change on Women in Pakistan and Afghanistan." Paper presented at Midwest Political Science Association Meeting, Cincinnati, Ohio, April 1981.

———. "The Politics of State-Sponsored Tourism Development." Paper presented at the American Society for Public Administration Annual Meeting in Denver, Colorado, April 8–11, 1984.

Srinivasan, R. "Computers in India." Speech delivered at the East-West Center, October 25, 1984.

Wan Fu. "The Present Situation and Prospect of China's Tourism." Speech delivered at the Kunming International Travel and Tourism Conference, November 25–28, 1981.

Selected Interviews

Afzal, Javaid. Regional Manager, Lahore PTDC. August 4, 1977.

Ahmed, Muneer-ud-din. Planning and Development Officer, Pakistan Department of Tourism Planning Service. September 9, 1977 and October 10, 1977.

Araneta, Gregorio. Philippine Undersecretary of Tourism. June 1977.

Bagatsing, Ramon. Mayor of Manila. May 26, 1977.

Buan, Eryl. Associate Dean, Asian Institute of Tourism. January 18, 1977.

Butt, Fuad. Developer of one of SEMA projects in Swat. Lahore. July 29, 1977.

Cacdac, (Colonel). General Manager, Philippine Convention Bureau. March 14, 1977.

Chalisey, Kanchan Mala. Deputy Mayor of Kathmandu. October 17, 1984.

Choy, Dexter. September 4, 1984.

De la Fuente, (Ms.). Director, Philippine Convention Bureau. March 14, 1977.

Edgell, David. Office of Policy Analysis, U.S. Travel and Tourism Industry, Washington, D.C. March 1984.

Faust, Charles. Staff of the U.S. Senate Committee on Commerce, Science, and Tourism, Washington, D.C. March 1984.

Ghory, Shireen. Director, Department of Pakistan Tourism Services. November 16, 1977.

Gurung, Harka. Former Minister of Tourism, Nepal. December 19, 1984.

Holden, Peter. Executive Director of the Ecumenical Coalition on Third World Tourism. Honolulu. November 13, 1984.

Inattulah, (Mr.). PTDC Peshawar Manager. August 12, 1977.

Khan, Jameel. Joint Secretary, Ministry of Tourism, Islamabad. August 15, 1977.

Khan, Maqsood Ali. District Manager, PIA. September 26, 1977.

Khan, Sardar Mohammed Afzal. Assistant Manager, Lahore Intercontinental. October 1977.

Krishnan, N. C. President, Indo-American Chamber of Commerce. November 5, 1984.

Lim, Narzalina. Undersecretary of Tourism, Philippines, 1987.

Mahmood, Hussein. Pakistan Resort Developer. October 27, 1977.

Meerza, (Mr.). Deputy Secretary, Pakistan Ministry of Tourism. August 15, 1977.

NEDA official working with tourism, Philippines. March 23, 1977.

Official. Philippine Consulate in Hawaii. October 29, 1984.

Officials. Pakistan Hotel and Restaurant Association. Karachi. October 1977.

Panzo, Jerry. Public Relations Director, Hawaii Visitors Bureau. September 6, 1984.

Paul, Manu. Maori activist. Honolulu. November 12, 1984.

Personnel. Central and field offices of the Philippine Department of Agrarian Reform. 1976–1977.

Personnel. La Union Tourism Field Office. Bauang, La Union, the Philippines. May 1977.

Personnel Manager. Philippine Tourism Authority. June 1977.

Portugal, Vic. Assistant Director. DOT Research Statistics Division. June 1977.

Principal. Administrative Staff College. Lahore. July 19, 1977.

PTDC Resthouse Manager. Miandam, Pakistan. August 19, 1977.

Qureshi, M. D. Saeed. Managing Director, PTDC, Pakistan. November 1, 1977.

Raja, Farooq. Manager, Peshawar Intercontinental Hotel, Pakistan. August 13, 1977.

Ramusan, Mitz. City Tourism Coordinator, Marawi City, Philippines. May 1977.

Riaz, (Mr.). PTDC Manager, Saidu Sharif, Pakistan. August 9, 1977.

Saladdin, (Mr.). Manager, Pakistan Tours Ltd. November 1, 1977 and November 4, 1977.

Salem, Mohammed. External Publicity, Ministry of Information and Broadcasting, Pakistan, 1977.

Sath, Aziz Ur Rehmon. Owner, Hotel Palmir, Lahore, Pakistan. August 9, 1977.

Secretary of the Hotels, Restaurants, and Clubs Association, Karachi, Pakistan. November 1, 1977.

Seneviratne, Maureen. Travel writer, Chiang Mai, Thailand. April 29, 1984.

Shaha, Rishikesh. Former diplomat and politician and author of books on the history and politics of Nepal. December 1984.

Shamin, Sardar. Indus Hotel, Pakistan. October 29, 1977.

Shoemaker, Thomas. Lobbyist for Travel Industry of America, Washington, D.C. March 1984.

Tinoco, (Ms.). Manila City Hall Attorney. March–May 1977.

Tourism Coordinator. Legaspi, the Philippines. January 1977.

Walji, (Mrs.). Pakistan Tour Agency owner. October 10, 1977.

Weidman, Kent. Diplomat-in-Residence, East-West Center. November 1984.

Williams, James. Congressional Liaison, U.S. Travel and Tourism Administration, Washington, D.C. March 1984.

Index

About the Author

Linda K. Richter, an enthusiastic tourist herself, is associate professor of political science at Kansas State University, where she teaches public policy and administration, Southeast Asian politics, and gender politics. She is the author of *Land Reform and Tourism Development: Policy-Making in the Philippines* and more than 40 articles on Asian politics and tourism, has testified twice before Congress on the Philippines, and serves as an Associate Editor of *Annals of Tourism Research*. She has been fascinated with Asian politics and travel and tourism all her professional life and has done field research in India, the Philippines, Pakistan, Thailand, Nepal, China, and Sri Lanka.

Production Notes

This book was designed by Roger Eggers.
Composition and paging were done on the
Quadex Composing System and typesetting
on the Compugraphic 8400 by the design
and production staff of University of
Hawaii Press.

The text typeface is Sabon and the
display typeface is Compugraphic Palatino.

Offset presswork and binding were done by
Vail-Ballou Press, Inc. Text paper is
Glatfelter Offset Vellum, basis 50.